ASIA AND THE WEST

AMS PRESS
NEW YORK

Asia and the West

Maurice Zinkin

ISSUED UNDER THE AUSPICES OF
THE INTERNATIONAL SECRETARIAT
INSTITUTE OF PACIFIC
RELATIONS

1953
CHATTO & WINDUS
London

Library of Congress Cataloging in Publication Data

Zinkin, Maurice.
    Asia and the West.

    Reprint of the 1953 ed. published by Chatto &
Windus, London.
    Includes index.
    1. East and West. I. Title.
CB251.Z5   1978   950   75-30091
ISBN 0-404-59574-X

First AMS edition published in 1978.

Reprinted from the edition of 1953, London, from an
original in the collections of the Ohio State University
Libraries. [Trim size of the original has been slightly
altered in this edition. Original trim size: 12 x 19 cm.
Text area of the original has been maintained.]

MANUFACTURED
IN THE UNITED STATES OF AMERICA

TO MY WIFE

The Institute of Pacific Relations

The Institute of Pacific Relations is an unofficial and non-partisan organization, founded in 1925 to facilitate the scientific study of the peoples of the Pacific area. It is composed of autonomous National Councils in the principal countries having important interests in the Pacific area, together with an International Secretariat. It is privately financed by contributions from National Councils, corporations and foundations. It is governed by a Pacific Council composed of members appointed by each of the National Councils.

In addition to the independent activities of its National Councils, the Institute organizes private international conferences every two or three years. Such conferences have been held at Honolulu (1925 and 1927), Kyoto (1929), Shanghai (1931), Banff, Canada (1933), Yosemite Park, California (1936), Virginia Beach, Virginia (1939), Mont Tremblant, Quebec (1942), Hot Springs, Virginia (1945), Stratford, England (1947), Lucknow (1950). The Institute conducts an extensive programme of research on the political, economic and social problems of the Pacific area and the Far East. It also publishes the proceedings of its conferences, a quarterly journal, *Pacific Affairs*, and a large number of scholarly books embodying the results of its studies.

Neither the International Secretariat nor the National Councils of the Institute advocate policies or express opinions on national or international affairs. Responsibility for statements of fact or opinion in Institute publications rests solely with the authors.

National Councils

AMERICAN INSTITUTE OF PACIFIC RELATIONS, INC.
AUSTRALIAN INSTITUTE OF INTERNATIONAL AFFAIRS
CANADIAN INSTITUTE OF INTERNATIONAL AFFAIRS
COMITE D'ETUDES DES PROBLEMES DU PACIFIQUE
INDIAN COUNCIL OF WORLD AFFAIRS
JAPAN INSTITUTE OF PACIFIC RELATIONS
NEW ZEALAND INSTITUTE OF INTERNATIONAL AFFAIRS
PAKISTAN INSTITUTE OF INTERNATIONAL AFFAIRS
PHILIPPINE COUNCIL, INSTITUTE OF PACIFIC RELATIONS
ROYAL INSTITUTE OF INTERNATIONAL AFFAIRS
IPR INTERNATIONAL SECRETARIAT 1 *East Street, New York 22, N.Y.*

AUTHOR'S NOTE

It is very difficult to make adequate acknowledgment to those who have helped me over this book. There have been so many of them, and their ideas have been absorbed over so long a time.

Those who have had most effect in forming my mind, and whose ideas I have plagiarised most extensively, are my service contemporaries, Robin Keith, John Bowman, Bobby Dalal, J. F. Hosie, N. M. Wagle, George Wyndham, Hari Singh. But I owe a large debt also to some of those under whom I have worked, David Symington, V. Isvaran, H. M. Patel, Sir Jeremy Raisman, the late Sir Akbar Hydari, M. K. Vellodi; or with whom I have been in close contact otherwise, Sir B. and Lady Rama Rau, Mrs. H. R. Stimson, Mr. M. Ayub, Mr. M. Ikramullah, General Sir F. Tuker, Lt. Col. W. A. C. H. Dobson, Sardar K. M. Panikkar.

More recently, I have had the advantage of learning how capitalism works at its best from Sir Geoffrey Heyworth and of drawing on the great knowledge of the East of Mr. Roger Heyworth.

I owe a debt to Professor Mitrany for early encouragement, to Mr. A. S. B. Olver, of Chatham House, for reading the typescript; to Messrs. Lever Brothers & Unilever Limited, for giving me the leave in which to write and to the Institute of Pacific Relations both for sponsoring this book and for having, over many years, published the results of the specialised research on the East, without which a book as general as this one could not have been written at all.

For assistance in research I must express my gratitude to the Unilever Research Department, and especially to Mr. K. Lacey and Miss Wolf. Without their untiring efforts, the book could never have been completed in the time. And, like everybody who has worked at Chatham House, I have developed a great respect for the unfailing helpfulness of the Librarian and her charming staff.

My greatest debt of all, however, is to my contributor, Guy Wint. Only a misplaced modesty, indeed, has made him ban the appearance of his name as a co-author. From the original idea to the reading of the proof, the book is, in essence, as much his work as mine.

THE NEW ASIA

To the student of Asian affairs, the signs of ferment among the Asian peoples have long been discernible, indeed clear; but it is the course of world events since September, 1939—even more since the fateful Japanese attack on Pearl Harbour in December, 1941—that has brought the New Asia into being at a speed that few, even of the profoundest observers of international affairs, could have foreseen.

And, as a result of the speed of the rise of the New Asia, the urgency that it presents has become a matter of paramount importance, not only to the new governments that have arisen in the course of the last few years in that vast sector of the earth's surface, but equally to the West. The peoples of "Monsoon Asia", with whom this study is concerned, comprise nearly two-thirds of the population of the earth. For the first time for centuries they are conducting their own affairs with independence and a growing sense of the inescapable part they are called upon to play in the future of the world.

For independence, in an unsheltered world where every development in any single part of it has its immediate reflection elsewhere, is heady medicine for the peoples of Monsoon Asia; it brings new problems with it that superimpose themselves on the economic and social problems which their previous rulers, often alien, have been for so long trying to solve. Independence, as such, brings a spiritual release, but it does not achieve the economic and social millennium— these are determined by other forces, and the eternal problems of ignorance, poverty, usury and debt, land-hunger and the revival of cultural and community life remain.

For what we see in Asia to-day is not only a political revolution; it is an economic and social upsurge, a rising not solely against alien rule, but an upsurge against privilege and want; and it is upon their success against these age-old problems of Asia that the governments of New Asia will stand or fall.

Political thought and political practice in the New Asia are sharply divided, but the economic and social problems remain common to both; it is probable that Delhi and Peking, as representing the two main centres of Asian development and thought, will rank among the chief political centres of the world and provide the nuclei from which stability in this vast area can radiate. To the achievement of this stability, so important to the West, the West has much to contribute.

But there is much the West must understand, in order to make its contribution effective; advanced western political systems cannot suddenly be imposed on the peasant society of Asia—nor can the application of Western technology by itself create an immediate increase in the standard of living.

Capitalism is too frequently identified with "imperialism" or "exploitation"; it is indeed often regarded as a specifically Western invention, with the result that nationalism in Asia, in its turn, is too often regarded as specifically anti-European and anti-capitalist—the more so since their societies are traditionally accustomed to some form of collectivism, or in many cases to governmental enterprise.

Equally, however, none of the governments of the New Asia can afford to disdain any means whereby the lot of the common man, upon whose support they now depend, can be lightened.

Any study, therefore, that seeks to lay bare the root problems of Asia, their causes and historical growth and their relation to the West, in terms that both Western and Asian readers can readily appreciate, must be welcomed. I believe that this book is a valuable contribution to that purpose.

GEOFFREY HEYWORTH

London
9th November 1950

CONTENTS

CONTENTS

INTRODUCTION

It has been suggested that, when the history of this century is seen in perspective, the main events of the last decade will seem to be, not the war or the changes it has caused in Europe, but the happenings in Asia. In every major country of Asia there has been revolution. The classes which controlled their governments in 1939 are no longer in power. The non-Asiatic powers whose rule during the past century so profoundly affected Asiatic history have changed their aims and methods of operation, and their power in the continent has also undergone radical change.

The key areas of Asia are China, India and Japan. The outside powers are the U.S.S.R., America and Great Britain; France and Holland play a lesser part.

During the 19th century and until the outbreak of the last war, all affairs in Asia were dominated by the impact of Europe. Until two or three hundred years ago, Europe and Asia were roughly level in their degrees of technical advance, and nearly level in the efficiency of the organisation of the societies. Then, suddenly Europe forged ahead. In every political structure there is a power centre and there is a set of political ideas about how society should be organised. Because of industrialism, because of its application to warfare, and because of the new social structure which industrialism brought about, the West European countries became very much stronger than the Asiatic. A power disequilibrium between the two areas had developed—not unlike the economic disequilibrium to-day between the dollar and sterling areas.

As the West European countries, with their new power, pressed on the Asiatic countries, these one by one cracked, fell into disorder, and were annexed politically by the Western countries. The West did not set out on a deliberate tour of conquest. As a rule it went to the East to trade, and its blind weight broke the Eastern countries. The weakness of the Asian governments was not only military; their prevailing political ideas did not allow them to organise the type of society which could resist the western powers.

One eastern government was able, by borrowing both technique and political ideas from the West, to reorganise its society so quickly that it was able to appear to the West as a workable and viable state.

This was Japan. Until the turn of the century Japan would have been no match for the Western countries in a straight-out power struggle. But they did not try to overthrow it because it provided a political structure which was at least tough and strong enough to fit in to the system which the West had more or less involuntarily created in Asia. This is an interesting proof that Europe was not bent on conquest for its own sake. It was trying, more or less consciously, to create political systems which would stand the wear and tear of the industrial age.

As the result of this expansion by Western Europe, a chain of Western Empires was created across South Asia. Great Britain controlled India, Burma, Ceylon and Malaya; the power which it thus exercised in the Indian Ocean sheltered the smaller imperial systems of the Dutch in Indonesia and the French in Indo-China.

Not only did Europe sit on top of the political life of these countries. Their economies were shaped, not primarily by forces evolved within themselves, but by forces from Europe. In their cultural life they produced little that was original, at least until near the end of the period; their effort went either to defending the culture of the past from the new influences of the West, or to receiving, adapting, and trimming these influences. During this long period of western ascendency in South Asia, there was of course change, just as there was change in Europe itself, but the change was an evolutionary one within the peculiar and well-defined civilisation which this imposition of Western rule on Eastern lands had created.

The influence of Western Europe extended still further East. China, whose historic contribution in creating Asian civilisation was equal to that of India, lay for a time equally helpless against the West. China was not actually conquered by the Western countries. Why should they have wasted military effort when China was willing to yield up its ports to Western control? By this act China became, like the rest of Asia, a victim of "imperialism". And, like the other countries, it exposed its economic life and its cultural life to the transforming influence from the West. It was passive. It seemed broken.

Two other outside powers operated in Asia during this time, America and Russia. The American influence was the same as the European, but was its shadow. On the whole America retarded the West in spreading its actual political sway (though it annexed the Philippines) but reinforced it in its cultural and commercial sway.

The Russian influence was quite different. Russian policy everywhere on its borders has been described as "gradual aggression". Russian expansion was slower but more purposive than that of the West; it was exerted, not across the oceans but across its land frontiers which were contiguous with those of China. Russia aimed, far more consciously than the West, at building a permanent Empire. Russia pursued its Asian policy by fits and starts, usually in the periods after its expansion had been checked in Europe. It knew how to recede; but no Russian recession could be counted on as permanent.

Such, in broadest outline, was the picture of Asia as the result of the West European onset.

As the result of the last war, West European power has receded from Asia. American power, operating in ways quite different from European power in the past—operating often ineffectually—has intensified. Russian power has continued to operate, menacingly, unremittingly, and at the moment seems to enjoy more hope of glittering result than at any previous time in history.

The withdrawal of the West European power was sudden. But the system which it had supported had been archaic for some years before the war broke out. The heart of the system was British rule in India. During the century of British ascendency, "national" India had matured and was ready to take over the state machinery and operate it without British participation. The British had read the situation correctly, and were preparing their departure, not without pride in having prepared India for self-government. They expected, however, to move out by slow degrees, since this would ease the transition, both in Great Britain and India.

The trends of the age were accelerated by the war. The Indian national movement was galvanised into new gigantic heaves, which convinced the home government in London that a rapid and complete abdication was necessary if India was not to be permanently hostile. In fact it proved impossible for the British to extricate themselves from the Indian sub-continent without partitioning it in the process: hence the birth of Pakistan. In the rest of the "imperial" territories in South Asia, it was the attack by Japan which precipitated the emancipation. The western functionaries were forced out by the Japanese in Indonesia, Indo-China, Burma, and Malaya. The Japanese in their turn were forced out again; but in the upshot the local nationalist parties won so much power that the former rule could not be re-established, except in Malaya.

B

The British withdrew voluntarily and rapidly from Burma. The Dutch, after futile efforts to recover their position in Indonesia, yielded to the inevitable and abdicated. The French are still fighting the revolution in Indo-China, but have announced that they are doing so because the national party, led by Ho Chi-minh, is Communist, or near-Communist. To the Annamite government of Bao Dai (which is non-Communist), the French will hand over most of their authority.

To-day the Western European countries retain in South Asia certain trading bases, such as Hong Kong, and certain backward territories, such as Malaya; but there are no more Empires.

Their power has also been withdrawn from China. The foreign concessions in the ports were retroceded to the Chinese national government during the war.

The consequences of these changes are very great.

In the huge territories from Aden to New Guinea which were formerly under the control of the Western European powers, a new instability has been introduced. Until the Japanese attack in 1941 these countries had basked in a security unfamiliar in Asian history. They may not have enjoyed material well-being; but for decades they had been sheltered from the gales of the world and had had a stability and peace which were novel in their history. This was now ended. The power which had given the protection was withdrawn. In its place was left a number of new foci of power—in Delhi, in Karachi, in Rangoon, in Batavia. The question is whether these new centres of power can maintain tranquility in their countries, and whether they can be internationally so organised that the countries live at peace with one another.

In another way also there was change. The Asian countries, emancipating themselves from the political control by the West, had developed a set of ideas about the way in which they desired their societies to be reorganised. National emancipation thus brought in a period of rapid social and economic reform. But reforms of this kind may lead to political outbreaks of a very wild nature. The new governments in Asia are thus subject to pressures more profoundly revolutionary than any Europe has ever known; for in Asia all the revolutions, national, economic, and social, are taking place at once.

Two tasks therefore face the world. One is to organise international security in the vast area in Asia from which the sheltering power of the West European imperialists has been withdrawn. The other is to strengthen the governments of the succession states so that they do not break up from weakness or internal stresses.

The Asian countries will not try to perform these tasks in a closed Asian world. The great conflict of ideas in the world outside Asia intrudes into Asian politics. Asia is torn by the struggle. On the one side are governments and parties which desire to continue the process begun by the West European governments in Asia—namely, to build up the Asian countries as liberal democracies tinged with a moderate socialism. On the other side are governments and parties which see in Communism the only hope for overcoming the economic crisis in the Asian lands. The struggle between them is dominated by this economic crisis. It is a crisis of under-production, under-employment, stagnation, over-population and worsening poverty.

In the struggle between Communists and non-Communists, each side looks for support outside, to America or Russia. They do not want, except as a last resort, the backing of outside armies; that would run counter to their nationalist feeling; but they are ready to accept economic aid, technical aid, diplomatic aid.

Russia and America are willing to be invoked. Watching the conflict in Asia, they know that their own position in the world will be strengthened or weakened by the way the battle goes. So they seek ways, by discreet use of their influence, or by direct intervention where this is safe, to weight the chances in Asia of the governments or parties which seem their natural allies.

America's first experience in this cold war has not been happy. It began to wage it at the very moment when British power was withdrawn from India, and it had become clear, even to the non-expert, that Asian stability was undermined. (American opinion had tried in the previous years to hustle on the British withdrawal). The key of American policy was to make a Kuomintang-American alliance, or axis. Round this axis the non-Soviet countries of Asia would revolve. American observers on the spot always doubted the chances of this policy succeeding; the American White Paper analyses in great detail the story of its failure. Having backed the Kuomintang so completely, so disastrously, the Americans could not back the new regime; and now the Korean War has finally killed the hope of the China alliance. China has made its choice, and it is not America.

America now faces the problem whom to back next. One school in America would like to throw American power behind Japan.

Japan has an impressive history. During the war its aim was to substitute Japanese power for West European as the organising link in China and South Asia. That was the meaning of the Asian "Co-Prosperity Sphere". It was to be the old Western empires in Asia, run under new Japanese management and with new ideas. Japan's bid failed, but it so nearly succeeded that some Americans believe that Japan would still be the best ally of America in its campaign to exercise influence on Asian affairs. Certainly Japan, in spite of its present difficulties, cannot be written off. Its assets are still impressive. The unity of its people, their discipline and skill, the restless enterprise of its governing classes, and their readiness for everything new, may enable Japan, if given any chance at all, to play again a part in Asia. As an ally in actual war Japan would have obvious uses, though its exposed position would entail equally obvious obligations. But in peace, in a cold war, Japan is too special, too remote, to be the lynch-pin of the new Asia which is emerging. Despite the very real increase in economic equality and political freedom which has resulted from General MacArthur's reforms Japan's democracy is still too imbued with patterns of thought and behaviour special to Japan to be able to provide an inspiration for others.

The Key area is not Japan, but the Indian Sub-continent, and above all India itself. Alone among the major countries of Asia, India and Pakistan have a middle class whose whole mode of thought is democratic. Elections and parliaments and cabinets obedient to the will of the people are to them not something imposed from outside but something for which they have fought and in which they have grown up. The 1952 general elections in India, moreover, with their freedom and their orderliness, have shown that there at least these ideas have gone beyond the middle class to the people. Half the electorate voted, in politically more conscious Peninsular India the figure was two-thirds. In a country where authority at every level above the village has always before flowed from above, some 90 million people, a number equal to the whole population of Great Britain and France combined, exercised their new power, and discovered that it was power by defeating no fewer than 28 Ministers. In India power has passed to the people; and the people know it. It is a revolution, the more world-shaking for having been non-violent, and with which in our time only the Russian and perhaps the Chinese Revolutions can compare.

In the Indian Sub-continent, therefore, defenders of freedom do not have to be sought, or bought; they are there. India and Pakistan may be neutral in the cold war. They cannot be neutral about the freedom and democracy on which their States are based. They are not allies of the free world; they are part of it.

They are, however, poor, and for half a century now, except in a few favoured areas like Sind, they have been getting poorer, as population rose quicker than income. The stability which their governments have established after the strain of Partition is a miracle; but, in a world where so many countries are getting richer, they cannot hope permanently to remain stable, unless their people too can look forward to a better life. For this their governments need help, quite limited help, less than has been given to Japan or Chiang Kai Shek. If freedom and democracy are to be established in Asia, that help must be given, not with conditions attached, to buy friendship, for the friendship is already there; but freely and from a full heart, in discharge of the obligation which has been placed upon all of us to help a brother in distress.

The help given, to be effective, must be given without thought of reward. Yet, the bread cast upon the waters is sure in time to return. The Indian Sub-continent, and in particular India, dominate the whole area from Aden to New Guinea. If they go all Asia will go with them. If they can give their people food as well as freedom, factories as well as democracy, then Communism will be stopped on the Chinese borders more effectively than by many divisions. Asia is determined to be richer, even if it means liquidation on the Chinese scale, but it would prefer its bread without bullets. There could be no better investment for America than to help India and Pakistan in showing that liquidations are not essential to welfare.

This book is intended as a contribution to the study of the Asian background against which such a policy must be planned.

PART ONE

Chapter I

EASTERN VILLAGE AND WESTERN CITY

Mahatma Gandhi's saying that the heart of India is in its villages is equally true of the whole of Monsoon Asia. By contrast, the heart and civilisation of the West are in its cities—in Rome and Jerusalem and Paris. [1]

In Europe city life is very old and many European towns still stand on their ancient sites. The villages, however, are usually new. The reasons for this are largely technical. Europe is an area with many good harbours and navigable rivers, and in the days before railways, water transport was universally cheap and fairly easy. A fairly extensive commerce was thus made possible and towns naturally grew up at the main fords and river mouths. The villages, on the other hand, are new, sometimes because there was only enough population to clear the forests at a fairly late date, as in much of Eastern Europe; sometimes because implements were not adequate for the marshier lands until the early Middle Ages, as on most of England's clay; sometimes because it was not until nation states grew up at the end of the Middle Ages that it was safe to move the village site from the top of a defensible hill to the valley.

Western life has indeed never been organised on the basis of the village as a unit with an organic life of its own. It has always been the city which has aroused men's deepest loyalties. Jerusalem was eternally a bride to her lovers the Prophets. No conquest of Alexander's could move his tutor Aristotle from the belief that only as citizen of a polis could man express his whole nature. The Roman Empire itself was primarily a confederation of municipia, in which the idea that the will of the prince is the supreme law came in only in the time of decadence. The political ideal was always a small unit in which every free man could have his say in the assembly, every

[1] The West (or Europe) here, and in similar contexts throughout, is a cultural and not a geographical concept. It means the countries of city corporations, free association, and Biblical religion; it therefore includes Hollywood but excludes the Nazis.

[2] This is, of course, not a full explanation of a very complicated historical phenomenon. It is only an attempt to suggest some of the main causes.

man of note a share of office. Even in the fall of the Roman Empire the bishop in his cathedral town continued to provide an urban rallying point, so that not even the Vikings were able to reduce Europe utterly to self-sufficing villages, though it is true that in the 9th and 10th centuries the combination of Viking and Saracen attacks very nearly destroyed European trade completely.

The classical Western concept was of a group larger than the village and thus too large for everyone to know everyone else, yet small enough for everybody to be inspired by a common devotion. The Middle Ages gave a new twist to this concept. They invented the corporation, the group which was more than the sum of its members and yet less than the whole of the community. The corporation asked only for a part of the loyalty of its members and was thus able to come between the individual and the State without necessarily creating a conflict between the State and itself.

The possibility of belonging at the same time to several corporations taught men to look at themselves from many angles. For example, when Christianity was spreading in barbarous Europe, tribal loyalty was so all-embracing that whole tribes would become converted because their chief so decided. But the mediaeval European learned to see the Church as one organisation among others. To-day Western men see themselves as simultaneously members of many corporations with many loyalties. A modern Englishman is not only a member of the English nation, but usually also a member of a Church, a trade union, a co-operative society, a political party, perhaps even a football club. Each corporation is entitled to some of his loyalty, but none can claim to transcend the loyalty due to the others.

Men who thus organize themselves through a series of different groups can never be completely dependent on any one group, not even the State. The strength of freedom in Europe has always resided in the diversity of its institutions. Gleichschaltung is a totalitarian trick.

If the cities in the West engendered a free society, the villages produced a society of an entirely different kind, unorganised, servile, dead. There are exceptions, like the Swiss and the French communes of the 12th and 13th centuries, but they are very much exceptions.

It is true that in the early days of Greece and Rome, or in Anglo-Saxon England before the Danish invasion, the village was relatively free and self-governing. But in the eras which have created Western civilisation—the Hellenistic Age, the Roman Empire, the 13th and

14th centuries—the village had hardly any vitality of its own at all. The land of Italy under the later Republic was engrossed by large landlords who ran their latifundia not by the labour of peasants living in cottages but by slaves living in barracks. In England the Norman conquest enslaved Saxon and Danish peasant to alien lords. Through most of mediaeval Europe the peasant had to settle his disputes in the barons' court, to farm under his steward's directions. He could neither leave his land nor marry his daughter without his lord's permission. He could only defend himself beneath his lord's banner. His hovels were burnt and his womenfolk raped in private wars which brought his lord no more discomfort than occasional genteel imprisonment. Personal freedom for the European peasant even in Western Europe is often no older than the 15th century, while east of the Rhine it was the great achievement of the 19th century. All over Europe the village is not the unit either of administration or of tradition.

Personal freedom has, moreover, not, in the West, been accompanied by economic independence. The English villein had become a free man by 1500 and spent the next 300 years losing his land to enclosing landlords. The Junkers of Eastern Germany made their estates efficient by evicting their peasants. The small subsistence farmer so typical of Asia survives to-day nowhere in Western Europe.

Freedom in the West has come from the towns. The countryside was capable only of jacqueries. It was the towns which brought freedom to the village through the liberty they offered to the fleeing serf. The borough and its struggle for self-government is the basis of every European attempt to obtain freedom before the French revolution. Wherever the towns had no importance or lost their importance, as in Germany after the Thirty Years' War or in Russia by the 16th century, the result was totalitarianism.

The nature of these towns, and the ways by which they have changed Western society, are therefore of crucial importance, for it is they and their effect which historically differentiate Europe from Asia.

The key to the difference is that in Asia the cities were never long-lived, as in Europe. Their economic basis was not commerce. They were not the architects of civilisation. The only partial exception is China.

Outside China, to-day's great Eastern cities are new. Until the last century the cities of the orient were no more than the homes of the craftsmen, the armies and the courts of its kings, changing their site with every dynasty or royal whim. East of Persia, only Patna is a capital to-day and was a capital when Rome was young. Mohenjo-Daro is as old as Jerusalem, but it has been a ruin for two thousand years and more. The great towns of the orient to-day are ports and industrial centres which grew up in the Victorian Age. Bombay and Calcutta, Singapore and Hong Kong are contemporaries of Leeds and Manchester, Lahore and Harbin and Osaka of Detroit and Chicago. [1] Even the exceptions, like Tokyo, are themselves not very old. Tokyo has been important only since the beginning of the 17th century. Delhi was only raised from a provincial town by alien conquerors in the 13th century and depends to this day for its prosperity primarily upon university students and government officials, and not upon the economic activity of merchants and workers. Of the great past cities of the East there remain only tombs and temples; Angkor and Anuradhapura are dead as Xanadu.

The reason why China is a partial exception is itself interesting. Like Europe, China has great navigable rivers, though unlike Europe it has not got many. Such rivers as the Yellow River and the Yangtse do not dry up in the hot weather nor do they become raging torrents for very long in the rainy season. In consequence towns like Chungking, Nanking, An-Yang have histories as long as those of European towns, for they too are ports and forts and market centres performing an economic as well as an administrative function. But its economic importance has not been paralleled in China by the political fecundity of the European city, because from the beginning China was ruled by a central authority too strong for it to be possible for the towns to squeeze autonomy out of it and because the Chinese merchant ranked too low in the social scale for him to have the sort of ambition which makes merchants into Lord Mayors of London or Grand Pensionaries of Holland.

The East has known neither the City State nor corporations. Therefore there has been no such growth of diverse loyalties as in Europe. On the wall of one of the palaces of the Red Fort in Delhi there is written: "If there be heaven upon earth, 'tis this, 'tis this, 'tis this". But no poet has sung the praises of Delhi itself. No

[1]A few figures will illustrate this point admirably. Singapore was founded in 1819, had a population of just under $\frac{1}{4}$ million in 1900 and is to-day nearly a million; Hong Kong was founded in the mid 1840's, had a population of $\frac{3}{4}$ million in 1900 and is to-day over 2 million. Lahore rose from 90,000 in 1872 to 672,000 in 1941; Calcutta from a little over $\frac{1}{3}$ million in 1866 to over $4\frac{1}{2}$ million (for the whole urban area) in 1951.

Eastern city stirred the devotion of its inhabitants until such imitations of Western cities as Bombay and Shanghai came to arouse a Western-style loyalty among their citizens. No associations of citizens had arisen, for there were no citizens. There were only subjects and monarchs. Except among the Buddhists, there were no churches. The holy man was withdrawn from worldly affairs; where the religious faith engendered a social organisation, it was secular and associated with the State; the Muslim Caliph is the best example. The true Eastern city has always been a collection of civil servants, soldiers and artisans all dependent upon the whims of power. Nanking under Chiang Kai-Shek has provided an admirable modern instance.

It follows that the towns in Asia could provide no focus of resistance to arbitrary authority. The capacity to resist has, in Eastern society, resided in the village only. If the Eastern towns are all new, the villages are very old. The loess farmers of Shensi, the rice growers of Bihar, the shifting cultivator of mid-Sumatra, have been farming the same land in the same way for two or three or even four thousand years. The village could, if need be, function without any external authority at all. It alone had a political organisation separate from that of the State. The village elders, sometimes elected, sometimes nominated, sometimes attaining their position by an indefinable combination of age, inheritance and personal influence, performed all the tasks which in the West were the part of the lord of the manor and his bailiff. They settled disputes, dealt with petty crime, decided who would be allowed to reclaim the wasteland. In Java or Upper Burma, they reallotted holdings as families changed in size. They saw to the upkeep of the village temple or mosque, controlled the relations between the village craftsmen or servants and the other villagers. Often even the distribution of taxes among the households of the village was left to them. It was only in degenerate days—for instance, the last fifty years of Maratha rule in the Deccan—that tax-assessment was left, not to the village council, but to the village headman alone. Even then, the State itself did not dare to do the assessing directly through its own officers.

In the old style village the State hardly interfered at all. It usually provided no regular civil courts, though the district officer might act as arbitrator in a case of particular difficulty or when one party had bought his interference. It left to village authority such offences as cattle trespass, boundary disputes and faction fights, which constitute almost the whole of village crime. The village could never rely on the State more than partially, even for defence. Though it was the shining merit of a good King that in his days a woman with a baby in her arms could travel with a bag of gold and without escort from end to end of the Kingdom, such Kings did not often happen. The village had to be ever prepared to defend itself against bandits, raiders and unpaid troops. Chinese villages have been building walls and buying off outlaws—and officials—as corporate units within the last thirty years. The State indeed was important to the Eastern villager not so much for its preservation of law and order, which was arbitrary and uncertain, but for its economic functions, its water control through dykes and irrigation and wells.

The State normally collected its taxes on the principle of what the traffic would bear. If it failed in its duty of protection, this did not mean that the taxes became any less. The Eastern State, in so many ways so inefficient, was always an excellent tax collector. Its refusal to leave any surpluses to fructify in private hands was responsible for the lack of capital which has over the centuries kept Eastern productivity so low.

The Eastern village was left to run itself; but this did not make its life idyllic. Village elders can be as oppressive, as obscurantist, and as stupid as any official. The Government in its hunt for revenue used such methods as giving taxpayers the alternative between meeting an exorbitant demand or having a troop of horsemen billeted on them. In the village, however, public opinion necessarily had great force, if only through its embodiment in custom. The elders had reached their position by conforming, not by having new ideas. They were the solidest Confucians, the most pious Muslims. They were not likely in their old age to go in for new-fangled innovations, or to make life difficult for themselves with their neighbours by flying in the face of village opinion. A criminal knew what severity he could expect, a creditor knew how much severity he could apply, a householder in trouble knew in what ways his neighbours would, and in what ways they would not help. And beneath the village organisation there were minor self-governing bodies, such as caste or clan councils, who decided what aid was due from a man to a poor relation or what standard of work a craftsman must keep up or be fined.

The village world was, moreover, a free world. There was untouchability but no serfdom; slavery was rare outside the houses of the great. There were of course exceptions. The Malay chief, or, in India, the Rajput noble could and did indulge in extremes of cruelty to their peasants, stealing their wives, torturing them, killing them, with no hope of redress for the victim; the Japanese samurai was entitled to cut down without further ado any peasant whose attitude he found insufficiently respectful. But these were abuses of power, not of property, the acts of a lord, not of an owner.

From these basic differences between East and West in the relation of town and country proceed many of the characteristics of the two different types of civilisation.

In Europe, what gave the cities their importance was their economic life, not their political position. It was the city of London, with its trade, which absorbed Westminster, not Westminster which absorbed London. For this economic importance, moreover, cities have been indebted but little to the sweat of a dominated peasantry. The churches of Venice or Florence were not built out of peasant land revenues.[1] The cities of mediaeval and Renaissance Italy lived by the silk they made, the spices they traded, the banking and insurance services they furnished. Holland and the Hansa grew great on herrings.

In Asia, always with the partial exception of China, cities grew rich because their lords were powerful. In Europe cities became powerful because their lords were poor. The combination of their wealth and the lords' poverty enabled them to buy their freedom. Thus they discovered what Asia has been discovering only in our own day, that wealth comes from abandoning self-sufficiency, accepting whole-heartedly the division of labour and concentrating production in those places which have the greatest natural advantages.

This specialisation produced the great wool towns of Flanders, the banking of Florence, the cotton manufacturing of Manchester. From it has developed the wealth which has created the capital which has transformed the world. But before this capital could perform its life-giving miracle, the towns had to fulfil a second function. It was not enough for them to provide the opportunities for money to be made, they had also to give the atmosphere of security in which the men would be willing to save. The merchant and craftsman could put by their money and invest in enterprises whose return would be slow because they were organised in boroughs and protected from the greed of their needy lords by their

[1]It is not suggested that the riches of Venice were therefore more moral than those of Eastern cities. Much of Venice's wealth came from trading in slaves and from looting the Empire of Byzantium.

walls as well as by their charters. They knew that their taxes would be limited to those they were prepared to vote for in the town council and could not be increased merely because their monarch had another daughter to marry. Contrast this with the situation in Asia. The preference of the Eastern merchant for gold and silver, which he could hoard, over productive investment is not a result of any peculiarity of the Oriental mind. It is the natural reaction of every sensible businessman to the knowledge that any apparent possession of wealth would bring down upon him a tax-collector eager to squeeze out every collectable penny. In the East there was the feeling also that it was morally wrong for merchants, who ranked in public esteem below peasant, priest and warrior, to possess any large sums of money. [1]

It was the capital created by the commerce and craftsmanship of Western towns which has made possible the Industrial Revolution, and the increasingly expensive achievements of scientific research. The lack of security for capital in Asia explains the lack of capital available for investment and that in turn explains Asia's technical backwardness. That is the great economic consequence of the difference in the status of the towns in Europe and in Asia, but there is also a spiritual consequence more profound though less obvious.

In the Western town all men started equal, at least in the early centuries. There was no aristocracy of birth resting upon military prowess and monopolistic offices as there was in the countryside. Any man, if he was successful in his business and respected by his fellow citizens, could aspire to anything. Wool merchants, bankers, goldsmiths, sons and grandsons of labourers, who owed nothing to clan feeling or force of arms, could be Lord Mayors, commanders of militias, exacting creditors of the Crown itself. Thus trade and industry established the social value of their functions, and thus were created the great commercial dynasties.

But in Asia until the most recent time, real opportunity did not exist. There is no Asian equivalent for the Fuggers, Counts of the Empire, the Medici, Grand Dukes of Tuscany. In Asia government was carried on by the appointees of the monarch or the lord. In

---

[1]One may compare the position in France or Italy in 1946 when the capitalist did not know what would happen to his currency, how much he would be assessed for war profits or whether he would not be nationalised out of hand. He bought dollars where the Eastern merchant had customarily bought gold. But the eagerness to hoard, the refusal to invest was the same. And Chinese merchants have shown in recent years that the East too can appreciate the safety of a draft on New York as against a gold ingot under the floor.

China they were scholars, in Japan soldiers, in the Malay lands or in the Rajput states of India they were the local nobility. Nowhere were they merchants, nowhere did they fail to look on businessmen with disdainful dislike.

In the Eastern towns, the lower classes were beggars, hangers on, soldiers, hewers of wood and drawers of water for the court and the rich. The artisans and skilled craftsmen were too few and too dependent upon noble patronage to have any aspirations to self-government or to influence.[1] But the Western towns both required a much larger proportion of skilled men to man their industries and were small enough for these skilled men to be able to attain influence and authority. There was no royal army, as in the East, to make rioting useless. No royal magistrate held power by delegation, nor election. The only organised force was a city militia and the larger part of this was formed by the lower class itself. Sometimes the artisans could hope for election to the city council. Thus the Western town workman was conscious of his power to influence and change the political authority under which he lived. There could hardly be a greater contrast than with the Western peasant, who accepted the vagaries of his rulers with the same resignation as he accepted the weather.

In the West city and country benefited each other by mutual exchange. The Western city bought its food and its raw materials by the sale of its products, its cloth or herrings or imported furs. No such compulsion weighed on Eastern towns for they could obtain their needs from taxes and had no need to trade. The Chinese Grand Canal was first built to enable tribute rice to be brought to the capital. The Western village was steadily drawn into a wider economy which embraced first the whole nation (by 1600) and then the whole world (by 1850).

The consequence was that in the West the countryman was always in touch with the larger world, in Asia he was not. In the West the countryman was ready to migrate to the towns or to emigrate overseas. He could adapt himself to the changing modes of life brought in by the Industrial Revolution. In Asia the peasant could conceive no other way of life than the agricultural. It was bound up with his reverence for his ancestors, his hopes for his descendents, and his faith in his gods. He did not think of it, as an American

[1]They were often quite tightly organised under the caste in India or into guilds in China, but their organisations aspired only to the control of their own members, not to authority over the community as a whole.

share-cropper does, as just another, and rather unsatisfactory, way of earning a living. Only the fairest promises of a recruiting agent or the direst poverty have been able even in the quite recent past to move him from his land to factory or plantation, however little land he might still have and however deep in debt he might be. And so the towns and industries of Asia have remained unbuilt until our own day, and the wide open spaces overseas have been filled with Europeans. Australia and New Zealand so much nearer to Asia than to Europe are to-day European lands, because the need of the Western city for trade produced a willingness to venture for which there is nothing comparable in Asian society.[1]

The final and most important consequence of European urban life was the growth of the middle classes. This is a purely European phenomenon. Perhaps the most fateful thing about the middle class was the type of mind which it engendered. This mind was practical. Its interest was in physics, not metaphysics, economics not theology, law not jurisprudence. This type of mind is the result of the peculiar conditions of urban life. In a countryside there are usually only two classes, the landed and the landless, the one in favour of the status quo, the other either submissive or revolutionary. But in the towns there is room for an infinite gradation. It is this play of levels which has given the Western city-dweller, and through him all Western society, his flexibility and curiosity of mind, his admiration for skill and appreciation of success, the weight he gives to tradition and the readiness with which he innovates.

This urban class, these urban traits and urban professions, have been lacking in Asia. The West has brought them to her. It is no accident that the Renaissance began in Florence and Venice, the Reformation in Geneva and Wittenberg, that Amsterdam led 17th-century science or Shakespeare wrote for a London audience, while the scholars of the East have so often been Confucian literati retired to their village homes, its theologians so often Brahmin monks in their remote monasteries, its poets writers of epics that every village schoolboy knows.

The Asian village has been free; the European town has been

[1]There were occasional periods when it appeared as if a similar willingness to venture might develop amongst Asian merchants also. Indian merchants and explorers civilised and traded with all S.E. Asia for a time and some Chinese voyages extended as far as the coast of Africa. But the Muslim conquest and the decline of Chola power destroyed India's S.E. Asian trade and hostility of the later Mings to all Chinese overseas connections greatly curbed the adventurousness of the Chinese merchants.

enterprising. From this enterprise have come, over the last few centuries, the freedom of thought, the eagerness for knowledge, the capacity to save and to invest which have first transformed Europe and are now transforming the world.

Chapter II

THE PEASANT WORLD OF ASIA

Asia to-day is still a predominantly rural continent, as it has been for many centuries. The great apparent Westernisation of Asia in the last century has but scratched the surface—though a relatively small part, notably Japan, has been more profoundly affected.

Conditions vary from country to country in Asia, but there is a certain uniformity in its peasant civilisation. To grasp what is happening in Asia to-day, it is necessary to bear in mind the broad details of this rural society. The aim of this chapter is to paint its picture, though only in the most general terms.

Three-quarters of the population of Asia is to-day still rural and the percentage is dropping only very slowly (Table 1).[1] The percentage of the population directly dependent on agriculture (Table 2) has even in some places increased with the decay of the old handicrafts.[2] The farmer dominates society. Men who are not farmers are mostly providers of services to farmers, not themselves producers. They are government officials or lawyers, not factory hands or metallurgists.[3] Japan alone has followed in the footsteps of the West sufficiently to reduce the percentage of her people engaged in agriculture below half.[4] This is a change comparable with that in France which was five-sixths rural in 1819 and is rather under half rural to-day.

Asia is not merely predominantly agricultural, it is specifically peasant. The unit of farming is tiny. The farmer's aim is to produce from his own land enough to keep his family. Their food almost always comes from the holding; even to-day the clothes are quite often made from home grown cotton; the houses are built from local bamboos or local mud; the fuel is dung cakes of the cattle or the firewood of the waste. Sales of produce, though they may

[1]In this, and certain other chapters, tables will be found at the end.

[2]E.g. Census of 1911 in India showed $5\frac{1}{2}\%$ of the population engaged in industry. This had dwindled to 4% by 1941.

[3]India's 350 million people include only two and a half million factory workers.

[4]The reduction is from 78% in 1873 to 44% in 1937.

sometimes be considerable, are marginal. The farmer sells only when he needs money to pay his rent or his taxes or the money-lender's instalment, or to buy the goods the village cannot produce—salt and iron and, increasingly, factory made cloth.[1]

Nowhere in Asia is there anything comparable with the 200–400 acre farm business of Canada, mass-producing wheat for a world market, or the heavily capitalised tenant farms of England organised for maximum yields of milk or barley for town schools and town brewers.

The reason for the smallness of holdings (Table 4) is not only the over-population, though that is often very important. It is also that Asia is a cereal and not a livestock area and that lack of capital and mechanical ingenuity has kept Asian implements so primitive. With such implements the area that can be managed by one family is strictly limited. For rice, outside labour has to be employed at transplanting and harvest—even on a three-acre farm. For wheat or millet, oil seeds or cotton, the size of farm is normally governed by the area which can be ploughed by one pair of bullocks.[2]

These technical limitations have meant that even where land was available, the unit of cultivation has remained small. It was often as low as $2\frac{1}{2}$ acres even in the under-populated Sind of the 1890s.

Tiny holdings, lack of livestock, independence of the market and religious principle, combined to make the life of the peasant of most of Asia purely vegetable, made up of rice and wheat meals, bamboo houses and dishes. Many people do not eat meat or fish or eggs at all. Hindus and Buddhists have a religious objection to taking life and even those who have no such religious taboo can very rarely afford any but cereal foods. The Chinese loves pork but most families can only kill one pig a year. Fish is unprocurable except on the sea coast and by the great rivers. Even milk is not drunk over most of the area, either because, as in China, the peasant does not like it, or because, as in India, his cattle belong to draught breeds whose cows give but little. Everywhere the great crop is grain (Table 5). In Indo-China rice is actually 86% of everything that is grown. Grass,

[1]In comparatively untouched areas like the Lao country of N.E. Thailand, such sales will not exceed one-fifth of the crop. In a fully commercialised area like Lower Burma they may reach three-quarters. A fair average might be one-third.

[2]This varies from 7 acres up to perhaps 20 according to conditions. Sometimes even these crops are worked by hand, e.g. barley in Japan, and then it is impossible for one family to manage more than 7 or 8 acres.

so important in Europe, is almost unknown in Asia.[1] So the beasts must pick up their living as best they can on the stubble and dyke edges, in the woods and commons; to grow food specially for them would use land which is needed for their masters' food. So great is the competition for land in Tongking or South China that men do with a hoe what animals could do more easily with a plough, because the food of a labourer takes less field space than that of a buffalo.

Centuries of subsistence farming have made the peasant reluctant to depend for his daily bread on anyone but himself. Normally he would only devote his commercial crops to the small areas which are left after his needs for food have been satisfied. Table 5 shows how tiny as a result is the proportion of the land growing commercial crops in almost all these countries. It is rare for either a higher monetary return or the possibility of using labour more intensively to condemn the peasant to complete dependence on the market.[2] The large native output of rubber in Borneo and Sumatra is possible only because rubber there uses land and labour not immediately required for food.[3]

Coal and steel consumption are the index of economic modernisation. In the vegetable and self-sufficing civilisation of Asia, there is little room for either (Table 6). No peasant in Asia has a coal fire or gas oven. Only in Japan and in Malabar has electricity been taken to the farm. Cart-axles and ploughs are still made of wood and only the ploughshare and the sickle-blade are steel. The wooden wedge and the bamboo tie are still more usual than the iron nail.

Peasant self-sufficiency at its best gives everybody something, but it never gives anybody very much. In India in 1872 only one cultivator in ten was totally landless. In Japan or North China even to-day, the mere agricultural labourer is very much the exception.[4] But on the other hand, large farms are almost unknown. To own 140 acres, the average size farm in America, makes an Indian or a

[1] In France one-third of the area is under grass: in Great Britain normally over one-half: in Japan it is one-thirtieth and in India less still.

[2] Jute requires 1000 people to the square mile, mulberry trees will keep four peasant families to every three acres.

[3] These are still largely lands of shifting cultivation and rubber can be grown on the land which is temporarily fallow recovering its fertility. Also there is no interference with rice growing since the rubber can be tapped at the time when there is nothing to do in the rice fields.

[4] In Japan there are only 540,000 labourers out of an agricultural manpower of 17,360,000.

Chinese a gentleman living on his rents. In all Tongking only 250 owners out of 900,000 have over 90 acres. In Japan, only one owner in 100 has as much as 25 acres. [1]

The equality in Asia is, however, an equality in poverty. Agriculture everywhere is a seasonal occupation with days when there is nothing to do except watch the crops and the animals grow. But in Western mixed farms, with its superimposition of the rhythm of animal life upon that of the ripening of the grain, leisure has been reduced to a minimum. In Asia, with its overwhelmingly cereal farming, there are months of utter idleness, with nothing to do but go to a wedding, or lie on a string bed and smoke, or revive one's local faction-fights.

Take for example the small rice-grower in Tongking. He needs for every acre 13 days for tilling, dressing and manuring, 18 for preparing the seed-bed, transplanting and irrigating, 20 for cleaning, manuring and stirring the water, 16 for harvesting, ridging, drying and winnowing, 10 for finally husking the rice. The total for an acre is only 77 days of which perhaps 20 will be done by the women-folk; and 60% of the peasants of Tongking have no more than one acre. This is particularly low, but everywhere in Asia the figures show that the farmer has five or six or more months of enforced idleness. The average Javanese holding, for instance, needs only some 65 days man's labour a year. The Korean farmer works only 100 days; the Japanese only 140. Even in the Bombay Deccan where holdings are comparatively large, five months of idleness is normal.

This does not mean that the peasant is lazy. The high proportion of the work done by women is not the result of any Oriental sense of male superiority. It is simply that though at certain times, for example between harvesting one crop and ploughing for the next, nothing needs to be done, at other times, notably at harvest, every pair of hands has to be pressed into work. To manage one acre of tobacco requires a family of four and then outside assistance will be needed for the trenching. But there will still be half the year when the family have nothing to do.

The extreme smallness of the area which the Eastern peasant can cultivate unaided is partly the result of the extreme simplicity of his implements. This simplicity has made many hands necessary to work a small area and thus has helped to produce a growth of population which has in turn, by making labour the cheapest of all the factors

[1]One may compare France, the most peasant land in Western Europe, where sixteen properties in every hundred were over 25 acres in 1908.

of production, prevented any such improvement in the technical equipment used, as has happened in the West. In parts of India when millet is harvested, each stem is pulled separately from the ground: in Europe the scythe has been used for centuries. In Japan the green-fly are picked off the tobacco one by one with a blob of bird lime on the end of a stick: in Europe the farmer would rather let the greenfly live. And one combine-harvester can do the work of a whole Chinese village.

The enforced idleness of the Eastern peasant has for him many compensations. It places a very high value both on leisure and on being his own master. He is far more inclined to look upon days without work as holidays than as unemployment. And he finds no difficulty in filling the days when he does no work to his own complete satisfaction. There are always births, deaths and marriages to be celebrated. In India one not only invites one's relations to a wedding, one sends them the fare money with which to come. There are religious festivals to be attended, pilgrimages to be performed, village amusements to take part in. The Burmese has his regattas, the Hindu his caste-dinners, the Japanese his trip to Fujiyama. There are village politics, perhaps even a little litigation over a boundary or an insult. In the old days, and to some extent still today, there were the village crafts. The women spin and weave, the men go to the jungle to hunt or collect charcoal. It is on the whole a life which has, over the centuries, made the peasant happy, for though he can work himself painstakingly if he has to, he is not enough of a Victorian to consider work a moral virtue. His general attitude to the relative values of work and leisure is nicely summed up in the story of the Chinese boy who offered to give up opium-smoking for a day to save the money to pay a labourer to take his place at the harvest.

A society so narrow and contented has a natural resistance to change and this resistance has been greatly reinforced by the system of inheritance. In England the custom of primogeniture drove younger sons to make their fortune in the city or the Colonies. In Asia the rule is to divide property between all the sons, though for a generation or two the heirs may farm together as a joint family. This explains why, in healthy periods of society, lawlessness is rare in Asia. It explains also why the large estates which have, on occasion, been built up by fortunate officials or successful land-grabbers are so soon fragmented. The landlord in Asia does not normally own a lot of property. Except for the British created Indian zemindars, there is no equivalent of the great feudal estates of Europe. In Yunnan a man lets out his land to tenants if he has more than 5 acres. In the United Provinces of India, a Rajput will let if he has only 2. For in Yunnan to wear a blue gown and not to work is a sign of distinction, and a Rajput is dishonoured if he touches a plough.

The very smallness of the Asian landlord makes him more, not less, grasping than were the great nobles of Europe. In Europe the incomes of the great landowners were too large to make oppression a necessity. Their education was sufficiently good to give them ideas of duty to their tenants, at least in England. The Eastern landlord, on the contrary, is simply an investor who wants a maximum return. This is true whether he is a retired peasant or a Shanghai stockbroker who thinks land safer than Chinese Government loans.

The equal rights of all heirs explains also the extreme lack of mobility in oriental society. The sons of the rich and of the ruined move, the rest stay in the village, and division amongst heirs leaves few who are either rich or ruined. Those few may go to the towns or to the plantations, but the migration is too small to make any impact upon the great mass which stays behind. There has been no movement of population in Asia which has changed the face of a whole area in the way that Ireland was changed by immigration to America in the 19th century. A few of the most surplus of the poor go off to find work elsewhere, a few of the best educated of the rich become professional men or officials in the cities. The peasant pioneers quite effectively, as he has shown in Lower Burma and in Manchuria, but he does so because he is poor and not because he regards adventure as a good in itself. That is why it is Europe which has inherited the earth.

Asia has paid for the cheerful tenant and social balance of small peasant agriculture in missed opportunities as well as in low productivity.

TABLE 1

PERCENTAGES OF POPULATION, RURAL AND URBAN

Country			1910 (or thereabouts)		1930 (or thereabouts)	
			Rural	Urban	Rural	Urban
British Malaya	..	..	75	25	70.5	29.5
Indo-China	..	..			90–95	5–10
Japan	..	..	50.4	49.6	35.5	64.5 (1935)

PERCENTAGES OF POPULATION, RURAL AND URBAN—*contd.*

Country				1910 (or thereabouts) Rural	Urban	1930 (or thereabouts) Rural	Urban
Korea	..	..	..			88.3[*]	11.7 (1936)
Indonesia	..	..	..			92.5	7.5
Manchuria	..	..	..			80	20 (1935)
Philippines		..	..			90	10
Thailand	..	..	..	90.65	9.35	89	11
CONTRAST							
U.S.A.	..	..	..	54.2	45.8	43.8	56.2
Australia	..	..	..	51.3	48.7	35.9	63.8

N.B—The change has in many European countries been comparatively modern. In 1880 one can still find percentages comparable with those of Asia, 84% in Sweden or Canada, 80% in Austria, 70% in Germany. The failure to transform has been in the last 80 years.

Sources: Karl J. Pelzer, *An Economic Survey of the Pacific Area,* Institute of Pacific Relations, New York, 1941, pp. 13, 15.

S. Chandrasekhar, *India's Population,* New York, 1946, p. 30.

TABLE 2

PERCENTAGE OF POPULATION DIRECTLY ENGAGED IN AGRICULTURE

Country	Percentage engaged in agriculture, forestry and fishing c. 1940	Percentage engaged in trade and industry and mining c. 1940
India	67	16½
Burma	70	20
Thailand	83	9
Japan	44	30
China	70–75	10–15
Indonesia	70	15
Indo-China ..	71	6
Malaya	61	23
Ceylon	65	23
Philippines , ..	76	8
Korea	77	11
CONTRAST		
Australia	19	40
Great Britain ..	6	56
France	35	29

Sources: Pelzer, op. cit. p. 15.

Indian and Burmese Census Returns.

Report II, Preparatory Asiatic Regional Conference of the I.L.O., New Delhi, 1947, Chapter I.

TABLE 3

NUMBERS ENGAGED IN FACTORIES WORKED BY POWER

Country						c. 1900	c. 1940
India ..	..	..	..	..	..	444,000*	2,487,000
Burma	..	..	..	..	..	31,000	90,000
Japan	..	..	..	..	..	422,000	2,937,000
China	..	..	..	..	..	Negligible	1,204,000†
Ceylon	..	..	..	..	..	35,000	398,000
Indonesia	..	..	..	..	..	Small	173,000
Indo-China		..	..	..	..	12,000	120.000
Philippines		..	..	..	..	35,000	398,000

*British India only.
†Official estimate for 1930 in 29 cities.

Sources: *Large Industrial Establishments in India* (Indian Statistical Abstracts),
1942.
J. L. Christian, *Modern Burma,* Berkeley, Calif., 1942.
G. C. Allen, *Short Economic History of Japan,* London, 1948.
C. Robequain, *The Economic Development of French Indo-China,*
London, 1944.
Philippines Census and Statistical Year Book.
N.B.—The figures are not exactly comparable e.g. the Indian figures are
for factories with more than 20 employees, the Japanese for those with
more than 5.

TABLE 4

AVERAGE SIZE OF AGRICULTURAL HOLDINGS

Country	Average Size of holding (in acres)
Korea	$3\frac{3}{4}$
Cambodia	$2\frac{1}{2}$
Burma	10
Java	$2\frac{1}{4}$
All China	5
Kwantung and Kwangai	Under 2
Fukien, Chekiang, Kiangsi	2
Japan	$2\frac{3}{4}$
Manchuria	7*
Tonkin	$2\frac{3}{4}$
Cochin-China	$22\frac{1}{2}$†
East China	$1\frac{1}{2}$
Yunnan Plain	1
Central Siam	10
S. and N.E. Siam	4
India	5
United Provinces	$3\frac{1}{2}$
Madras	$4\frac{1}{2}$
Bengal, Bihar, Orissa, Assam	3
Bombay	12
CONTRAST	
Denmark	40
France	20
U.S.A.	145
Rumania	16
Poland	$14\frac{3}{4}$

*This figure may seem surprising low. It is explained by the smallness of the holdings in the old settled areas in Liaoning.

†Cochin-China is untypical because there, alone an Asia, there are no large rice-growing estates.

Sources: Report IV, Preparatory Asiatic Regional Conference of the I.L.O., New Delhi, 1947.

TABLE 5

CROPS IN 1935 IN MILLION ACRES

Country	Total crop area	Area under rice	Area under wheat, millet, barley, maize	Area under commercial crops (oilseeds, jute, cotton, tobacco tea)
British-India ..	226	80	77	37
N.E. India ..	42	$32\frac{1}{2}$	2	5
Japan	15	$7\frac{1}{2}$	4	$\frac{3}{4}$
S. China ..	111	$46\frac{1}{2}$	40	$8\frac{1}{2}$
Burma	$18\frac{1}{2}$	$12\frac{1}{2}$	$1\frac{1}{2}$	3
Java and Madura	21	$9\frac{1}{2}$	$5\frac{1}{2}$	$1\frac{1}{4}$
France	18	–	$3\frac{3}{4}$*	$\frac{1}{2}$

*Wheat only.

Source: V. D. Wickizer and M. K. Bennett, *The Rice Economy of Monsoon Asia,* Stanford, Calif., 1941.

Statistical Abstract from British India, 1929/30 to 1938/9, seventy-first number, London, 1942.

TABLE 6

CONSUMPTION OF COAL AND STEEL, 1938

Country	Coal	Steel
	In thousands of tons	
India	27,020	1,200
Japan	44,890	7,362*
China Proper	4,700	166
Burma	420	45
British Malaya	500	
French Indo China	500 (1936)	
Korea	3,000 (1936)	Under 100
France	67,500	4,416

*Including Manchuria 484,000 tons and Korea 100,000 of which part came to Japan.

Sources: Statistical Year Book of the World Power Conference, No. 4, 1936/46, London, 1948.

British Iron and Steel Federation Statistical Abstract, Vol. II.

India Statistical Abstract.

Chapter III

THE STANDARD OF LIFE

The productivity of peasant Asia with its tiny holdings and primitive equipment cannot but be low. Two or three acres do not leave much over after the family has been fed and clothed to provide a surplus with which to pay the taxes and make the savings which are required for social services or industrial development. And the position is made worse because over most of Asia techniques are so primitive that yields are half or less than half those obtainable by intensive farming in Western Europe or Japan (see Table 7).

The high Japanese yields in particular are in sharp contrast to those obtained in the other countries. They are partly the result of the ancient practice of using nightsoil and of treating every plant with individual care—practices which account also for Chinese yields being rather higher than those of the remaining countries in the list. But they are mainly the result of the application of modern artificial fertiliser and modern agricultural research to Japanese fields on a scale which has not even been contemplated in the rest of Asia. The difference between, say, Japanese and Indian out-turns is the difference between an agriculture which has been transformed by the impact of Western science and one which continues unchanged in the old peasant ways.

Not even a Japanese yield, however, on a holding of Asian size can give a standard of life in any way comparable with that of the modern West, though it does not compare too badly with that of the Western peasant in the days before the Industrial Revolution. The real income per occupied person of the agricultural population does not exceed 150 International Units anywhere in Asia.[1] It must again be emphasized that this is not a particularly Eastern poverty. The figure for agriculture for England in 1800 is 121; for Sweden in 1870—138; for Italy in 1901—183. But that is no consolation for the Asian patriot who compares his standard of life not with the West of 50 or 100 years ago, but with the West of to-day. A century and a half of scientific discovery and mechanical develop-

[1] One I.U. equals the purchasing power of one U.S. dollar in 1925-34.

ment has raised the standard of life in a way previously unimaginable. The average income in Switzerland in 1929 was 1147: in Australian agriculture in 1935-6 it was 1408. Closer at home in Asia itself there is Japanese industry to point the moral that it had 959 International Units per head as early as 1934.[1]

Translated into monetary terms, these figures mean that each Indian rural dweller had £3 15s. per year in the early thirties, each Chinese about £4,[2] each Javanese only about £3, each Filipino farm family £13 per year in 1938. These estimates give full credit for the value of the house and for food produced on the farm.

These figures are most intelligible if translated into terms of actual goods. An example may be taken of an Indian rice farmer with 3 acres. This is the average in N.E. India. The farmer's crop in a normal year will be about 3,500 lbs. He probably has a wife, two children and an old mother—families in Monsoon Asia average from four to five people. The average rice consumption in India in 1938 was 14½ ozs. per day. This would represent 1,600 calories for the adults and 1,200 for the children. (In England under rationing it is 2990). Rice consumed in a year would thus be about 1,650 lbs. 120 lbs. is required for seed. That leaves about 1,730 lbs. If the farmer has a landlord, he will take the usual half-crop and pay the taxes. Then nothing will be left whatever to the tenant. He needs a margin to buy clothes or salt or kerosene, purchase a new bullock or pay for his daughter's marriage. He can obtain this only by cutting the already low food consumption of the family or going into debt. Tenancy, however, is a relatively new and still very patchy evil in Monsoon Asia. We may therefore assume here that the farmer has the 1,730 lbs. available to sell. He might, at to-day's high prices, get Rs. 20 per maund of 82 lbs; for 19 maunds this is Rs. 380. His land revenue is probably Rs. 30. He is therefore left with Rs. 350 (not quite £30). Indian prices are to-day no lower than British, so £30 a year is roughly the equivalent of the income of a British working-class family with only 10/- a week left after paying rent and food. In fact, the Indian farmer is in a rather less favourable position, for every five or six years the Indian farmer will have to

[1]Colin Clark, *The Conditions of Economic Progress*, London, 1940.
[2]Ta-chung Liu from whom this figure is taken, points out that if one allows for the difference in structure between Chinese and American society, it would be about £9 in American terms. Similar adjustments need to be made in the other cases.

buy a new bullock, which may cost £40. The marriage of a daughter
may cost him £50.

To sum up, at to-day's prices, and assuming that the farmer is not
in debt and has no rent to pay (as was usual in the old days, and, with
the abolition of zemindari, will again be true for perhaps two-
thirds of the land), the farmer is about as well off as an English
agricultural labourer before the war, perhaps even slightly better off.
At pre-war prices, which were as unfavourable to him as to-day's
are favourable, his 19 maunds would have fetched only Rs. 62
(1934) and after paying his land revenue, even assuming some
remission for low prices, he would have had only about £3 left.
A tin of kerosene would have cost him 4/-, a sari for his wife perhaps
10/-, a pound of sugar or a box of matches 1d. or so. He was thus
not at all well off. If both his bullocks were to die at once he would
be driven into debt. But at least each member of the family got a
garment a year. There could occasionally be some light in the hut.
Even a visit to the 4d. seats at the cinema two or three times a year
would not be impossible.

Such men as the 3-acre rice farmer in India rank in status with a
London bus driver or a miner at the coal face, and 4 or 5 acres would
rank him with a maintenance electrician or a head clerk. He lives the
life he loves in a countryside that has been familiar to him for
generations. He can marry a daughter or bury a mother (in China the
more important of the two) without getting into more debt than he
can hope to pay off in a year or two. He can send his son to the high
school in the nearest town, and hope to see him one day a clerk or a
lawyer or even a sub-inspector of police. When he grows old, he
can hope to make his peace with God by pilgrimage to Benares, perhaps even to Mecca. In youth he can face a fine of 40/- and £5 costs
for assault and battery in a clan faction fight without being ruined.
His sons and daughters are sought in marriage, his opinion is sought
in disputes. It is he whom the Government official tries to persuade
to use a new seed or a new fertiliser, he who is elected to the committee of the co-operative society, who helps to build the local
school, and has credit enough to be able to build his new well with
Government money borrowed at 5%. There are no riches or hope
of riches in this life, but there is enough to eat and somewhere to
live, sturdy independence and the respect of one's neighbours.

So long as the villager lived in a world where few were richer
than himself, no one asked for more. Now, however, the spreading
knowledge of greater wealth and higher standards which capitalism

has made possible in the West are shaking the old contentment to its foundations. For there is no quick method of attaining the higher standards which the peasant is now learning to want and his frustration turns easily into an envy corrosive to all settled government.

TABLE 7

YIELDS IN QUINTALS (APPROX. 220 LBS.) PER HECTARE (2.47 ACRES) (PRE-WAR)

Country			Wheat	Rice	Cotton
India	..	..	7.1	13.4	1
Burma	..	..	5.4	14.3	1
Siam	..	..	—	15.3	2.2
China	..	..	10.5	24.3	2.1
Indonesia	..	..	—	16.6	—
Indo-China	..	..	—	11.2	1
Malaya	..	..	—	16	—
Ceylon	..	..	—	9	.7
U.S.A.	..	..	8.7	24.7	2.4
CONTRAST					
Japan	..	..	18.9	36.1	2.2
Great Britain	..	..	23.1	—	—

Chapter IV

BANKRUPTCY

OVERPOPULATION

The alarming feature of the peasant economy of Asia is not simply that it is desperately poor. It is that in recent decades, and in most countries of Asia, it has been growing poorer. It is a changing, dynamic economy. But it has been changing for the worse.

The contentment of the Asian peasant was always precariously balanced. His holding never gave him more than a bare living, and every natural calamity has always in the past meant starvation for the many. The growth of population and the impact of the West have between them, in the last hundred years, so upset the delicate balance that most of the Asian countryside is now bankrupt. There are still many fortunate individuals in Upper Burma or Siam, Sumatra or Bombay to whom the old economy continues to give happiness and a living. Not everybody is a tenant or a debtor, not everybody's holding is of an uneconomic size, but those who are thus fortunate are to-day a much smaller proportion of the whole than they were a hundred years ago.

The bankruptcy is new only in its scale and geographical scope. In China it has all happened before, every time the population has risen above the capacity of the land to sustain it. The words of Li Ku'ei (who was a minister of Wei in N. China in 400 B.C.) would not need to be made very much blacker to describe the conditions of to-day.

"A farmer having a family of five usually cultivates about 100 mow (perhaps 10 acres) from which he gets 150 piculs of millet. From this total one tenth is taken as tax. 135 piculs remain. A family of five will consume 90 piculs for the whole year. The remainder is 45 piculs, which can be sold for 1350 cash. On religious services 300 cash must be spent, on clothing for a family of five 1500. Therefore the deficit at the end of the year is 450 cash. Nothing is put aside for such emergencies as sickness, funeral expenses, and extra taxes".[1]

[1] *China,* United Nations Series, University of California, Berkeley, 1946, chapter on "Economic Development" by Wu Ching-ch'ao.

To-day the position is worse. The holdings are smaller, the amount eaten is less, money has to be found for landlords and moneylenders as well as for a tax collector satisfied with one tenth. Everywhere the decline of handicrafts, tenancy, debt, overpopulation have ruined the countryside. The effect of the decline of handicrafts has been well shown by Dr. Fei Hsiao-tung in his study of Haihsienkung in E. China. In spite of attempts to revive them through the co-operative movement, the decline is probably irretrievable. The average holding of an owner is $1\frac{1}{2}$ acres. The average yield is 51 bushels of rice. Of this the family eats 42 bushels. The rest sold in 1935 for 20 dollars. [1] But the minimum expenses were two hundred dollars. This village had been ruined by the decline of its local handicraft, silk, which in the 1920's had brought in 300 dollars a family, enough to meet all expenses and leave a small margin. In 1935 it brought in only 45. [2]

An example of the ruinous effects of tenancy is provided by the Tongking peasant. He farms a hectare which he double-crops (this is a rather favourable example since only half the land is double-cropped). His land brings him 6,600 lbs. of paddy; he pays 3,300 as rent; his expenses are 880; he is left with 2420, lbs. or about 1,700 lbs. of rice which is just enough to feed a family of five. Nothing is left over even for salt or a plough-share or the fish pickle dear to the Annamite heart. [3]

The effects of debt are more complicated. Debt may rise out of some natural calamity, above all from famine which causes men to sell land and children for a few baskets of rotten rice, and China had 1828 famines between 108 B.C. and A.D. 1911. [4] The sale of land at ridiculous prices was so widespread in the Bengal famine of 1943 that Government had to pass special legislation to permit its redemption. Debt may also rise from the improvidence of men who borrow for to-day's pleasures without considering how to repay. [5] It may rise simply from their incapacity to make ends meet. The families which Professor Buck investigated in Szechwan in 1942 had an annual income of 1454 yuan, an expenditure of 1791. Once in debt, the peasant's position is hopeless. No crime, from cheating to forgery, is too sordid for the moneylender intent on exploiting his

[1] Dollars always means U.S. dollars, unless otherwise stated.

[2] Facts from Fei, Hsiao-tung, *Peasant Life in China*, London, 1939.

[3] The different attempts at land reform and rent control are described later. See Chapter 12.

[4] W. S. Thompson, *Population Problems*, London, 1932, p. 51.

[5] Malcolm Darling, *The Punjab Peasant in Prosperity and Debt*, Oxford, 1932.

D

debtor's distresses. The debtor becomes a tenant on his own land. His position is distinguished from that of other tenants only by his willingness to pay a higher, and uneconomic rent, to stay on his ancestral earth. In West Khandesh in India, I have myself seen Bhils owning 15 to 20 acres of black cotton soil, bringing in crops which were worth £40 or £50 at 1940 prices (four times that at 1951 prices) who have become the absolute bond-slaves of their creditors. They surrender to them their crop without knowing its price, sign for them blank promissory notes, borrow from them food for the family within a few months of harvest, borrow seed for the new season, borrow the few pence required to get drunk or to go to the cinema on market-day.

Debt leads to tenancy, tenancy to debt; the decay of handicrafts by depriving the peasant of any source of income except his land, makes the circle irretrievably vicious. And the end is the terrible fate of landlessness in a society where all status, all security of employment, all happiness in the present and hope for the future, depends absolutely on the possession of land. The man without land finds himself without work for six or seven months of the year; he can hope for a wife for himself and spouses for his children only in families as ruined as his own. From the landless came most of the million and a half dead in the Bengal famine. It is the landless who suffer the consequences of the shortage of women in the Punjab. The landless man seldom dares to assert his rights against his fellow-villagers who still have land. His grievance may be failure to pay his meagre wages, or refusal to let him use the village well because he is Untouchable. He is the whipping boy for all the frustrations of the police; he is always available to plead guilty since he cannot afford a lawyer and thus he swells the percentage of convictions on which so many of the police think promotion depends. If starvation compels the landless man to borrow, he pays 50% or 100% a month, and in Cochin China, for example, work done in satisfaction of a few weeks' old debt is reckoned at 20 cents instead of the normal 35, and sometimes for 90 cents borrowed in the morning a piastre must be returned in the evening. In England before the Moneylender's Act, the labourer might pay 1d. in the shilling per week. In Asia to-day the debtor's position is even worse.

The growth of tenancy and debt show a peasant society which is on the way to collapse. But the coming into being of large numbers of landless labourers reveals that the society finally has collapsed. Tables 8, 9 and 10 give an idea of how far the process has gone in those of the different countries of our area for which figures are available.

From these figures it is clear that there are great differences in different areas in the extent to which the old society has ceased to enable its members to live the good life. The worst pressure points are India, S. China, Lower Burma and parts of Indo-China. Areas like Thailand or Cambodia are still relatively comfortable. Indonesia, or rather Java and Madura, is worse off than the figures given in the table suggest, for although the number of the absolutely landless and of regular tenants is small, the number of those who have only a garden may be as high as one-third.

Behind this collapse lies an increase in population incommensurate with the increase in the cultivable land. In these ancient fixed societies, each member of each generation wishes to do as his fathers did before him; and what they did, overwhelmingly, was to farm little plots of land. The Asiatic farmer recovered from the waste or hacked out of the jungle just enough to satisfy his needs: the most primitive, the Sakai of Malaya or the Baiga of Central India, with a million acres of forest to choose from, has been content to burn off for his millet or upland rice just two or three acres. Thus, if the family has more than one son, the next generation needs more land. No Asian peasant ever took a 5,000 acre Crown lease as the early settlers did in Australia. All the Australian farmer had to do as numbers increased was to increase the intensity of his exploitation of the land by changing over with time and the increase in numbers from sheep farming to cereal farming and from cereal farming to market gardening. The limitations of his technique compelled the Asian peasant to begin with the methods of market gardening.

This need for land has led to desperate results, even in the past. The stability of the population of Japan between 1600 and 1870 was achieved partly by infanticide.[1] The recurrent civil wars and breakdowns of civil authority in China have been plausibly interpreted as due to periodical increases of population. In India's eventful history there have always been wars and famines bringing down the population whenever it has swollen beyond the ordinary.

In the days before the West brought to Asia its effectiveness against famine and disease, the Malthusian checks were successful in keeping the population down. At the end of the 18th century, and in the more untouched lands as late as 1900, populations were

[1]Abortion has recently been legalised in Japan subject to very meagre safeguards.

still well within the capacity of the Asiatic lands to carry them, as Table 11 shows. The enormous growth which has occurred since is shown by Table 12.

This increase in population has not been due to some special Oriental philoprogenitiveness. It is not the result of Eastern sexuality or a heathen addiction to polygamy. Indeed the percentage of growth has been lower than in the West. India's population increased three fold between 1750 and 1941, but the population of the United Kingdom increased over five times in the same period in spite of large emigration. Even the population increase in Manchuria was less rapid than that in the United States, where the population rose from 5,300,000 in 1880 to 147,000,000 in 1948. India's rate of increase is to-day about the same as Holland's. The West rails at the improvidence of Eastern birth rates. But in 1894 Germany's birth rate was 36 compared to India's 34.

Asia's present problem is an old one in human history, and the West has only been preserved from its impact in a particularly painful form by the great discoverers and the Industrial Revolution. English real wages dropped by half between 1730 and 1800. Ireland had to send half of her population overseas to attain her present measure of prosperity.

Indeed the history of the Highland island of Tiree presents the East's difficulties in a nutshell. In 1769 it was comfortably balanced at a moderate standard of living with 1676 people and a flourishing handicraft industry in kelp. The improvement in medical care at the end of the 18th century and the beginning of the 19th brought the population up to 6,500 in 1846, but at the same time the kelp industry found itself no longer able to compete and collapsed. The standard of living went down to starvation level and the people were only able to save themselves by emigration. To-day the population is down again to 1,000 and the people once more live in reasonable comfort. The East has reached the stage of 1846. Its difficulty is that the remedies which lay open to the people of Tiree are no longer available. The people of Tiree had Glasgow factories and Canadians farms to which to migrate, but for the modern citizen of Asia the doors of other lands are shut. And except in Japan, the factories which should give the landless work have yet to be built.[1]

Except in China, the problem of surplus population is quite

[1] The excess population in Asia is of course much larger than it was in Europe. Even unrestricted migration would make little contributions to the solutions of the problem.

recent in Asia, and it has not become desperate until the last half century. Before that when there was still empty land waiting for the babies to clear when they grew up, their arrival was welcome enough. The first Census Commissioner in Burma talked of the "wonderful" increase in Pegu and Martaban since the commencement of British rule. In some areas there is land still. Sind found room for many thousands of Punjab refugees in 1948. The Lungkiang province of Manchuria has only half its arable land under cultivation.[1] In North and North East Thailand only 7% of the land is utilized at all. 3 million acres have gone out of cultivation in Lower Burma since 1938. There are only 20 million people in the 700,000 square miles of the outer provinces of Indonesia. This was because, until recently, the Javanese were reluctant to emigrate. Even in the relatively heavily populated Sumatra and Celebes, with nearly 50 people to the square mile, 70% of the land is still forest.

In such areas the old life still goes on contentedly. In the extreme case, New Guinea,—which scarcely has a peasant economy in the normal Eastern sense—it may perhaps last for centuries. But such cases are now the exception. The way in which the land has been filled up is shown for China and India in Tables 13 and 14.

As the figures for India are reasonably reliable whilst those for China are extremely approximate, it may be worth while expanding a little on the Indian position. There are still to-day a few places with spare land, such as Bastar State or the Eastern Assam Valley. But they are very few and extremely remote. Substantially India and Pakistan too, with the exception of Sind,[2] are full, full as they have never been before in their history, full without even the narrow safety-valve once offered by emigration to Malaya and Burma, Ceylon and East Africa. What 50 years ago was a menace only in the occasional Dacca or Gorakhpur is now the nation's most terrible threat; for no peasant state can be stable in which the peasant has not the land to provide him with what he needs to eat.

In the last seventy years in India cultivation has increased by perhaps one-twelfth[3]; population has increased by nearly three-

[1]Karl J. Pelzer, *Economic Survey of the Pacific Area*, Part I, Institute of Pacific Relations, 1946, pp. 99, 139.

[2]In Sind there are still 20 acres for every plough and schemes for 2 barrages to bring under cultivation 5 million acres within the next decade.

[3]Assuming that cultivation in the 1880s in unsurveyed areas was roughly in proportion to that in surveyed areas; for some parts of India this may be an exaggeration, in which case the increase in cultivation may be a little higher than one-twelfth.

quarters. Where there were 1½ acres per head, now there are only ⅔.

The districts in Table 14A were selected at random and do not include any samples from the particularly crowded districts of E. Bengal or the Madras river deltas, since district changes and the Permanent Settlement make it difficult to give figures which would be both trustworthy and comparable.

The point which stands out is that everywhere there has been some increase in cultivated land, but that it has been adequate to meet the growth in population only in special cases. This comes out most clearly in the figures for provinces as a whole. There has been hardly any change in the area of cultivated land in Bombay since 1885, in Madras since 1913. Even in the Punjab, with its great canal colonies, the increase in cultivation has only been one-quarter, while the increase in population has been one-half. In Bihar, in the crowded Ganges plain, the population went up between 1921 and 1941 from 29 million to 36 million, but the cultivated area went down from 26 million acres to 25.

To sum up. The old-settled areas in India like the Ganges plain were full by 1880: most of the rest of India was full by 1914; and only the exceptional jungle or irrigable desert was left for the last generation to occupy. Now, outside the Sind-Rajputana desert and the tribal jungles of Orissa or N.E. Assam, there is nothing left. The Indian subcontinent has been filled to the brim and for the babies not yet born some other occupation will have to be found than peasant agriculture. They cannot all go into industry or become clerks and engine drivers. Those who continue on the land, necessarily the vast majority, will also have their lessons to learn for the land will be able to carry its burden only by the use of the most modern research and the maximum of fertiliser.

This will in itself bring profound changes. For a peasant who learns to use Gammexane and artificial insemination and the latest wheat-strain from Pusa ceases to be a peasant, and becomes an agricultural technician. The Government will be forced into new attitudes. It will not be able to leave it to the peasant to work out his own rescue. There is not the time for this. Both India and Pakistan know it. Have not the political troubles of the last 30 years coincided with the period of saturation, and were not the comfortable districts quiet during the most violent political campaigns? The politicians and the civil servants have not forgotten their lesson.

The experience of China and India is not different from that of

Korea or Japan or Java, only more striking. Table 15 gives a few of the relevant figures.

This quiet process of internal colonisation has been going on all over Monsoon Asia for centuries and it has greatly speeded up in the last hundred years. The settlement of Lower Burma and Cochin-China between 1860 and 1920 is comparable, though on a smaller scale, with the settlement of the American Middle West at very nearly the same time.

The end of the frontier has, however, now come in Asia as in the United States, and it is an ending portentous of future change. The productivity of the old economy was always low.[1] It could not be otherwise where a man cleared from the waste only what he needed for his own subsistence, and where capital investment was only a twentieth or a thirtieth of what it is in the West.

The collapse of the old economy has reduced this productivity still further. More sons to inherit means smaller holdings in the next generation; Table 16 shows how many families to-day do not have the 3 acres of rice-land or the 10 acres of dry farm which are necessary for a decent living on Asian peasant standards. However, the reduction in the size of farms below the minimum necessary for efficiency involves a positive increase in costs.[2] Division amongst heirs involves steady increase in fragmentation until fields become a mere patchwork and the peasant spends half his working life going from one plot to another.[3]

The result of all these trends is that perhaps four-fifths of the peasants of India or China or Japan are living below the poverty line, with never enough to eat or to wear or to keep them out of debt. The bankruptcy of the countryside is emphasised by the comparative prosperity of those callings in the towns, which have been created by

[1]To take an extreme instance, in the Outer Provinces of Indonesia man has always been employed, yet the Netherlands East Indies Government estimated in 1939 that average income per head in agrarian families was less than £3 10s od.

[2]In Japan in 1934 costs were 69 yen per tan (about ¼ acre) of rice on holdings under 1 acre; and 48, two-thirds as much, on those over 12½ (*Asahi Shimbun*, Tokyo, June 28, 1934). In China a worker produced an average of 2,042 pounds of grain on farms of 1½ acres, 4,560 pounds in those of over thirteen (Gerald F. Winfield, *China: The Land and the People*, New York, 1948).

[3]E.g. In Szechwan plots average 80 square yards. In India it is not unusual for a single acre to be split into 15 or 20 fragments. There is similar extreme fragmentation in French Canada when there is no primogeniture. It is worth while remembering that in England primogeniture forced the younger sons to go away to earn their living. This was especially true of the west of England.

Western influence. In Tongking in the 1930s a farm labourer earned
5d. a day and was employed for seven months in the year. But an
electrician in Saigon got 2/6 a day and was employed the whole
year round. A woman harvester in Gorakhpur in India got perhaps
3d. a day for three months, while a woman weaver in Bombay got
1/3 a day the whole year round and a bonus as well when the mill
made money. The only hope for Asia lies in bringing to the countryside the methods which have produced these comparatively high
incomes in the towns.

THE IMPACT OF THE WEST

The second main cause of the pauperisation of the East has been
the impact of Europe. The impact of the West on the East has taken
two forms. Each has been almost equally disruptive of the stability
of the old peasant society. The first form of the impact was to make
it appear that the poverty of the East was preventible. The wealth of
Western societies revealed to the East that its low standards were
the result not of the will of God, but of the inefficiency of its own
techniques. That would in itself have been enough to create a
ferment in the Eastern mind.

The second form of the impact was to introduce to the East not
only new methods of production but also new modes of thought.
All the disturbing elements of Western civilisation with its emphasis
on liberty and progress, equality and change, were injected into a
society already in economic crisis.

The impact was the more tremendous because out of the twenty
centuries for which West and East have been in contact, for nineteen
it had been the East whose ideas influenced the West. It had been the
West and not the East whose economy was upset by Eastern trade.

The interaction of East and West is to-day so central to the general
situation in Asia that a brief historical review must be given of the
relation between the continents.

The Romans were the initiators of East-West trade on any scale.
Its Eastern trade caused a drain of money to Asia. There was thus
a steady decline of prices in the Roman economy and a consequent
drying up of commerce. This was one of the causes of its exhaustion
and final collapse. Later in Byzantium, the import of silk from the
East in the 6th century helped to dazzle the barbarians and hold off
the Mussulman for the centuries during which Byzantium converted
the Slavs to Christians. Silk culture spread to Italy in the 12th
century, and was one of the foundations of that primacy of her

cities which produced Dante and Giotto, St. Peter's and the Renaissance. But though the mediaeval West thus learnt to make for itself the silk whose import had contributed so heavily to Rome's ruin, it needed more than ever the spices which alone could make tolerable the salt and half-rotten meat of winter. The desire to circumvent the Arab middleman in spices inspired the search for an alternative way to the East, which took Christopher Columbus to America, the first Englishman to Moscow and Vasco da Gama to India. But this competition of the merchants was a struggle within the Western world. The profits the Western merchant made were at the expense of his own people, not at the expense of his Eastern supplier. The successful pepper rings were in London rather than Cochin. Not until the 16th century did the West trade directly with the East at all. Venice and Genoa made their profits in trading with Cairo and Aleppo, not in direct commerce with India or China. And even when a Western trader had firmly ensconced himself in the East, his influence on its populations remained negligible.

Eastern influence on the West remained unquestionably stronger than Western influence on the East until about 1700. Eastern trade turned Portugal for a time into a great power. Twice it drove England and Holland to war. Trade introduced to Europe in the 17th century cotton and tea that were to have so all-conquering a future. But though the East thus continued dominant, there were signs of change. The West gained control of the coast-land of Ceylon and half a dozen places in India and Indonesia. The East began to lose control of its own international trade. The merchants of Malacca or Surat were disappearing from the high seas; increasingly the Western ships made the profits on carrying Coromandel cottons to Burma, indigo to China, Chinese pottery to Java.

As late as 1800 an observer might well have agreed that Eastern influence on the West was still much deeper than Western influence on the East. True, there were by then patches of Western rule in Bengal and Bihar, Ceylon and Java; the East had no corresponding control in Europe. But Western rule did not mean comprehensive influence. It changed nothing except the colour of the receiver of taxes. Religion and thought, the way of life of merchant and craftsman and peasant were still untouched, still flowing in the channels that had been worn for them by centuries of use. In the West, on the other hand, the search for spices had had the most universal and unexpected effects. It had led to the discovery of America (for Columbus stumbled on it while searching for a way to India); to

the opening of maritime bases in South Africa; to the discovery of
Australia. Mercantilist economics were a response to Eastern
demands for bullion. 18th-century fashion was inconceivable without muslins and silks, ivory and lacquer and tea. The Encyclopaedists
were spurred to their attacks on the divine right of Church and
King by Chinese this-worldliness and Chinese views on the mandate
of Heaven.

In 1793 the Emperor Chi'en Lung said to Lord Macartney "The
Celestial Empire possesses all things in prolific abundance and lacks
no product within its borders. There is therefore no need to import
the manufactures of outside barbarians in exchange for our own
products".[1] He spoke for all Asia and for 2,000 years of history.

It was only the 19th century that was to make his answer seem the
ridiculous pomposity of an anachronism. But already it showed a
certain lack of perception. The reflective Asiatic may have argued
that for 2,000 years Asia had given and Europe had taken. This was
a rational arrangement in trade, for Europe had nothing to offer.
But in other respects, Asia might have done well to borrow. Roman
Commercial Law, Newtonian physics, 18th-century chemistry,
might have been no small returns for Hindu algebra and Chinese
political thought. The proper pride of Asia in its own achievements
had degenerated into obscurantist arrogance long before its weakness was finally exposed in the 19th century.

The East had failed to see the changing of the times. The Tangs
had ruled from Samarkand to Peking. Their poetry and their
painting and their 40 million people had made their China a State
beside which the Europeans of the Dark Ages, fighting for their
lives against the barbarian Viking, might have seemed as the
African tribesman seemed to the Europeans of the last century. The
glories of Gupta sculpture and Gupta literature, the extent of Gupta
sway, had contrasted with a Roman Empire shaking to pieces under
the hammer blows of invading Huns and Germans. But in 1800 the
Tang and Gupta Empires had been dead a thousand years and more.
Meanwhile the West had more than caught up on the East which, for
the first time in its history, had been truly unchanging. In the West
the period between, say, Charlemagne and Arkwright had been one
of the great leaps forward of man's progress. In India and China in
the same period there had been but a short step, and that backward;
and outside conquest, Muslim in India, Mongol in China, was only
part of the explanation.

[1] G. F. Hudson, *The Far East in World Politics*, London, 1939, p. 13.

The advance of the West began about 1200 at the time of St. Thomas Aquinas, the growth of the University of Paris, the institution of Henry II's new Assizes, and the building of the Sainte Chapelle. Thus the new techniques of the West had but three centuries behind them when the first Europeans went exploring in Asian waters. But there had been enough time for the West to acquire sufficient experience in practical matters to give it unanswerable power. The East took another three hundred years before it so much as realized what it lacked. Not till the days of the Meiji Restoration and Mahatma Gandhi did the East either imitate Western technique successfully, or attain enough consciousness of its own weakness to impose upon itself the restraint, and the avoidance of provocation, which are so necessary for a weaker power dealing with a stronger one.

The most obvious European superiority was in weapons. In the beginning, in the 17th century, it was the superior manoeuvrability of Portuguese and Dutch ships, increased still more by the invention of the fore and aft rig in the 16th century, and the greater accuracy of their cannon, which gave them the victory in every sea fight, from the first great battle off Diu in 1509 to the taking of Macassar in 1666. Then it was the better discipline of European and European-trained troops, drilled to wheel and advance in formation and to obey orders even in battle, and the greater range and accuracy of their artillery, which made of a few dozens or hundreds of men the arbiters of Empire. [1] Already in 1503 Duarte Pacheco's 100 Portuguese enabled 8000 Cochinese to stand off 60,000 of the Zamorin's men. In the great battles of the 18th century in India, when half the country was the cockpit of French and English ambition, there were never more than a few hundred Englishmen or Frenchmen involved. Law had only 780 Europeans at Trichinopoly.

More important even than European training or European weapons was European discipline and European unity. In the East for every Salabat Jang who called on the French, there was always a brotherly Nizam Ali to appeal to the English; if one claimant to Johore would not cede Singapore, Raffles could always recognise another. In contrast with this division among the Asiatics, the English or French or Dutch presented a united front. Sir Philip Francis might try to ruin Warren Hastings at home, but he did not desert to Tipu. Albuquerque was never confronted with a captain who would not fight, like Holkar who rode off the field on the fatal day at Panipat

[1] As Bernier, the 17th-century traveller, said.

when the Marathas lost the lordship of India. Conquest was easy for
the Europeans, not because of some inherent inferiority in the
Eastern fighting man—Indian and Gurkha, Japanese and Karen,
have disproved that on a hundred battlefields since—but because the
East lacked an adequate chain of command, a proper drill-book for
its armies, and modern gunsmiths.

In trade, too, European technique early outstripped that of their
Eastern rivals. The Eastern trader, however big—and Howqua of
Canton was worth 26 million dollars in 1843 [1]—traded as an individual or private partnership; and only under Government pressure did
the traders organise themselves into a comparatively regular, continued and responsible partnership such as the Canton Hong.
The East India Companies, English, Dutch and French, on the other
hand, represented the European discovery of the possibilities of the
joint-stock, with its separation of the functions of saving, or risk-
taking, and of management. The Dutch East India Company began
with a capital of £540,000 subscribed for ten years certain, the second
Joint Stock of the English Company (1617) raised £1,600,000. The
stock might be held by anyone who wanted to speculate with a little
of his money without having to risk his whole future—a London
wool-merchant or a Yorkshire landowner, a Harlem herring fisher
or an Amsterdam banker. There was no need for the whole body of
individual subscribers to know or trust each other, for the decisions
on what risks exactly should be taken with their money were made
by Courts of directors of less than twenty men, men chosen for
their experience and weight, well-qualified to decide whether to
take the risk of sending out woollens to Canton to sell at a loss, or
to take the equally severe risk of rousing the wrath of mercantilist
politicians by sending out bullion. Actual management was further
delegated to a man on the spot who, since he could be chosen for
ability and not simply for his shareholding, could be a Coen or a
Clive.

No Eastern merchant, limited to his own resources, choosing his
managers from his family, could compete on level terms with such
organisations. The Eastern State did not take the interest in the
traders' welfare which the Dutch and British governments took in
the Dutch or English East India Companies. Eastern governments
would never have dreamt of giving to merchants a charter like that
by which the States-General enabled the Dutch East India Company
to make war and peace, build fortresses and annex territory, as well as

[1]H. B. Morse, *Chronicles of the East India Co.*, Oxford, 1929, vol. 4, p. 59

to monopolise all trade from the Cape of Good Hope to the Straits of Magellan. On the contrary, Eastern monarchs were inclined, as in Tongking and Siam, to make a royal monopoly of any item of foreign trade from which they thought money could be made.

There thus arose a connection between trade and political power unknown to Monsoon Asia. European Companies became instruments of national policy; in return they made of their country's strength a means of attaining their own desires. This interplay is shown well in Dutch history in Asia. The Dutch in pre-Company days had made their large profits in the East by coming into contact as little as possible with the Portuguese. But the States-General, eager to weaken their enemy the King of Spain, who was then King of Portugal also, insisted that the Portuguese should be fought. Thus Holland acquired its empire. But the Company gained little profit. The English and French East India Companies in their wars with one another were able to draw on all the force and ability of their homelands. Suffren fought the Royal Navy in Indian waters in the 1780s. Wellington commanded at Assaye.

There was an ambiguity about these European companies in the East. The Companies saw their servants as their branch managers, whose task was to make their branches pay. The Clive they liked to see was the writer filling in his ledgers. But their servants in the field saw themselves as holding the flag high in a heathen land, missionaries of their country's civilisation; Clive saw himself as the defender of Arcot, earning deathless fame. The Companies were quite prepared to see their servants accept such humiliations as were inflicted by the Japanese on Dutch merchants at Nagasaki, or by the Chinese at Canton, because there the Companies made money. Their servants, however, fancied themselves better as Presidents of governments or Governors of provinces, even though the armies and navies which they had to maintain were bankrupting their companies. East India Stock stood at 191 in 1753, and at only 140 in 1760 after Plassey had given Bengal to the Company. Buxar in 1764 gave the Company the Diwanni of Bengal, Bihar and Orissa, but in 1772 it had to apply to the Crown for a loan of £1 million. The Dutch East India Company's dividends averaged 30% from 1708–17; they were only 14% between 1768 and 1777—after the final assertion of Dutch authority over all Java. In the 1770's the Dutch Company made 50% on turnover in Bengal and Surat where it had no political power, but the cost of its Eastern Empire left it with a debit balance of some £10 million by the mid-1780's.

The conquest of India and Indonesia resulted from a time lag between Europe's discovery of one great instrument for far-flung trade, the limited company, and its discovery of another instrument, the telegraph. The chain of command in the companies was clear. There was never any open disobedience by their servants. But when orders took six months to pass from Europe to the East, and when protests against the orders could not reach the home office for another six months, it was always possible for the company's officers in Asia to argue that circumstances on the spot were not those which the Directors had had in mind when framing their instructions.

These differences of view between the European merchant adventurer resident in the East and his employers at home survived the invention of the telegraph. In 19th-century Shanghai, the Yangtze Valley was regarded as vital to the British Empire; but the Foreign Office was never converted to this view. The profound knowledge of the India Office always seemed a little old-world and out-of-touch to the harassed official in India. But once the telegraph had been invented, the Foreign Office and the India Office could enforce their views. The Yangtze Valley was not annexed. The reform in India went forward at the British Cabinet's pace. Before the days of the telegraph the time factor ensured that the view of the man on the spot would normally prevail. Neither he nor the Company could face the paralysis that would have resulted if he had always waited for orders before taking action. Wellesley, faced with what seemed to him an immediate French threat, could not stop to worry over his Directors' views. Again and again decisions which could not be undone had to be taken without asking for orders at all. When Charnock had a dispute over Customs dues in 1686 and decided to take Balasore he could not wait a year while he asked London for permission. When the discontent of the Governor of Jacarta (Batavia) gave Coen a chance to outflank the tergiversations of the Sultan of Bantam and the intrigues of the English he had no time to ask Amsterdam.

Since the Company's servants had to make great decisions on their own responsibility, largely unaided as well as uncontrolled from home, they had to be men of an initiative equal to the task. In consequence the balance of the interest of the companies swung ever more strongly toward conquest and against profits. The preservation of the prestige of their Company seemed to its agents on the spot a higher duty than the preservation of its profits. Their temptation to use force grew, too, as the superiority of Western technique grew ever greater. By the time the 18th-century frigate had replaced the Portuguese galleon and the 18th-century guns the 16th-century brass cannon, no Eastern government could stand up to the smallest of Western expeditions. The Peshwa, head of the Mahratta confederacy, was beaten in 1818 by a force of 2800 men; China was beaten in the Opium War without England's using any ship larger than a gunboat. Japan was opened by four ships of which the most powerful was a steam frigate.

The techniques that gave the West its victory are not very romantic—joint stock companies, drill, cannon founding, obedient commanders, ships that could sail against the wind. But behind them lay the whole of the West's political and scientific tradition.

TABLE 8

LANDLESS LABOURERS AS PERCENTAGE OF TOTAL AGRICULTURAL POPULATION

Country	
Korea	3.8
Cochin-China	75
Cambodia	Negligible
India	20
Ceylon	44
Thailand	Small
Indonesia	30
China (Yunnan)	30
China (Kwangtung)	50
N. China	Small
Japan	3
Malaya (Malays only)	Negligible
Manchuria	7
Burma	40

N.B.—The figures vary in date. Those for Japan are for December 1948. Those for India are taken from the 1951 census; it must be remembered in addition that many owners only have pocket-handkerchiefs of land and have to supplement their incomes by labour. Those for the other countries are for different dates in the 1930s, but conditions there are probably much the same to-day, except in Burma, where the disturbed conditions of the last few years have made possible widespread squatting. The figures for Indonesia are Hasselman's for Java in 1903. They would now be somewhat higher.

TABLE 9
PROPORTION OF OWNERS AND TENANTS

Country	% owners	% part owners	% tenants
India	85	—	15
Burma	59	—	41
Thailand (except the Menam Valley)	90	—	10
Menam Valley	70	—	30
Japan	36	37	27
China: Wheat Region	65	18	17
South China	27	27	46
Szechwan	47	22	31
All China	46	24	30
Tonkin	99	—	1
Annam	90	—	10
Cochin China	64	—	36
Korea	20	25	55
Ceylon	75	—	25
Manchuria	37	35	28
Indonesia	90	—	10
All Philippines	49	16	35
Philippines (Province of Bulacan)	21	14	65
Philippines (Mountain Province) ..	95	3	2
COMPARE			
U.S.A.	42.3	28.3	2

N.B—In cases where there are no figures for part-owners, that does not mean they do not exist, merely that they are not separately recorded in the figures.

Sources: For Indonesia: Hasselman's figures for 1903; the number of tenants to-day would be considerably higher.

India. Census of India Paper No. 1, 1952. The 1931 Census Report gave owners as 45% and tenants as 55%. The change would appear to be the result of the abolition of Zemindari which is taking place, and which has already made the Zemindar's tenants feel they are owners. The percentage of land under tenancy is higher than 15%, as many who have returned themselves as owners rent land also.

For Japan: Andrew J. Grad, "Land Reform in Japan", *Pacific Affairs*, June 1948, New York. The percentages give the position before the land reform of 1948.

For the Philippines: *The Yearbook of Philippine Statistics*.

For China: Wheat Region and S. China, Karl J. Pelzer, *op. cit.*, p. 110.

For Szechwan: J. Lossing Buck, *An Agricultural Survey of the Szechwan Area,* Institute of Pacific Relations, New York, 1943.

For all China: Gerald F. Winfield, *op. cit.,* p. 279, quoting Dr. Tsui of the Nanking University College of Agriculture.

For the rest: Report IV to the Preparatory Asiatic Regional Conference of the I.L.O.

TABLE 10

AMOUNT OF DEBT IN MILLIONS OF £

Country			Date	
India	..	..	1938	1500
Burma	..	..	1930	40 (Including seasonal advances)
Japan	..	..	1938	350
Thailand		..	1935	10
Kwantung		..	1933	Two-thirds of peasants in debt.
Cochin-China	..	..	1933	Debt virtually universal

Sources: Report IV, Preparatory Asiatic Regional Conference of the I.L.O., New Delhi, 1947.

Andrew J. Grad, *op. cit.*

J. S. Furnivall, *Colonial Policy and Practice,* Cambridge, 1948.

James M. Andrews, *Siam, Second Rural Survey,* 1934–5.

Chen Han-seng, *Agrarian Problems in Southernmost China,* Shanghai, 1936.

TABLE 11

POPULATION IN RECENT PAST

Country					Date	Population
India	..	..	..	..	1750	130 million
Java	..	..	..	..	1815	4½ million
China	..	..	..	..	1766	180 million
Japan	..	..	..	..	1804	25½ million
Ceylon	..	..	..	..	1827	885,000
Burma	..	..	..	..	1800	Under 3 million
Philippines	..	..	..	..	1800	Under 2 million
Siam	..	..	..	..	1900	5 million
Malaya	..	..	..	..	1900	800,000
Manchuria	..	..	..	..	1890	10 million

TABLE 12

POPULATION TO-DAY

Country	Population (in millions)	Date of census or estimate in Col. 2.
India	357	1951
Burma	17	1948
Thailand	17	1948
Japan	80	1948
Indonesia	76	1948
Malaya	6	1948
Ceylon	7	1948
China	463	1948
Philippines	20	1948
Manchuria	43	1943
Indo-China	27	1948
Pakistan	75	1951

TABLE 13

GROWTH OF PRESSURE ON LAND IN CHINA

Date	Population (in millions)	Mow under cultivation (in millions)	Mow per head
1661	105	549	$5\frac{1}{4}$
1766	182	740	4
1872	339	820	$2\frac{1}{2}$
1931	420	1,249	3

N.B.—The easing of the position after 1870 is due to the opening up of Manchuria and Inner Mongolia.

Source: China, United Nations Series, University of California, Berkeley, 1946, chapter on "Agriculture" by A. Kaiming Chiu. The figures are necessarily very approximate.

TABLE 14A

GROWTH OF PRESSURE ON LAND IN INDIA

District	Population 1881	Population 1941	% Increase approx.
	To nearest thousand		
Malabar (Madras)	2,261,000	3,930,000	75%
Azamgarh (U.P.)	1,531,000	1,823,000	20%
Gonda (U.P.)	1,167,000	1,720,000	50%
Chanda (C.P.)	543,000	873,000	60%
Raipur (C.P.)	1,093,000	1,516,000	50%
Bilaspur (C.P.)	715,000	1,549,000	120%
Darrang (Assam)	272,000	736,000	170%
Khandesh (Bombay) ..	1,028,000 (1872)	2,240,000	120%
Ratnagiri (Bombay) ..	1,019,136 (1872)	1,373,466	25%
Upper Sind Frontier (Sind)	90,000	304,000	235%
Montgomery (Punjab) ..	380,000	1,600,000	340%

District	Cultivated 1884-5	Cultivated 1937-38	% Increase approx.
	Acres		
Malabar (Madras)	911,000	1,750,000	95%
Azamgarh (U.P.)	869,000	1,000,000	5%
Gonda (U.P.)	1,168,000	1,240,000	60%
Chanda (C.P.)	653,000	1,065,000	60%
Raipur (C.P.)	1,965,000	2,165,000	10%
Bilaspur (C.P.)	1,102,000	1,920,000	70%
Dawang (Assam)	227,000	660,000	190%
Khandesh (Bombay) ..	2,447,000 (1872)	3,700,000	50%
Ratnagiri (Bombay) ..	1,429,000 (1872)	1,800,000	25%
Upper Sind Frontier (Sind)	270,000	800,000	200%
Montgomery (Punjab) ..	272,000	1,605,000	500%

These are mostly districts which were relatively empty in 1880. Azamgarh, with its 5% increase, is the one which is typical of most of the more heavily-populated areas—the Ganges Valley, for example, or the Cauvery Delta.

ASIA AND THE WEST

TABLE 14B

Province			Population In millions to nearest quarter million		Cultivated In acres to nearest quarter million		
			1881	1941	1884–5	1913–4	1937–8
Madras	..	..	31	49¼	27	43	41½
Bombay	..	..	16½	21	32½	43	41½
Punjab	..	..	18¾	28½	25	28	31
Assam	..	..	5	10¼	1½	7½	8
Central Provinces	..		10	17	14	20¼	28¼

The increase in cultivation in both Tables 14A and 14B is probably overstated in most cases, as the earlier figures do not appear to include an estimate for cultivation in unsurveyed areas.

TABLE 15

GROWTH OF PRESSURE ON LAND IN OTHER COUNTRIES

Country	Early Date	Acreage Cho.	Date when near maximum first reached	Acreage Cho.	Recent Date	Acreage Cho.
Korea	1910	2,465,000	1918	4,342,000	1936	4,427,000
Japan	c. 1720	2,980,000 La.	1915	5,922,000 La.	1943	6,000,000 La.
Java	1900	3,800,000	1929	7,600,000	1929	7,781,000

N.B.—In interpreting these figures, allowance must be made for more intensive use of the land in different countries. Thus, in Java, the irrigated area increased from 450,000 acres in 1895 to 3 million in 1920. The index of acres actually cultivated went up from 96% in 1929 to 111% in 1938. 15% more of the land had been put under double-cropping in nine years.

TABLE 16

PEASANTS WITHOUT ENOUGH LAND FOR SUBSISTENCE

(Figures For 1930s Unless Otherwise Stated.)

Country*	Percentage owning under 1 acre (to nearest %)	Percentage owning under 3 acres (cumulative figure)
Japan	49 (under $1\frac{1}{4}$)	92 (under $3\frac{1}{2}$)
Tonking	63	94 (under $4\frac{1}{2}$)
Luts'un, Yunnan	50	83
China (1926)	45 (under $1\frac{1}{2}$)	69 (under 5)
Punjab	20	64
Bengal	43 (under 2)	60 (under 5)
Java (1903)	33 (under 35 hectare)	71 (under .71 hectare)
Philippines	23 (under $2\frac{1}{2}$)	

*All these areas are largely rice-growing, except for the Punjab and N. China.

Sources: Shiroshi Nasu, *Aspects of Japanese Agriculture*, Institute of Pacific Relations, New York, 1941.

Pierre Gourou, *Land Utilization in French Indo-China*, Institute of Pacific Relations, New York, 1945.

India Famine Inquiry Commission, *Final Report*, Delhi, 1945.

Fei Hsiao-tung and Chang Chih-i, *Earthbound China*, Chicago, 1945.

Karl J. Pelzer, *Pioneer Settlement in the Asiatic Tropics*, New York, 1945.

Chapter V

REVOLUTION

Asian society is now undergoing a process of more revolutionary change than ever before in history, because the two forces hitherto discussed, the filling up of the land and the impact of the West, have lately been working in ever closer unison and with ever greater effect to dissolve the old, stable peasant society.

The pressure on the land has only recently become explosive; only recently has the Western impact acquired explosive force. The explosion has now finally been set off by the inextricable mixture of the two which has occurred.[1] Without Western medical knowledge and control of famine and horror of infanticide, the increase of population would have been very much smaller; and the resultant impoverishment would not have been nearly so severe if it had not been for the effect of such Western ideas as nationalism and the sanctity of contracts with moneylenders in destroying the balance of society. Equally, the East would have continued for very much longer in its complacent contempt for the Western barbarian if it had not been for the desperation caused by the growing realisation of the poverty and powerlessness inseparable from an unchanging and overpopulated countryside.

The reaction of the East to the West has not been everywhere the same. In each country there has been revolution. But the revolution has taken different lines. In some countries of Asia, the spirit of the West has been successfully understood and caught. This is what happened in India. Sometimes it was the material techniques of the West which were taken over. This is what happened in Japan. Sometimes the Eastern community has shown itself too weak to be other than a *corpus vile* on which Western methods have had their way unchecked, enriching it as in Malaya or exploiting it, as in

---

[1] In 1800 the West held only part of India and Ceylon and Java. The rest of India and Ceylon were annexed and China was first forcibly opened up, between 1800 and 1850. The conquest of Burma, Indo-China, the Outer Provinces of Indonesia and Malaya happened almost entirely after 1850 and so did the opening up of Japan and Korea.

Korea. Sometimes, as in Tibet or Siam, remoteness or ingenuity have enabled an Eastern society to keep itself more or less untouched. For countries whose own countryside was descending into bankruptcy, it became a matter of life and death to discover the secrets which lay behind Western wealth and Western productivity. Since those secrets are spiritual as well as material, their adaptation to the needs of Asia has involved, and is involving, material and spiritual revolution.

These varying responses are the real history of Asia to-day. The next part of this book is an attempt to describe them in detail, country by country.

NOTE

Growth of population and growth of Western influence have characterised all Monsoon Asia in recent years. But form and effect have varied from country to country.

Western influence has sometimes been a liberalising force, bringing ideas of nationalism and of representative government and creating the middle class required to put them into effect. Sometimes it has had more unfavourable results, increasing wealth but only at a terrible cost in exploitation and uprooting. Everywhere and always it has tended to break up the accepted patterns of society. New classes have been created, factory labour or Western-style technicians whose struggle to remake society in their own image has been and will be profoundly solvent of all traditional forms. New methods of creating wealth have been introduced, so effective that people have become deeply dissatisfied with the easy and unproductive ways of the past. Horizons have been widened, making people realise that they are part of groups which go far beyond their village; whether the groups are religious, national or racial, the mere fact that a new loyalty is created is upsetting of the balance of society.

Population pressure too has had very varying effects. There is the desperate industrialisation of Japan, the chaos of China, the slow decline in welfare of the Indian countryside; all are in part at least the result of increased population. In certain areas, Siam, for example, or Lower Burma, it has even had for a time a beneficial effect, permitting the rapid bringing under cultivation of waste land.

The successive chapters of this Part are an attempt to illustrate the most important facets of Western influence and of population pressure from the experience of the different countries. In each country only the dominant facet, the one which its experience illustrates most clearly, has been studied; but that does not mean either that other facets have not also occurred in that country, or that that facet has not occurred in other countries. Most facets have been of importance in most countries; the individual country method of study has been chosen only because it permits a simplification which brings out the process of development more clearly.

PART TWO

Chapter VI

IMPERIALISM

THE ATTITUDES

When the last war revealed to Western Europe for the first time the full plenitude of American wealth and power, European reactions were very mixed. There was desire to know how America had achieved its success; there was the will to imitate American systems; above all, there was a sense of outrage. It seemed a moral offence that a people so materialist and so crude, so given to chewing-gum, to loud talk and freedom of behaviour towards women, should also be so prosperous and so able to impose its concepts on a not altogether willing world. Europe felt entitled to accept large free gifts from America as if they were a kind of expiatory offering by America to Europe's older civilisation. Later, as the fundamental oneness of all Western culture became clearer under Russian pressure, these attitudes have changed. There is more real understanding of what America stands for and what she has to contribute, in material welfare or social equality, to our common civilisation.

The years 1945–9 have thus re-enacted in miniature in Europe what has been happening over all the last century in Asia. But because the initial gap in wealth and strength between the West and Asia was greater, the transition by the East from an attitude of resentment to acceptance, from blind dislike or blind imitation of the West to discriminating assimilation, has been much slower. East and West had no community of race, religion or culture. Thus the shock to the East was the greater when it realised the disparity of its strength compared with that of Europe.

Asia's first reaction on finding itself so much weaker and poorer than the Europeans was to take refuge in the explanation, so soothing to its self-respect, that all its ills were the fault of the West. It supposed that its exploitation by the West was made possible only by a quite temporary superiority of weapons and of social system. It believed that the communities subjected to Western supremacy could catch up with the West if they freed themselves from Western dominance. Generalissimo Chiang Kai Shek blamed even Chinese student sloppiness on the "Unequal Treaties."

Later, however, Western culture came to be regarded as having more to it than mere technical superiority. In most of Asia, Western culture enjoyed increasing prestige. It was the key to greater material or political freedom. The seats of power were filled with Westerners or the Western-trained. The only way to authority or position in one's own society was to make oneself able to compete with the Westerner on his own ground. Confucian scholarship proved no qualification for the Chinese Customs Service. A candidate could present English without Sanskrit for the Indian Civil Service examination, but not Sanskrit without English.

The Asian faced in every sphere of life the West's placid assumption of its own invariable superiority. Slowly he came to accept the West at its own valuation, until the Russo-Japanese War of 1905 showed that Asia too could learn the new technique. The first world war showed the Asian that the new wealth could still be put to the old evil purposes.

The acceptance of Western values extended to so remote a subject as philosophy. The 19th-century Englishman assumed so firmly that Sankar Acharya could have nothing to add to Plato that no Indian University dared to give Indian philosophy a place in its courses equal to that of Greek philosophy in Oxford "Greats". Indians gave weight to their own thinkers only in so far as the West had first approved their teachings. The great influence of Sir Sarvapalli Radhakrishnan's *History of Indian Philosophy* in restoring the credit of the Advaita Vedanta with the ordinary educated member of the reading classes has been largely due to his position as an Oxford professor.

The substitution of the Western thinkers for native ones has given the educated Asian a sense of inferiority, and a feeling that he cannot think his past glorious, his art beautiful or his thought profound, until some Westerner has first affixed the seal of his approval.[1] To-day Indian sculpture is the pride of independent India; but in the 19th century it was English archaeologists like Cunningham who saw in the statues of Konarak or Khujraho one of the most magnificent sensual expressions of the human soul, while Indians themselves were filling their houses with the shiniest of coloured lithographs. The great Maharaja of Bikaner, who could

[1]This is perhaps less true of the Chinese than of other Asians.

still build for State purposes in the best Mughal tradition, bought only the most insipid of Victorian flower-paintings for his own private pavilion.

This upsetting of Asian taste and Asian self-confidence was not in itself exploitation by the West. But it produced a disturbance of Asian balance that helped to make Asia exploitable. A society that had been forced to recognise the inferiority of its standards and the bad taste of its judgments, was not a society which could face the world on level terms; it was too busy learning to think in the foreigner's language and to imitate his institutions. Not until the lesson had been learnt, not until the Indian could see in the flag the symbol of the State and not just of British rule, or the Chinese feel himself as much at home as an American in running an Exchange Bank, did the Eastern societies recover enough to stop copying and begin synthesising. Only then did they remember that their own past and their own traditions had something to teach. The balanced discernment in Mr. Nehru's book *Discovery of India* could have been achieved only when India was on the verge of independence; if it had been written earlier, it would have been either aggressive or apologetic.

Asia has now spent many years in this absorption and imitation and synthesis. During this time her contribution to the common part of the world's culture has been made from capital, not from the current income of thought. The Eastern ideas which have influenced the West in the last century have not been those of contemporaries but those of two thousand years ago, Buddhism and Vedanta, Yoga and Confucianism. The paintings and the sculpture which have filled Burlington House have been those of Sung and Gupta; the literature which has been read has been the *Tale of Genji* or Yeats' translation of the Upanishads.

There are now signs that at last the synthesis has been finally achieved, that Asia has attained once more that ease with herself without which no spiritual creation is possible. Synthesis has been achieved first in politics. In Burma the time for declaring independence was fixed by Buddhist astrologers, but the politicians drew up a constitution of the purely English cabinet-government type. Nehru's foreign policy relies partly on the Indian inspiration which for centuries gave Sanskrit names to the Kings of Champa or Sri Vijaya, partly on the dominant position of India in the Indian Ocean built up by the British. Sun Yat-sen was a revolutionary in the true European tradition of dramatic escapes and long exiles, yet he was always Chinese in his concern for the People's Livelihood. Cultural synthesis is still new and tentative. A novelist like Mulkraj Anand learns to use a Western form to convey an Eastern content. A Tokyo turner gradually stops going back to his village for the harvest.

When the synthesis is complete, it will be politically important as well as intellectually exciting. Self-respect requires giving as well as taking. A people can only be comfortable in the world, neither aggressive nor humble, when they know themselves creative. It is only a mingling of West and East that can ever make what the West has to teach acceptable to the Eastern masses. In the 19th century it was only the intellectual who was upset. The people continued to pay their land revenue undisturbed by the doctrine of "no taxation without representation". They let the tombs of their ancestors take up much-needed arable unmoved by thoughts of Bentham.[1] But the deep transformation on which Asia has embarked, the industrialisation and the compulsory primary education, the use of commercial fertiliser and the adult suffrage, requires not merely the leadership of the thinking, but also the co-operation of every citizen. That co-operation can be obtained only when the new wine is poured into the old bottles, when the abolition of untouchability is justified by quotations from the Vedas, when Jinnah makes a modern nation out of the Koranic sense of Muslim brotherhood, when the prestige of the Japanese Emperor is put behind democracy, or Siam is able to make education compulsory by using the monastic school.

The pouring has only begun, and sometimes the old bottle bursts under the strain. But it can already be seen that from this pouring is coming a revolution such as Asia has not known since first she took to rice-agriculture.

EXPLOITATION

The words "imperialist exploitation" have now many meanings. They include oppression by and general rapacity of the governing race, though for this meaning the accuser has more and more to point to examples half a century out of date. They include the sense in which Lenin used the words, the monopolisation of colonial industry and resources by the mother-country and the treatment of the colony as a market rather than a community of human beings.

[1] The average tomb in China seems to last for about three generations.

A primary reason for the appeal of Left wing politics in Asia is that the Left has attacked these policies and attitudes, whilst the Liberal has often seen in them (frequently enough quite rightly) only their beneficial results in increasing the country's power to produce wealth for its own and the world's benefit. But the true, the main meaning which the East gives these words, is something more intangible, more negative and also more penetrating. The Asian feels that his civilisation was caught at a temporary disadvantage in capital and inventiveness and social order, and that therefore for him free competition can never be fair. The worst exploitation to him results from the *laisser-faire* which leaves his society to face the advancing tide of Western ways with all its dykes unmended. What he demands from his Government is such "planning" as was done by Meiji Restorers in Japan—positive action which, in cushioning the shock of the collision with the West for his community, will enable him to enter the new world, not as a subject, but as a citizen.

The history of Western contact gives the East ammunition for all its charges; and the charges go home the more effectively to the Western mind because of a change in the West's own ideals.

In the past it has always been the conqueror's way to exact from the defeated the reward of his conquest. But when Europeans, who went to Asia in the first place not as conquerors but as traders, found themselves the lords of great empires, they felt the need for justifying their conquest morally. Thus they began the theories that their spring of action was to promote native welfare, and to prepare the peoples for self-government. These culminated in the theory of trusteeship, which has in the last hundred years transformed the relations of ruling and dependent peoples. No Magyar noble ever felt it necessary to apologize for having confiscated Slav land; but the British Government is uncomfortable under criticism which suggests that white men should not be allowed to settle in Tanganyika even on wasteland. The worth of victory is assayed, not by captives and loot as in a Roman triumph, but by the growth to wealth and freedom of the conquered.

It is by the West's own standards that an increasingly critical East has judged the West and found it all too often wanting. It is true that there has not been much of the first, the Nazi meaning of exploitation, in the West's rule in Asia. There were no Goerings scouring India or Java for art treasures to steal. Nobody tried to ship the handlooms of Dacca to England as the Germans stole everything from machinery to barges. There were no huge unpaid debts for requisitions of food and raw material. Isolated instances occurred. Warren Hastings squeezed the Begums of Oudh. The Dutch depopulated Banda to protect their spices monopoly. There were odd peculations.[1] Burke could rightly say that "our Indian Government in its best state is a grievance"; he could not have said it was an oppression. Even the Japanese in Korea made on the Koreans no German-style levies of clothes or food or art treasures, in spite of the Bismarckian quality of the methods by which they had conquered the country.[2] When the Easterner alleges that the East India Company cut off the thumbs of handloom weavers in Bengal, which is *not* true, or that the Japanese used opium and heroin to destroy Chinese resistance, which *is* true, the importance of the accusation is not the truth or untruth of the facts which it relates but the emotional attitude which ensures that the accusation will always be believed, because it provides a defence against those who see in Eastern weakness only Oriental inferiority.

Of exploitation in its Leninist meaning there has been much more. Some of it has been defensible. It is to the advantage of the whole world that the whole world's resources should be used to the maximum to provide that freedom from extreme want without which no other freedom is possible for the ordinary man. The starving have no dignity, only stomachs. To this increase in wealth the opening up of the world by the free movement of capital and of labour since 1800 has made a greater contribution than anything since the discovery of agriculture. The whole of humanity is better off for the new cities of the United States, the wheat of Canada, the wool of New Zealand: it is better off also, and in exactly the same way, for the rice of Burma, the rubber of Malaya, the jute of Bengal, the cotton mills of Osaka or Bombay, the coal of Fushun or the hydro-electricity of the Yalu.

There is no disagreement over the advantages of this increase in the size of the cake. The dispute between civilisations, as between classes, is over the size of the slices. If all the new wealth goes only to one class or one country, then the other classes or countries, though they may not be absolutely poorer, feel themselves relatively

[1] E.g. The Resident at Benares made £40,000 a year above his pay in the 1780's. Marshal Daendels, as Governor-General, sold to the State the palaces at Buitenzorg he had just, as Governor-General, induced the State to give him.

[2] In their earlier imperialist phase in Korea, the Japanese were more thorough. Hideyoshi removed the craftsmen of Korea bodily to Japan. This was really the only benefit which Japan enjoyed from Hideyoshi's adventure.

so.[1] It is still worse when the cake has got bigger and the native slice has at the same time got smaller. Forbes Royle said in 1855 that jute-weaving in Eastern Bengal "pervades all classes and penetrates every household; men, women and children find occupation therein". That was before Indian jute goods exports began. By 1925 there was a jute mill industry started by Scots enterprise which exported over £30,000,000 worth of gunnies alone. The cake was enormously bigger, but the East Bengali no longer had a share. The profits went to Britons and Marwaris, the employment mainly to immigrants from Bihar and the United Provinces. That is only the most striking example. Another is provided by the substitution of mill-made cloth, usually imported, for cloth hand-woven in the village. The piece goods India imported from Great Britain in 1913 would have employed three million families of weavers who instead were driven back into semi-idleness on the land. The first effect of the opening of Japan was the ruin of the Japanese weaver; Japan had to import her cloth until she learnt to make it in her own factories. The brighter colours, the cheaper price of the factory article was no consolation to those who lost their work.

The third form of "exploitation", the destruction of the balance of the old civilisation, is much the least simple.

The introduction of Western methods into countries where capital traditionally went into jewellery or hoards rather than investment, and where nobody was skilled in the new techniques, necessarily involved the bringing in of Western capital to provide the money, Western technicians to provide the skills. Japan itself had borrowed £150 million overseas by 1914; the only departments on whose efficiency the Chinese Government could always rely were those which were foreign-run, the Customs, Posts and Salt Gabelle. The Japanese Army and Navy, later so menacing, took their first lessons in war from German and British missions.

Equally it was the West which first introduced certain services, passenger travel to Europe, for instance, or endowment policies, and certain forms of organisation, Exchange Banks for instance, or Universities. Naturally therefore the business tended to go to Western institutions, for whom these new forms were not new, and equally they tended to employ by preference their own nationals,

[1]Chapter XIII on Manchukuo is a study in the extent to which it is possible to increase enormously the productive power and the wealth of a colony while drawing off all the benefit to the governing country and leaving the natives no better off, perhaps even worse off, than before.

since they already had the requisite skills and did not need a special and elaborate training.

Some of these services and forms of organisations were of great value to the East. The Indian Government could borrow in England at $3\frac{1}{2}\%$ where the Marathas had discounted their revenues with the Poona bankers at 30%. A British bank in Shanghai would give a Chinese business man a draft on London for a fraction of the commission he would have to pay a Chinese house to get a draft on Kunming. The Easterner paid less and got a wider cover if he insured with some great Western corporation, whose resources went far beyond those of any Eastern family or partnership business, whose actuaries could work out the correct premium to a decimal point, and whose world-wide interests rendered it immune from the risk of being bankrupted by any merely local disaster, however big.

There is here neither loot nor any failure to share advantages with the Eastern customer. The test of "exploitation" in this sense is therefore neither what services are being performed by foreigners, nor the size of the remuneration the foreigners receive for what they do, but how far similar native institutions are being given a chance to grow up, how far natives are being prevented from acquiring the foreigner's special skills; more positively, it is whether or not the Government positively encourages native institutions to develop, and takes active steps to see that natives are trained for every post they could reasonably hope to fill.

Outside Japanese areas, positive discrimination was the exception. The tram-drivers of Bombay were Indians, the engine-drivers of China Chinese, the Burman who got an adequate degree stood as good a chance of becoming a Forest Officer or District Engineer as any Englishman. An Indian could deposit his money in any bank he pleased, and as Indians learnt modern banking the deposits in Indian banks grew from 8 crores in 1900 to 633 in 1945. A Chinese could start a shipping company as freely as any foreigner, even in the international concession at Shanghai, and by 1939 there were one million tons of Chinese shipping. Rubber was of Western introduction in Indonesia, but by 1939 more of it was produced on native small holdings than on European plantations.

But there has been much of failure to give positive help, of lack of response to the demand that the scales shall be weighted in favour of local enterprise, as once the Navigation Act of 1651 helped British shipping against the then more efficient Dutch.

The Japanese gave that backing; such banks as the Yokohama Specie Bank, the Industrial Bank or the Bank of Taiwan had government support, and often direct government participation, from the beginning; no order was placed abroad without a Japanese student being sent with it to learn the technique of carrying it out; Japanese industry was given all the tariff protection it needed to be able to grow.[1] Until after 1918, however, the Japanese were unique. Elsewhere no protection, no assistance was given to the new Asian enterprises struggling to be born. Chinese tariffs were held at 5% by treaty until 1928. India was free-trade until after 1918, so much so that for 30 years from 1893 there was an excise duty on Indian cloth production because there was a revenue duty on Manchester imports. Foreign banks and insurance companies competed on completely level terms with local firms until the last decade; foreign shipping companies can still ply in Indian coastal waters, and were only restricted on Chinese rivers in 1946 (to the great disadvantage of Chinese trade).

Indeed such assistance as government had to give usually went to a foreign institution—if the government were a colony, normally to an institution of the home country. The K.P.M. was incorporated by a special Dutch statute in 1888, and to it went all the mail contracts or official passages of the Indonesian Government; when the Indonesian Government made an agreement with the Japanese restricting shipping competition in the thirties, it was the Dutch Japan-China-Java line which benefited, but the Indonesian as consumer and producer who paid the resultant higher freights. Again, the Chinese Maritime Customs, under Sir Robert Hart, banked with the Hong Kong and Shanghai, and many British Civil Servants and Army officers in India kept their accounts with Grindlay's or Cox and King's.

On the principle of free competition, governments were quite right to act as they did. For an Indonesian shipping line deliberately setting out to train Indonesian Merchant Navy officers, there would have been necessary both a government share in the initial capital, since Indonesian savings would not have been large enough to provide the amounts required unaided, and, initially at least, government management since Indonesians had no experience of shipping. To make use of Dutch savings waiting to be invested, Dutch maritime experience all ready to be used, was both simpler and cheaper. But the Indonesians saw, not the money saved for

[1]This point is dealt with at greater length on pp. 183–186.

education or health, but only the great modern industry in which they were being given no chance to gain experience, and the large payments for shipping services in their balance of trade which might have been used for machinery.

Equally, on a purely commercial basis, the Chinese Customs were quite right to bank with the Hong Kong and Shanghai; the money was safer, the business dealt with more efficiently, than would have been possible in any Chinese bank at the time. But the Chinese nationalist saw only that foreigners were being enabled to make a profit by relending their funds, that a chance was being missed of giving to Chinese a skill every nation needs in the modern world. Again, it was cheaper and more convenient for the Indian Government to buy its locomotives abroad, since the demand was fluctuating and the Indian engineering workmanship poor; but the Congressman saw only that the railways—his railways—were spending millions in England which spent at home might have provided work for the workless and training for the untrained.

To the Westerner these Asian complaints often seem hypocrisy. He counters with untouchability and the extortion of Chinese warlords: even in Korea the worst oppressors, the 83,000 landlords who took one-third of the total rice crop against the one-fifth that $1\frac{1}{2}$ million tenants got, were Koreans, and quite small Koreans at that, of whom only 300 owned over 50 acres. Sometimes of course it is hypocrisy; the bitter nationalist may be a landlord's son or a Chinese General. But often the complaints rise from an obscure realisation that the ills of his own society are within the Asian's power to cure by an act of State—untouchability can be abolished, landlords expropriated—whereas if he once falls too far behind the West he may never be able to catch up enough to be treated as an equal and thus enabled to preserve his self-respect. Equating poverty and difference with barbarianism is a universal sin, in the past indeed more common in Asia than in Europe. So attacks on foreign textiles and support for local cotton mills are the result, not of industrialists' subscriptions to party funds but of the knowledge that the displacement of the handloom by the cheap prints of Manchester spells impoverishment for the village, while mills in Bombay or Shanghai represent both society's resilience in adapting to Western impact, and an opportunity of other work for those whom machine-woven cloth makes workless. Attacks on Western exchange banks for the size of their profits and dividends are ridiculous—the profits of the Chartered Bank of

India Australia and China were only £460,000, the dividends of the Hong Kong and Shanghai only £800,000, in 1948; but whatever the more ignorant controversialists may actually say, the real gravamen of the attack is directed not against their profits, but against their use of Eastern deposits to buy Western securities. In an India which was dissaving in 1947 and 1948, in a China which has usually spent and not saved even the remittances of overseas Chinese, the nationalists dream of the industrialisation which would result if the Hong Kong and Shanghai's £24½ million of British gilt-edged, the Chartered's £42 million of London securities, were replaced by holdings of such local industrial stocks as the German banks used to take up in Germany. They forget, or have never learnt, the dangerous rigidity to which the German banks were thus reduced.

This third form of "exploitation" has therefore been particularly damaging to good understanding between East and West, because too often in the same action in which the Westerner has seen only the material benefits conferred by Western enterprise, the Easterner has seen only the danger to the spiritual balance of his society or the failure to confer other material benefits which he considers would have been of more use to him. Past rapacity is now a subject for fallacy and nobody any longer looks on any Eastern country as a market pure and simple, but the argument over the advantages brought to the East by Western capital and institutions and skill is one which is likely to be conducted with great heat for some time yet. Though as the East asserts its political and economic independence and thus becomes able to decide for itself what it will and will not take, it may be hoped that the fires of this controversy at least will be rapidly extinguished.

KOREA

The best example in Asia of the working of imperialistic exploitation is Korea. One can find in Korea all the typical features of Asian peasant societies—the low productivity, the debt, the lack of a social conscience in the upper classes, the pressure of population on the land. What distinguishes Korea from the other countries is the thoroughness with which the Japanese acted on the theory that the purpose of colonial rule is to benefit the imperial power. Industry was developed for Japan's benefit, a modern administration was installed—but to provide jobs for Japanese. The Korean language and culture were forbidden; but it was never made possible for the

Koreans to be at home in the culture and language of Japan. From the beginning to the end of Japanese rule, the governing motive in Japan's mind was self-interest.

Yet so fruitful are the new techniques which the 19th century developed that it is very doubtful whether the Koreans were in the end any worse off because of Japanese rule. Efficient administration and widespread industrialisation created so much extra wealth that the Japanese probably took no more than they had created in the first place. This section is an attempt to study this process in more detail.

Korea before the Japanese came was a purely peasant economy of even lower than usual productivity. Her native government was a synthesis of all that was worst in Oriental misrule. Japan gave her an industry and government of Western competence, yet the peasant grew poorer, not richer. The new health services reduced his death-rate, but the new industries, built to serve Japanese, not Korean, needs, could not absorb all the new hands. Taxes benefited the Korean farmer less, not more than before the conquest, for the budget was spent for Japanese purpose. Those who misruled the Koreans were no longer even men of their own speech. The Korean was, at the end of Japanese rule as at the beginning, an unproductive and oppressed peasant, deriving no benefit commensurate with the burdens it placed upon him from the superstructure of material welfare and good government the Japanese had built upon him.

Above all, the Korean remained a peasant. In 1920, 87% of the Korean population was dependent on agriculture. In 1938 the percentage of farmers was still 75.7%. The Korean was also both poor and philoprogenitive. Two-thirds of all holdings were under $2\frac{1}{2}$ acres. The birth rate was 32.4 in the years 1929–38.[1]

Poverty did not diminish under Japanese rule—for the Korean it increased. Cultivation did not keep up with population. Population grew from 14 million or so in 1910 to 24.3 million in 1940; but the rice area increased only from 1,353,000 cho in 1910 to 1,662,000 in 1930, and the area under other cereals only from 1,697,000 cho in 1910 to 2,631,000 cho in 1930. Between 1930 and 1948 there was not merely no further increase, there was actually a slight decline. The area cultivated in 1948 was roughly the same as in 1919. Improvements in farming[2] only partly compensated for this worsened

[1]The average death rate for the same period was 19.9.
[2]E.g. the increase in the area under double-cropping from 347,100 *cho* in 1930 to 460,300 in 1938.

situation. Debt was increasing. From perhaps 500 million yen in 1932 it rose to 700/800 million yen in 1940. The average debt per family was £11, a year's net income for a tenant. The peasant was losing his land. Nearly two-thirds was in landlord hands in 1940. The percentage of farmers who were tenants without land of their own rose from 37.7% in 1918 to 53.8% in 1932. Rents were going up and were very high. Rents of half the crop were common. Despite the increased borrowing, the standard of living was necessarily declining. Labourers' real wages were only two-thirds in 1940 of what they had been in 1910. The amount of food available per head went down from 2.032 koku in 1915-9 to 1.668 in 1930-3. The peasant got less of his beloved rice. His consumption in 1934-8 was .399 koku compared with .707 in 1915-9.

The individual Korean's share of the cake was thus getting steadily smaller. Yet the cake, and the Japanese share of it, was growing without ceasing.

The Japanese did much development but it was for their own, not Korean, purposes. Thus at annexation they took over for the State all Royal and public land and two-thirds of all forests. They then increased the amount of timber cut from 673,000 cubic metres in 1910 to 2,780,000 in 1939. But the timber went to Japan or Japanese construction, while the Korean peasant lost his rights of fuel and pasture. When the State had a grant to make of timber land it made it to a Japanese company, both because it was Japanese and because it had capital and skill which the Koreans had not; thus the Chosen Ringyo Kaihatsu Kabushiki Kaisha was given for nothing $1\frac{1}{4}$ million first-class acres in 1937. Moreover, owing to the Japanese control of State land and the Korean's own increasing poverty, more and more of the best parts of the land itself passed into Japanese hands. Initially in 1910 the Japanese owned no Korean land. In 1945 they were found in possession of 700,000 hectares—one-sixth of the cultivated total and considerably more than one-sixth of the more fertile areas.

It was the same with the alleged improvement of the Koreans' old industries of agriculture and fishing. The fish catch went up from $8\frac{1}{2}$ million yen in 1912 to 87 million yen in 1938. But the 30,000 Japanese fishermen, with their modern trawlers and all the best fishing grounds, were able to catch more fish than the 480,000 Koreans. All the big fish buyers and curers and canners were Japanese, and five-eighths of the catch went to Japan. The Korean must have got a little more than in 1912, but, allowing for the depreciation of the yen and the middleman's profit, it was not very much more. Similarly, the fertilizer made by Japanese companies, the improved seed discovered by Japanese research, the better agricultural methods propagated by Japanese experts, sent the rice crop up from 10½ million koku in 1910 to 24 million koku in 1938. Improved seed was used in five-sixths of Korea's rice land. But exports to Japan went up simultaneously from nothing to 9½ million koku, so that the individual Korean was left with less to eat, not more.

The largest increase in the size of the Korean cake was produced by Japanese industrialisation. By the late thirties this was proceeding so rapidly that imports of producer goods alone, without counting buildings or services or the other accessories of capital investment, were equal to a quarter of the Korean national income. This is as high a proportion as the *total* Russian investment, including building and depreciation, at the height of the Third Five-Year Plan. Altogether the Japanese had put in £300 million by 1940. 3,245 miles of railway were built, industrial production went up five times between 1922 and 1940, from 223 million yen to 1140 million; there had been no factories at all in 1910. Increases were particularly large in heavy industry. Electricity capacity grew from 1,700 kilowatts in 1910 to nearly 2,000,000 in 1943; aluminium from nothing in the early 30s to nearly 10,000 tons in 1943; chemicals and fertilizer from nothing to a production of 352 million yen in 1938 and a capacity of 500,000 tons per year respectively.

But all the fruits of this increased production went to Japan or for Japanese purposes. The total capital of all Korean corporations engaged in industry was only £1⅔ million in 1938. Total Korean savings were only 7½ million yen in 1933. The electricity went to industry or to the towns, not to the Korean peasant. Only one family in eight had electric light as compared with nine in ten in Japan. The best paid tenth of all jobs were reserved for Japanese, so that the number of Japanese engaged in industry and mining went up from none in 1890 to perhaps 130,000 in 1940. In 1945 hardly a Korean technician could be found who had even completed a middle school education. The Koreans did not so much as get the advantage of these subsidiary occupations which usually grow up in the shadow of great factories. There were no Korean lipstick or aluminium saucepan manufacturers, no Korean jobbing forges or garages. The Japanese industrialist made more money than in Japan. Profits in nitrogen in Korea were 30% against 10% in Japan. But

the Korean labourer received lower wages—the police had the
unrestricted right to flog[1] and treated trade unions as subversion.
There was no labour legislation, not even a Child Labour Law, until
after 1945.

Korea suffered from the third form of exploitation at its worst.
The Japanese Government never made any attempt to protect in
any way Korean native interests, and the balance of Korean society
was upset by Japan out of deliberate policy.

Korea had been earned by the war with Russia, and Japan saw
no reason why others than Japanese should benefit from the victory
which Japanese money and Japanese lives had won. The money for
the railways was debited to the Korean Government-General, but
many of them were built only to permit the quick concentration of
Japanese troops in Manchuria. The bank of issue, the Bank of
Chosen, was Japanese, with a considerable participation of the
Japanese state. The insurance companies were Japanese; the capital
of Korean companies amounted to only £7,000 in 1938. The 10,000
tons of shipping on the Korean Register were Japanese-owned.
The civil aviation and gold companies which the Government
subsidised so heavily were Japanese. For every task of the slightest
skill a Japanese was imported; the engine-drivers and guards on the
railways, the tram-drivers of Seoul, the foremen and mechanics in
the factories, were Japanese.

Above all, the government, with all that means in posts and
power and self-respect, was Japanese. The Emperor might.be made
Prince of the Shotoku palace, or 76 willing collaborators Japanese
peers, but everything that mattered went to a Japanese. In 1941, there
was only one 6th grade Korean amongst the 59 officers of the
Department of Agriculture and Forestry. In 1940 there were only
20 Korean judges out of 225—there had been 88 in 1909. The
school principals, half even of the primary teachers, were Japanese.
So were 12 out of 13 Provincial Governors. Only one-third even of
the ordinary police constables were Korean. The two divisions
stationed in Korea were Japanese divisions.

The incomes of Government-General and province, of country
and city, were spent for Japanese advantage. Every Japanese child
went to school. Only one Korean child in three went to school.
The University had 145 Koreans compared with 474 Japanese.[2]

[1]There were over 200,000 floggings between 1910 and 1920.
[2]Between 1945 and 1948 the S. Korean Government has claimed a rise in
literacy from 20% to 70%.

Out of a total budget of £40 million, Japanese officials, Japanese strategic railways, the service of Japanese-held debt, subsidies to Japanese companies and such like expenditure for the benefit of Japan, took perhaps nine-tenths. Education and health got under £2½ million and even of this much was for the Japanese.[1] There were nearly as many Japanese in high schools as Koreans, and they filled the city hospitals.

One million Koreans emigrated to Japan. But both there and at home the Korean remained unskilled, poor, powerless and despised. The Japanese were not risking the growth of a native middle class adjusted to the West and its techniques such as made the Congress and the Muslim League in India and the Kuomintang in China. The leadership of free Korea has had to come from exiles.

An attempt may be made to estimate how much of the Korean national income the Japanese succeeded in these various ways in abstracting. In 1938 net production was about £100 million. Roughly half was exported to Japan, against which about half the imports were production goods. Net production available in Korea was about £75 million. From this must be subtracted about £25 million from budget expenditure in Korea which benefited only Japan or Japanese. There must be a further subtraction for incomes of Japanese resident in Korea and for interest on Japanese investments in Korea kept in Korea for re-investment or as dividends to Japanese resident in Korea. This cannot have been less than £10 million.

The Japanese thus took about 12/- in the pound of the Korean national income. Yet so productive is the Western style of capital development that it is doubtful if the Japanese took out much more than the yield of what they themselves had put in. Increasing population would have brought increasing poverty to the Korean, even without the Japanese, and that increasing poverty was not made worse by more than perhaps 25% by Japanese rapacity. Japanese greed in Korea does, however, show up how comparatively favourable is the record of European countries in Asia. At no time, for example, did more than some 2/- in the pound of the Indian national income go to Great Britain, and even that was mostly for purposes which are necessary by the most fervid national standards, payments for railway debt or imported machinery, for example. Exploitation, moreover, so vital to the exploited, has never been of more than marginal importance to the exploiter. India never contributed more

[1]By contrast, in 1948 30% of the budget, excluding transport and communications, went to nation-building services.

than 6d. in the pound to the British national income, or Korea more than 1/- in the pound to the Japanese, and much, even of such contribution as was made, was for services rendered. It was not the fault of the Japanese that the Korean increased in numbers beyond the capacity of the land to bear. It was his fault that in his development of Korea's other resources, he reserved none of the fruits of his efforts for the Korean in whose country they were being carried out. It is perhaps poetic justice that the end of Japanese aggression was to leave the Korean in full possession of the investments which were the result of two generations of Japanese effort.

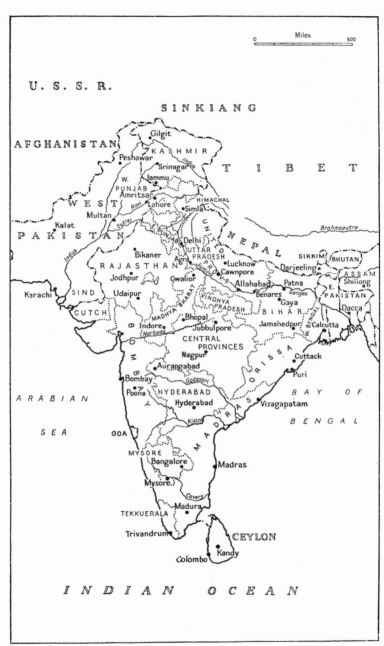

India and Pakistan (after partition)

Chapter VII

INDIA

INTRODUCTION

India is one of the great classical Asian economies, where increase in population has produced a pressure on the land as severe as it has anywhere in the world. This pressure is indeed now so severe that the whole Indian economy is most precariously balanced. The standard of life has been declining and very great economic effort will be required if the trend is to be reversed.

The two features which India shows more clearly than any other Asian country are, however, neither poverty nor population pressure, but firstly the disintegrating effect of Western legal concepts on a peasant countryside, and secondly the ferment of new intellectual life produced by the introduction into the East of the political ideas of the West. Eastern society had been governed by custom, status and equality—Western law was rigid, contractual and changeable. Eastern thought had been dominated by other worldly religions whose primary concern was with a man's own soul. The dominant beliefs of Western politics are that this world can be changed and that it is as valuable for a man to try and change the world for the better as it is for him to try and save his own soul. Much of Western politics, indeed, rest on the assumption that he who ignores the salvation of the community cannot hope to save his own soul.

Both Western law and Western politics were thus major instruments of change, though in different ways. Western law disrupted the Indian countryside. Western ideas made Indian politics dynamic instead of static. Under their influence, Indians came to believe that the ills of this world are not always tribulations sent from heaven. Sometimes they are the result of human incompetence and can be got rid of by a change in methods, and the men who use them.

The combination has been revolutionary. This chapter is an attempt to study what has happened in more detail and in its full setting.

SOCIAL CHANGE

The West has always boasted most proudly of the law and order which it has brought to its dependent territories. India is an example of how high a price to pay for Western order Western law may be. Increasing population would in any case have presented her with most serious problems. Those problems have been greatly aggravated by the protection the anglicised legal system has given to money-lender and landlord. Politically this legal system has been of inestimable advantage and has provided many of the concepts upon which the new free and liberal India is being developed. But economically, however necessary it was for the new towns, in the countryside it has been an almost unmitigated disaster.[1]

It has already been argued that in the old days before the British there was ample land for all. The peasant might be grievously oppressed. In a famine he might starve. He might be unable to buy anything not produced in his own village, but he had the great compensation that he had little need for the money-lender and the money-lender little use for him; for land is poor security when there is more than enough of it.[2]

It is not only important that the peasant's economic self-sufficiency made it unnecessary for him to have recourse to the money-lender. It is equally important that his lack of any marketable security kept down his expenditure on social occasions. Everywhere in the world the amount spent on such functions as weddings and funerals is governed by the need to keep up with one's neighbours. So long as nobody could borrow for such purposes, weddings and funerals necessarily remained cheap and because they remained cheap there was no need to borrow. It was a beneficent circle.

The peasant had then another protection against over-borrowing. The money-lender was dependent on his debtors' goodwill, not as under English law, they upon his. Courts were slow and irregular and not very good at enforcing their decisions; the rule of Dam-dupat—that interest beyond the amount of the principal went in reduction of principal—prevented the snowballing of debts; mortgages expressed as conditioned sales were recognised for all time as mortgages. Public order, and therefore the enforcement of

[1] The political consequences of the introduction of English legal ideas are discussed in Chapter XVIII.

[2] The *Khandesh Gazetteer* points out that few thought of buying land in pre-British days, and the *C.P. Gazetteer* tells of the surprise of the peasant who found that under the British his *Malguzari* was a saleable asset.

all decrees, depended upon the village officers and the village servants. An extortionate money-lender would not merely be obstructed, he would be beaten and quite likely murdered, as happened still in the 1930s in Sind.

The coming of the British changed everything. The new circumstances they created in the countryside at once provided a dozen reasons for borrowing and provided an adequate security which could be offered to potential lenders.

Once railways were built it became relatively easy to bring food into a famine-stricken area. The peasant, therefore, instead of starving now borrowed money in order to be able to buy from the grain dealers' stocks at the grain dealers' exorbitant price. The British Government fixed the land revenue at a definite cash amount instead of a somewhat flexible share of the crop. Over a period of years, the average amount payable was considerably lower than previously, but since it was not increased in good years, it was not decreased in bad ones either. And the peasant, who had not the habit of saving for bad times, had either to borrow to pay the revenue or else lose his land. Above all, it now became possible to borrow for every form of social extravagance. The thriftless pledged their land in order to marry their daughters in adequate style, and the thrifty had no option but to follow suit or be socially disgraced. In a world where marriages are arranged and a girl's chances may be severely damaged if it is known that a second-cousin drinks an occasional glass of beer, no father can afford not to live up to the standard of lavishness of his neighbours.

A new will to borrow was thus created in the peasant, but it could not have been satisfied if there had not been a parallel creation of a new willingness to lend in the creditor. Under the old system the money-lender could not afford to lend more than the value of one year's crop, for the crop was his only security. Such small debts even at 50% can be paid off easily enough by all but the most impoverished. But when the British introduced into the Indian countryside the clear cut conceptions of property which Western Europe had inherited from the Romans, they provided the peasant with something mortgagable—his rights in the land—and the peasant duly mortgaged. 70% were in debt in Bengal, 87% in Sind and 85% in the Assam Plains in the early 30s. To give to the Indian peasant a mortgagable asset was not in itself bad. For him to be able to borrow with greater ease in a famine, or to buy a bullock, was a net economic advantage. But unfortunately English law brought to India not only its concept of property, but all the ideas about contracts which had grown up to suit the commercial needs of London. They were not very well suited even to the English countryside. They were disastrous for the Indian countryside.

It may be worth developing a few examples at greater length. It was a basic idea of English law expressed as early as 1677 in the Statute of Frauds that the Court did not normally go behind a written contract, and certainly did not permit it to be modified by a collateral oral understanding. But collateral oral understandings were the very life's blood of all Indian agreements. The peasant would execute a sale deed on the assurance that the money-lender would treat it as, in fact, a conditional mortgage. The peasant would agree to a high rate of interest in the document, because he knew that the custom had always been that interest was waived in a bad year. He would sign a promissory note for more money than he actually got without troubling to have the note read to him, because he knew he could produce half the village to testify to the actual amount he had received. He would accept an onerous contract knowing that Hindu law permitted only simple, not compound interest, and would not let the debt increase above twice the original loan. Above all, underlying his agreement to any contract at all, was the belief that he could never be dispossessed of his land, save for non-payment of land revenue.[1]

Every one of these understandings of the peasant was unenforceable in a Court under British law.

He could lose his land with the utmost ease for "all property whatsoever is liable to attachment or sale in execution of a decree." (Civil procedure Code, 1859, section 205). There was no limit to the Court's capacity to enforce the rate of interest expressed in the bond, for Act 28 of 1855 had repealed the usury laws and provided that the Courts should decree the rate of interest contracted, and the Courts usually interpreted this to mean they were precluded even from considering whether the rate had only been agreed to under coercion, fraud or undue influence.

Not even the peasant's person was safe. For the Civil Procedure Code of 1859 had given to the creditor the right to proceed against either the property or the person of his debtor at his own, and not the Court's discretion.[2]

[1]In 1895, the Note on Land Transfer and Agricultural Indebtedness could still say "The idea of their lands being subject to sale in satisfaction of a bond debt or running account with a money-lender has occurred to few of them".

[2]The result was, of course, to reduce the debtor to slavery.

The peasant's whole basic assumption that every contract must be subject to custom and equity and the private agreements of the parties was false. No Court went willingly behind the documents in order to get at the facts, and the Evidence Act even gave a presumption of correctness to the money-lender's account books—instruments even a raw member of the Central Government should have known were usually fraudulently kept.

The law thus gave the money-lender every advantage, and he made full use of his opportunity. For he realised more quickly than the peasant how great was the cash value which the new dispensation, with its law and order, its increasing population and its exports of cotton and opium, was giving to land.[1]

The money-lender realised more quickly than the peasant also how simple the new Civil Law had made the transfer of land.[2]

The peasant could not conceive that the land which his ancestors had held for generations was just another debt. The money-lender understood that the law had made it as transferable as a bullock, as marketable as a maund of salt, so he lent and lent and cheated and cheated—until he could foreclose and foreclose.

Sir Thomas Hope, introducing the Deccan Agricultural Relief Act in the Bombay Legislature in 1879—no subversive Radical this—described his methods:—

"As Mr. Pedder expresses it: 'The passing of a bond by a native of India is often of no more value as proof of a debt he thereby acknowledges than the confession by a man under torture of the crime he is charged with. That the money-lenders do obtain bonds on false pretences: enter in them larger sums than agreed upon; deduct extortionate premiums; give no receipts for payments and then deny them; credit produce at fraudulent prices; retain liquidated bonds and sue upon them; use threats and warrants of imprisonments to extort fresh bonds for sums not advanced; charge interest unstipulated for, overcalculated on in contravention of Hindu law, these are facts proved by evidence'."

The peasant, not understanding, co-operated in the evil work. Not knowing his risks, he saw only that a cornucopia of wealth

[1] In Khandesh where in 1820 land had been valueless, in 1880 good land was fetching £7 an acre.

[2] Regulation I of 1793, 3.9. for example provided as follows: "The Zemindars are privileged to transfer to whomsoever they may think proper by sale, gift or otherwise, their proprietary rights in the whole or any portion of their respective estates without applying to Government for its sanction to the transfer, and all such transfers will be held valid".

was pouring over him; what matter that it was but lent. He borrowed for weddings, he borrowed to buy land, he borrowed to go to law—in 1900 one Bengali in 74 was engaged in a law suit. And he never hurried to pay back. In the cotton boom of 1861–5 he shod his bullocks with silver, but he did not pay his debts. So the debt piled up, and the money-lender made his false entries; and then came the horrible, the society-shaking shock. The money-lender went to Court, perhaps as the result of some such crack in prices in Gujerat as that which followed the end of the American Civil War.

The Court, bound by its own narrow view of an inappropriate law, had no option but to give the money-lender his decree. And so from decree to execution, from execution to the land passing into the money-lender's hands and the shaking of society which comes from the stability of peasant ownership being exchanged for the shiftlessness of rack-rented tenancy, was but the shortest of steps. And it was a step made the shorter by the corruption with which the Civil Courts were surrounded. Bailiffs were bribed not to serve summonses, clerks not to advertise sales, so that the money-lender could first get an *ex parte* decree and then buy in the land for half its price. And every Civil Court in fixing dates for adjournments would always consider the convenience of the money-lender's lawyer rather than a debtor who might have had 50˙miles to walk to come to Court at all. [1] It is a situation which has sometimes made it difficult for decent District Officers to see in Civil Courts anything but an instrument for transferring the property of the poor into the hands of the rich.

The justice of the State necessarily came to seem to the peasant remote, incomprehensible—the bought perquisite of the rich and the cunning. For the Civil Court not merely did not do justice in fact, it did not even appear to be trying to do justice. The peasant understood neither the language nor the law nor the procedure. So his cases went by default; in the Bombay Deccan in 1874, 150,000 warrants for arrest for debt were being used to take away the

---

[1] I have had personal experience of all the evils here described. The words of Ibbetson, Deputy Commissioner of Rohtak in 1891, are however worth quoting for the admirable way in which they describe one facet of the situation. "My heart burns within me when, as I go through the villages, I am appealed to daily by persons suffering wrong. They go away sadly either to endure the known wrong rather than the certain but unknown evils of a suit, or to borrow money, or having borrowed it, to suborn false witnesses and concoct a story by the dim light of ignorance of our law, convinced that the plain truth will be rejected on some ground or other that they do not understand."

independence of the Maratha farmer who had a century before lorded it in Delhi. Even the criminal law was weighted against the peasant. His little offences, faction fights or minor riots, brought upon him the whole weight of the State and its police. But the money-lender's crimes, cheating and malversation, false entries in account books and the intimidation by thugs of recalcitrant debtors, were treated as private affairs—contracts to be fought out in a Civil Court or non-cognizable crimes to be pursued by the complainant at his own expense. And even if a bold peasant did risk his money on bringing a case, he would be met not only by the better lawyers and smoother witnesses of the money-lender's longer purse, but also by the invincible ignorance about the conditions of the countryside of the Civil Judge, and all too often also by his invincible belief that false account books and promissory notes were neither cheating nor forgery, but the ordinary incidents of a money-lender's business.[1]

It was not without reason that the peasants of Allahabad, who had faced with equanimity Maratha and Mughal and Englishman, fled in panic when they heard the High Court was coming. Many centuries of experience had taught them the meaning of oppression; they knew and valued the rough equity of the village panchayat; but this elaborate and impartial injustice they found odd; better the old ways. So the peasants despaired and brooded and broke into exasperated revolt, riots in the Deccan in the 1870s, a rising in Chota Nagpur in 1899–1900, the rebellion in Bihar in 1942.

The slow decline in the support given to the British Government in the countryside was quite largely due to its failure to face the problem of debt. The failure was not in any way due to ignorance. Every good Collector reported the facts. Sir Thomas Munro had spoken of them already in 1822 and they were still being described in official reports in the 1930s.

The Government deserved to lose support, it did so little to solve a problem of which it was fully informed. There were exceptions. Protection was given to the aboriginals whose trust had touched the heart of every officer who dealt with them, and to the Punjabi from whom so much of the Army came. So also in Bombay where the Deccani peasant's refusal to suffer his wrongs quietly had made law and order itself dependent on their remedy. Protection was given also to the great landlords whose maintenance was con-sidered a political necessity and whose past glories and present embarrassments touched the imagination. Even these measures

[1]Personal experience.

G

were taken late. Nothing was done for the Central Provinces aboriginals, for example, until 1916[1] after they had already lost their land in the plains, or in the Punjab[2] until 1900 when over a quarter of the province had already gone to the moneylender. The earlier Acts, the Chota Nagpur Tenures Act of 1869 or the Deccan Agriculturists' Relief Act of 1879, only came after the civil court had had a generation or more in which to do its work.

Where Government did move it was very successful, and its very success placed in dark relief its failure to find general remedies, for the action it took to protect special classes could have been made of general application.

For example, it prohibited the alienation or mortgage or letting of aboriginal land without the Collector's permission. To-day in these areas Bhils and Gonds and Santals, whole-heartedly improvident and agriculturally incompetent though they have always been, still own their own land to an extent that induces the envy of their more advanced, and therefore more unprotected, neighbours. In the Punjab the attempt to prevent land passing to non-agriculturists was so successful that by the early 1930s only a quarter of the mortgages entered into were to non-agriculturists. The amount of land cultivated by tenants-at-will nevertheless went up from 6½ million acres in 1880 to 20 million in 1938, but that was because the law made no attempt to prevent alienation of land to fellow-farmers, and it is no Communist discovery that the money-lender who is also landlord or fellow-peasant is the most ruthless and land-hungry of them all. The Deccan Agriculturists' Relief Act had to be repeatedly amended to meet the dodges of the lawyers and the restrictive interpretations of the Courts, but it has preserved the Maratha as the most independent and upstanding of India's races. Most successful of all were the Encumbered Estates Acts and Courts of Wards Acts, which have made it virtually impossible for the great landowners to lose their estates. When they got into difficulties the Collector took over, under conditions which bore no relation to the English rules of the civil court. Repayments were based on what had actually been borrowed, regardless of the deed; the Collector could reject claims with which he was not satisfied; civil court decrees could be re-opened; only reasonable interest was allowed; the rule of Damdupat was enforced. As early as the 1880s in Jhansi debts of 11¼ lakhs were thus reduced to 7½. In the early days in

[1]C.P. Land Alienation Act, 1916.
[2]Punjab Land Alienation Act, 1900.

Bengal the great estates came under the hammer almost as quickly as they were formed, but these Acts have ensured that those who were Taluqdars of Oudh or Sardars of Gujerat fifty years ago are still so to-day.

It is therefore the odder that Government made no attempt to protect the ordinary decent peasant, whose loyalty was its backbone, whose discontent under worsening conditions was to provide the Congress and the Socialists with so dangerous a weapon. But it never did. In Bombay, for example, when Congress resigned in 1939, the Governor's régime which succeeded failed, except for very limited areas, to pass the executive orders needed to apply their Debt Conciliation and Tenancy legislation. That may have been just the caution of men unwilling to alienate any vested interest when engaged in a war of life and death—though the money-lender's inclinations, if any, have always been towards Congress. But there is no such excuse for a hundred previous years of inaction. For that the only explanation is the cynicism men get with age, the reluctance to interfere that comes when one no longer has the daily and hourly sight of wrong to drive its bitterness into one's marrow. Better to relax and remember the comfortable advice of Manchester, that Government's duty is *laisser-faire*, that any attempt to interfere with the beneficent natural law which removes ownership from the improvident to the provident, from the simple to the cunning, is as doomed to failure as trying to fix minimum wages for Lancashire children.

They might have been right if India had been like England, if the Bania had acquired in order to become a country gentleman. Such capitalists raised the output of English agriculture from 110 international units per head in 1800 to 590 in 1911.[1] But the bania, by his whole heredity and caste disposition, had no such ambition. He was a townsman, whose only interest in the land was his rack-rent. His tenants were always sucked dry, their land always the weediest and most eroded; and they paid perhaps £2 an acre (at 1935 prices) where an English farmer would have paid 30/- for land yielding four times as much and with farm buildings and maybe a piped water supply thrown in; the money-lender's tenant got nothing, neither bullock nor seed nor house.

How large was the problem, how many thus lost their land and sank to tenants or labourers, can be seen from the example of Bombay. There were 1,850,000 peasant proprietors in 1872, 2,344,000 in 1931; mere rent-receivers went up from 84,000 to

[1]Colin Clark, *op. cit.*

172,000. And this was before the Great Depression, which caused 40% of Madras Province[1] to be sold in the five years 1929–34, half—$5\frac{1}{4}$ million acres, the land of perhaps one million families—to non-agriculturists. A million Punjab acres were mortgaged between 1931 and 1936; in 1938 in the S.W. Punjab 40% of sales were to pay off debt, one-third were still making the sellers landless. And of those who still kept their land, many were insolvent, so much so that when debt conciliation was finally introduced in the 1930s, creditors accepted cuts that averaged nearly half their debt in order to save the other half.[2]

The whole of this disaster was not the result of the free hand that the law gave the money-lender, and the peasant's eagerness to borrow for unproductive purposes. Perhaps a third of the increase in debt from £200 million in 1911 to £1350 million in 1938 was incurred to meet real need. Agriculture is a slow process and somebody must provide working capital. But it was the other two-thirds that made the peasant's position so hopeless.

English conceptions of property not only gave these enormous advantages to money-lenders. It also created over half of India a class of landlords who were all too often even more parasitic.

Before the British came there was no such thing as a landlord in its English sense of the property. In Berar, where the British Government did not create landlords as an act of policy, as late as 1884 6,856,000 out of the 7,670,000 people dependent on agriculture were independent proprietors or members of their family. Property was strictly vested in the peasant, so much so that Mr. Fortescue, the Delhi Commissioner, could testify to a Parliamentary Select Committee that families who had absented themselves for years could return and re-occupy their land without any opposition. The law too was clear. Manu had said "The sages who know former times pronounce cultivated land to be the property of him who cut away the wood, or who cleared and tilled it", and the Prophet Mohammed "Whoever gives life to dead land, it is his". Above the peasant there were only tax farmers and feudal nobles and tribal leaders, men who had, not property, but jurisdiction, who exercised over the land the rights not of an owner but of a royal delegate. The fee simple was no more in the Zemindar in India than in the baron in England; but where the English baron extended his rights by

---

[1]The figures do not cover the districts of S. Kanara and Malabar.

[2]E.g. The average reduction in the Punjab was 45% and in the Central Provinces by August '38 debts of 684 lakhs had been reduced to 360 lakhs.

usurpation on the Crown, the Indian Zemindar could only do so by the still more harmful process of usurpation on the people.

The whole concept of land ownership as it developed in English or Roman law, with its absolute heritability, and its unfettered transferability, was totally alien to the Indian mind. The Zemindar was the holder of the delegated right to collect the land revenue, raised by Akbar's Revenue Minister, Todar Mall, to between a quarter and a third of the crop; it had ranged as low as one-twelfth under the old Hindu Kings. He might be a royal relation like most of the jagirdars in the Rajput States, or an heir whom the King delighted to honour like the first Raja of Orchha, or a tribal leader too powerful for the King to suppress, like the Raja of Ramnad; what he never was, was a country gentleman, a Mr. Darcy of Pemberton. The peasant himself could usually only sell within a limited circle; his family or his village might have a right of pre-emption, his village very often had the right to refuse to accept a purchaser it did not feel would fit into the community.

In a situation in which the peasant and the States retain so many rights, a Zemindar might be oppressive. He could not recover a full economic rent. He could put a man in a dark cell alone till he paid twice the dues he owed; but that was oppression and felt to be such, and therefore, except in the worst times, only occasional. He could not evict from his holding between morning and night a man whose ancestors had been there for a thousand years, and do so with a clear conscience and in the ordinary way of business, because somebody else had offered him 6d. an acre more on the rent.

The early English conquerors of India were, however, fired with the idea that what India needed to transform her was a class of men willing to give their capital to their estates, their charities to their dependants and their talents to their country. There have been many such in England, but they have been few indeed in India. From the ranks of the Indian Zemindars have come poets like Tagore, civil servants like Sir Jagdish Prasad, statesmen like Pakistan's Premier, Liaquat Ali Khan, cricketers like the Maharaj Kumar of Viziana-gram, but they have never produced a Coke of Holkham.

It should not have been expected of men of their ancestry. Some were descendants of officers of previous régimes who had made themselves semi-independent, like the Rajas of Pithapuram, sprung from a cavalry commander of Golconda; some bandits and thieves, like those Taluqdars of Oudh of whom Sleeman said they usurped four-fifths of the peasants' land between 1800 and 1850; but the majority were tax-farmers and the descendants of tax farmers, like the Maharajas of Benares, who had utilised the 18th-century weakness of the central power to collect more and more from the peasant and remit less and less to the Emperor.

Of such men British policy tried to make Cecils and Churchills. Its objectives and its weaknesses can be most fairly demonstrated in the case of the Taluqdars of Oudh. We find Lord Canning in 1858 arguing that: "The maintenance of a territorial aristocracy in India is an object of so great importance that we may well afford to sacrifice to it something of a system which, whilst it increased the independence and protected the rights of the cultivators of the soil, and augmented the revenues of the State, has led more or less directly to the extinction and decay of the old nobility of the country". The argument would have had force if it had not been that not one family in three amongst these men went back a hundred years and that Lord Canning himself had pointed out that most of their land and rights had been acquired by fraud and violence.

The error of creating a class of landed proprietors by confering property upon a miscellany of men to whom the rights of the State to collect land revenue had been delegated or sold, or by whom they had been usurped, was committed over most of Northern India and in a few areas in the South. But most of the evil was saved by the perception of Elphinstone and Munro who understood better the true state of Indian facts and who understood that the land revenue should be settled direct with the ryot, the actual cultivator.[1] The rest of India is Zemindar.

The Zemindar has been a landlord unremittingly, almost painstakingly bad. He has swallowed every remission which Government has given him and passed none of it on to his tenant. He has accepted permanent fixing of his own dues to Government and failed to fulfil the condition on which this fixing was made—that he should in turn fix the due of his tenants. The Zemindar's income was obtained at the expense of both the State and the peasant. In Bengal, the Government's share of the rents went down from nine-tenths in 1790 to one-quarter in 1903–4, and this limitation in Government's revenue goes far to explain the badness of Bengal's Government. The tenant, on the other hand, found himself paying a rent that was frequently

[1]Most of Bombay and Madras, Berar, Agra and most of the Punjab; Sind and part of the Punjab are a special case where there is a good deal of large landownership, but mainly as the result of grants or sales by the State of newly-irrigated land.

as high as half the crop, and showed a steady tendency to rise.[1]

Zemindar income was frequently very large, sometimes as high as £750,000 a year. In 1884 no fewer than 42 men each had over 130,000 acres, but few ever did anything for the land or its people in return for what they took out of the land. No Zemindar has given his name to a new strain of rice or pioneered with a new plough or a rust-resistant wheat. Lucknow is as full of landowners whose heart is in their politics and their lawsuits, their parties and their culture, as Threadneedle Street is of bankers whose first love is their prize bulls and their tractors.

Nor did Government confine itself to merely creating landlords. It also gave them powers which were appropriate rather to the farmers of the revenue that they had been, than to the property owners they had become. As early as 1799 in Bengal they were allowed to distrain summarily on both the person and the property of their tenants.

Government showed no such speed when it came to protecting the rights of the tenant—a tenant who had once owned the land himself and had only been reduced to tenancy by Government's action.

The first effective Tenancy Act in Bengal was passed in 1885. In Oudh Government never enforced the obligation to be placed on the Taluqdars to respect all subordinate rights and only gave the tenant protection by the Oudh Rent Amendment Act of 1921. Action elsewhere was equally tardy—1908 in Madras for instance, 1926 in Agra—and the protection given was never thorough. The landlord could, for example, evict the tenant from any land he wished to farm himself, and home farm lands, though they were usually let, were excluded from protection.[2] Yet the remedies required were simple enough—a provision that the tenant could not be evicted except for specified defaults, notably failure to pay his rent, and that his rent could not be raised except by a decision of a revenue officer for specified reasons, a rise in prices, for example, or in Government's demand on the landlord. And even so, the tenant was not always safe, for there were always holes in the law. In the U.P. nearly 700,000 tenants were evicted between 1939 and

[1] In the United Province, Government reduced its claim on him and the demand went down from 90% of the net assets in 1790 to 36% in 1929, but rents rose from Rs.1224 lakhs in 1893 to Rs.1881 lakhs in 1934.

[2] There were 7½ million acres of such land in the United Province alone.

1945 despite a great stiffening of the Act in the tenant's favour in 1939.

These figures are not just the result of a law which gave every advantage to landlord and moneylender. Neither landlord nor moneylender would have succeeded in obtaining so large a proportion of the gross yield of agriculture had it not been for the increase in population which filled up the land and deprived the peasant of the safety valve of going elsewhere and making himself a new holding out of the waste.[1]

The combined effect is to reduce the countryside to semi-starvation. The net income of agriculture, before deducting the cost of labour, was in the mid 30s perhaps £600,000,000 a year. Rent payments were around £150 million interest on debt about £200,000,000 (assuming the reasonable average interest of 15%). What was left for the peasant and the labourer and their families was $\frac{3}{4}$d. a day each; if we have underestimated by one-third it would still only be 1d! It is not surprising that food-grain consumption went down from 1$\frac{1}{2}$ lbs. per day per head in 1880 to 14 ozs. in 1936–8[2], that rents fell into arrears and debts stayed unpaid, that ends could never be made to meet[3], and that the peasantry more and more lost its only asset, the land which was its life. Indian agriculture had always been a means of living the good life more than just a way of earning a livelihood; now it provided neither life nor living.

So in Bihar and the Eastern United Provinces in 1942 there was the first serious revolt in over eighty years, and the Punjab massacres of 1947 were led by men who wanted the land even more than the lives of their neighbours. An Indian or Pakistani Government to-day walks ever on the brink of the precipice, and the path moves unceasingly beneath its feet, for there is no discontent so deep-running as that of the man who works as tenant or labourer on land that once was his, no tinder so ready to the spark of revolution as the soul of him whose dream of ownership has all the power of

[1]The figures for increase in population and filling up of the land have been given in Table 14a.

[2]The estimate for 1880 is that made in 1945 by Sir Manilal Nanavati, Deputy Governor of the Reserve Bank. That for 1936–8 has been obtained privately from the Government of India.

[3]An investigation in Bengal in 1935 gave average gross incomes of Rs.114 and average gross expenditures of Rs.116. As some 30% of the families were debt free, it will be seen that the bottom half must have been hopelessly bankrupt, and they did not include any families of landless labour.

recent memory, and who sees in those who now own his land men more cunning, not more thrifty, than himself.[1]

Only as the abolition of Zemindari and the curbing of the money-lender, which in most areas have been amongst the first fruits of independence, come gradually into effect, are the Governments scrambling back to safe ground.

THE CHANGE OF HEART AND MIND

Behind the westernisation of India's institutions lay a far more significant fact—the westernisation of its mind.

Great Britain's success in transmitting to India the essential concepts of Western liberal civilisation was perhaps its greatest contribution to world history. To have received these concepts was the greatest of all India's feats of absorption. Teacher and pupil share equal credit. The result is that India has been removed, probably permanently, from the ranks of the autocratic societies that have been the common form of society over most of the world's surface and most of its history. Once a nation has known ordered law and stable freedom, it never relapses entirely. Europe's long nostalgia for Roman law and Republican liberty is the best proof of this.

In the process of becoming westernised intellectually, India passed through two stages. The first was the attempt to copy the West completely. The second was to absorb what was important in the West while still retaining the best of its own tradition. The way in which the process took place can be seen clearly in individual Indian lives.

Mahatma Gandhi describes in his Autobiography how, as a student, he attempted to become completely an English gentleman; he even wore a top hat and frock-coat. But English gentlemen are not merely always courteous and considerate; they also drink whisky and eat beef, and the Mahatma could not imitate them in this. He therefore stated a synthesis. He rejected the respect for wealth and force which runs through so much that is bad in our Western civilisation, but he accepted the democracy, the eagerness to take action to relieve the suffering of the poor, the respect for the individual conscience, and the willingness to let each group get its own way, which constitute so much of the good. What he accepted

[1] Reform goes back well before independence; there was considerable restriction of the rights of both landlord and money-lender in the later '30's, for example. But the pace has greatly quickened in the last few years.

he married to certain aspects of his own tradition—the emphasis on moral force, the admiration for withdrawal from worldly desires, non-violence, the realisation that in India the poor meant above all the villager. Out of the combination of these concepts he produced the Congress Movement.

Pandit Nehru's life is a similar living example of the way in which India has made a synthesis of East and West. His father Motilal was at one time the complete Englishman of the successful barrister type, a man who would have been as much at home as a Bencher of an Inn of Court as in Allahabad. The son's political ideas, the passion for freedom that has taken him to gaol for so many years, the fervent nationalism, the emphasis on the secular state, even the tendency to an Asian Munroe doctrine, have obvious Western origins. But Nehru has also accepted non-violence, and the cult of home-spun cotton, from Gandhi. His *Discovery of India* shows how deep an inspiration to him is the sense of the glories of India's past. His synthesis has made him a great Prime Minister of India.

Jinnah was yet another example. There was a time in the 30s when he was living in London practising at the Privy Council Bar. Then he went back to India, taking with him all the understanding he had of Parliaments and politicians and constitutions and the British mind, a habitual use of the English language and English clothes; he added to that the appeal to the sense of brotherhood in Islam and separateness from all that is not Islam which always stirs Muslim hearts. Out of this synthesis came Pakistan.

At every level of Indian society, men have been making similar syntheses and combinations. They have absorbed new ideas and new ways and have synthesised them with the old so that they fit without shock and without sense of imitation. The first manifestation was the babu in patent leather boots, who sprinkled his talk with "Oh! my God" and looked down on "natives". That was the manifestation at the Kipling stage, laughable, pathetic. It started necessarily with externals. Over two or three generations there was a steady sifting of the new ways. It came to be understood that "looking down on natives" was a survival of tribalism which was out of line with the great concept of the brotherhood of man, and that this latter was the true foundation of Western civilisation. It was realised that punctuality was a greater Western virtue than was the wearing of patent leather boots, and that "please" and "thank you" said equally to inferior, equal and superior, were more symbolic of the Western spirit than "Oh, my God!"

To-day the result is seen in Pandit Pant, Prime Minister of the United Provinces, refusing entry to Hindu refugees to protect his U.P. Muslims; in the Hindu police protecting Muslims from attack; and in the way in which thousands of Revenue and Police officers have worked consistently overtime and so have kept the State moving forward through all the innumerable difficulties since independence. It can be seen in the provisions of the new Constitution for such diverse subjects as the abolition of untouchability, equal pay for equal work, or the right to education. It can be seen also in the rejection of the idea of village republics or the insistence on the need for a strong centre or the desire to make the planning of major industries a central subject. The members of the Constituent Assembly clearly understand what is best in the spirit of the West, and do not bother about its forms. They wear dhotis, not frock-coats, yet they understand the value of the committee system as making for personal friendships and the easy exchange of experience between political opponents; this is not understood elsewhere outside the Western Democracies. Above all, they have given India adult suffrage, for they have understood the great lesson of the 19th century, that the best protection for any class is the vote, and that an interested electorate can neither be bought nor permanently deceived.

Yet in all this completion of Westernisation—the Constituent Assembly is in a tradition which goes back at least to Macaulay— the Assembly has not forgotten what is valuable in the Indian tradition either, or that the electorate is entitled to have its prejudices considered as well as its principles. It has issued directives in favour of prohibition although Excise produced 25% of State revenues, for drink is regarded by most Indians as drugs are by Europeans. The Assembly has forbidden cow-slaughter, since the cow is still sacred to the countryside (though that is not the reason given by the Assembly for its action). State Governments have restored to village panchayats their minor jurisdiction, and have not seriously interfered with the traditional and Indian importance of the District Magistrate.

The westernisation of the mind of India was not the westernisation of the mind of the whole country. Essentially it was the middle class which became western in spirit; and this middle class was no more than about 5% of the population. But in the recent past, this class determined the social history of India, and still does so at the present.

It is for this reason that a society so overwhelmingly agrarian as the Indian is to-day nevertheless a dynamic one. The apparent conservatism of its peasant masses is politically deceptive. For though the masses in India may be conservative, all the leaders are men with the new ideas. The fight in India, and everywhere in Asia, is between the Left and the Further Left, and it is that which makes Communism so dangerous. There is no leader who wishes to keep the society as it is, or to permit the necessary changes to be a slow broadening from precedent to precedent. The moderate wishes to change without violence; he is willing to take time. The revolutionary wishes to do everything forcefully and at once. But even the Conservatives of the Congress are buying out the Zemindars at semi-confiscatory prices; even Pakistan wishes to see all heavy industry nationalised.

Chapter VIII

BURMA

One of the profoundest of Victorian beliefs was that economic freedom was a method of attaining greater production. Another was in the value of greater production merely as such. On both scores the Victorians were undoubtedly right. This is a poor world, and if people are to be adequately fed and clothed and educated, every ounce of production which can be obtained is needed. And it has yet to be shown that any other method is as effective as *laisser-faire* in releasing men's economic energies.

Most men are, however, creatures of custom who adapt themselves with difficulty to new ideas or new methods. The Victorians did not always realise that though the dynamic society they were creating did indeed produce great increases in material wealth, it did so only at the expense of disrupting the lives of millions who were unable to adapt themselves to a life of such rapid and constant change. This has been particularly true in Asia where so much of the dynamism has come from outside and the tradition of the local societies was peculiarly static. The clearest example of the way in which, in Asia, larger production has often been accompanied by social disintegration, is Lower Burma, and this chapter is an attempt to study the process in greater detail.

No country in Asia provides a more striking example of the strength and weakness of Victorian ideas of policy than Lower Burma, of the economic bound forward that comes from the letting loose of the unfettered energies of the individual, and the spiritual decay that comes from teaching the individual that the most effective way of loving his neighbour is to pursue his own self-interest. There is not even any need to look to Europe to point the contrast, for in Burma itself, in Upper Burma, there can be found a community which neither grew so rich nor lost so much of its soul.

As an achievement in settlement and economic development, Lower Burma ranks with Canada or the Argentine as a Victorian triumph.

The acreage under rice, the population, the trade figures (Tables

17, 18, 19) all tell the same story of expansion. The empty land of
1830—made empty by Siamese invasion, Talaing revolt and Burmese repression—grew enough rice in 1930 to feed its own 7¾
million people and 20 million more overseas; between 1872 and
1881 the population went up by 40%, between 1890 and 1910 rice
acreage grew by 160,000 acres a year; in the single district of
Toungoo cultivation went up from 60,000 to 475,000 acres in thirty
years (1884–5 to 1913–14).

Lower Burma provides us with a case-study of all the phenomena
which characterised 19th-century expansion everywhere, from the
Middle West to Australia. There is the concentration on the one
crop for which an immediate export market could be found. Rice
has always covered nine acres in every ten. The growth of agriculture was in response not to the old stimulus, the peasant's desire to
feed and clothe his family from his own land, but a new one, the
farmer's eagerness to produce enough to have a surplus to sell in
exchange for the fascinating new wares of the world's new mills;
two-thirds of the crop was exported in the 30s.[1] The technical
improvement which made the new stimulus effective was the 19th-
century's new capacity to carry goods in bulk cheaply for long
distances. The acreage under cultivation in Burma went up 2½
times in the 20 years after the opening of the Suez Canal.

The market was provided by the rise of great populations who
could no longer feed themselves—first in the West to which nearly all
Burma's rice went in the 1870s, then in the East where India alone
took 1½ million tons of Burmese rice in 1938–9. This great expansion
of urban hunger created the rice farms of Lower Burma as surely as it
did the great wheat farms of the prairie provinces of Canada.

The human beings who actually wrought these changes in Burma
were the product of another typical Victorian phenomenon—large
scale free movement of men from one country to another where
they thought they could make a better living in freer conditions.
Migrants flooded in from India, from the dry lands of Upper
Burma, from the hills of Karenni and from China, and by the 1930s
Burma had one million Indians and 200,000 Chinese.

There were in Burma, also in full measure, some of the less pleasant
features of the enterprising century. There was the absolute dependence of life on exports, the entrusting of all welfare, from the money
for a new turban to the resources for a new monastery, to the world's

[1]Production about 7 million tons of paddy which is roughly two-thirds as
much in terms of rice: exports 3½ million tons.

demand for a single commodity. Lower Burma has not even the diversity which Lancashire gets from her engineering and coal and chemicals. Above all there was the terrible susceptibility to boom and slump, to the upward and downward gyration of prices, which because output can only be contracted or expanded slowly, has in the last thirty years characterised food and raw material producing economies. A factory can be shut down or work overtime at a few hours' notice, but this year's rice crop depends on last year's decision to plant. So Burmese rice prices were in 1934 one-third of 1928, and to-day are six times pre-war. [1]

But more important than economic instability was social rootlessness. There was the growing willingness in every section of the community to treat society as an arena in which men fight out their battle for wealth. Government was conceived of as only a referee, and a rather inefficient referee at that, which interfered neither with rack-renting nor unbearable debt, neither with millers' combines nor cultivators' strikes. There was no Tenancy Act till 1939, no Land Alienation Act till 1941. In the great depression, the Burmese Government took none of the action to prevent widespread foreclosure that was taken in such countries as the United States and Poland. Its only positive interference in economic affairs was a little subsidisation of Indian immigration in the early 1880s in order to keep down wages. [2]

Government's inaction cannot be explained simply as the result of imperialism. The half of Lower Burma which was owned by absentees in 1938 was in Burman and Indian hands, not British. The £50 million which the Chettyars had invested by 1929 was perhaps four times the value of all British interests in Lower Burma. [3] Their

[1] What this means to the average individual farmer is shown by the following calculation. A Burmese tenant-farmer who in 1928 made Rs.70 after paying his expenses of cultivation except for family labour, and providing 1lb. of rice per day each for his family, in 1934 probably lost Rs.5 or Rs.10, and in 1948 may have made Rs.250 or Rs.300.

The extreme economic instability, compared with English industry, is clear. In England in the depression it was an unfortunate man who drew in money as dole less than half what he had earned when in work, and in the post-war inflation it has been a lucky job where a man earns more than 2½ times his pre-war money wages.

[2] *Annual Report on the Administration of Burma* 1882–3, p.141.

[3] In trading and banking and river transport, total British investment in Burma was about £50 million in the '30s, but only about a quarter of this was in Lower Burma. Helmut G. Callis, *Foreign Capital in Southeast Asia*, New York, 1942.

income from it was perhaps twice the British £5 million or so. Rice went mostly to India, cotton goods came mostly from India. Imports of all Burma from Britain were under £3 million, exports to Britain under £6 million in 1938-9; for Lower Burma alone they were only a million or so each way.

Not even the original motive for annexation of Burma by Britain was economic. Tennasserim was nearly given back in 1831 because it did not pay. British enterprise only began in Lower Burma twenty years after its annexation in 1852.[1]

The reason for Government's failure to control affairs was idealogical, not material. The civil servants who controlled policy were firm believers in the *laisser faire* of the leader writers of *The Times* and *The Rangoon Times*. Their mentors of undergraduate days had been Ricardo and James Mill and the busy life of a bureaucrat makes it difficult for him to keep up with the latest developments of economic theory. There were, too, inevitable difficulties in applying directly such economic doctrine as they remembered. The civil servant is interested not in theories, but in action, and therefore in his hands tentative conclusions of the classroom have a strong tendency to become rigid dogma in the field. The theories they used were intended for Christians and Englishmen at the beginning of the Industrial Revolution. They were applied unchanged to Burmese and Buddhists undergoing an agricultural revolution.

The intentions behind the policy were of the best. The civil service was composed of men in general deeply devoted to the interests of the country they were governing. But good intentions are no substitute for full understanding and the results of applying undiluted *laisser-faire* to Burma, without even the restraints which tradition and the power of vested interests enforced in Europe, were sometimes disastrous. Because the individual was given rights, the rights of family and village were destroyed. Because there was open door for immigration, there grew up unassimilable minorities. Because it was possible to get rich quick, men tried to clear more land than they could manage. Because of the insistence on the fulfilment of the written contract, debt became intolerable. The use of money as the most important of symbols brought in its train the

[1] Cobden alleged that the war of 1852 was fought and Lower Burma annexed to recover a debt of £750. The allegation is hardly fair to Dalhousie, but even had it been true, £750 was hardly an important sum for Victorian England.

great problems of a cash economy. It also brought the gangs of labourers unemployed for half the year and the peasants who slept in the streets of Rangoon for lack of a home. The new apparatus of Government brought railways and English education but also law courts and corruption.

Some of this was a direct consequence of Government's own errors; for example, all waste land was declared to belong to the government. Thus, individuals were enabled to buy the land on which the water supply of the village might depend, or which might already have been cleared by a squatter whose rights the surveyor was bribed to ignore; and the enclosure of the waste meant in Burma, as it once had in England, the cottager's loss of his right freely to gather fuel or graze his bullock.

Under Burmese law all members of the family had complicated rights in the land; but too often in entering up the Record of Rights only those of the actual manager were included.

As in India, however, the most serious of Government's errors was the introduction of a legal system which had only the most unpredictable relations with the living custom of the people. The High Courts were staffed with judges many of whom knew nothing of Burma, and who gave to the Dharmathats (written collections of Buddhist law) an authority which overrode against all precedent the living custom of the village. Thus, since 1899—and only since 1899—the eldest child has special rights of inheritance; yet the average villager continues to follow the custom which gives him no such right. No one knew what the High Court would decide in any given case, and litigation acquired the attractions of horse-racing; the rankest outsider could win. The lower courts were staffed with men whom the whole structure of the law tempted into corruption, for no longer was the law customary, carried from generation to generation in the heads of the village wise men, familiar, in so far as it concerned him, to every village adult. No longer was the judge's function arbitration.[1] No longer was legal argument conducted in the language of the people. The law was contained in codes made in India and written in English, many of them drafted in the period of bad draftsmen from 1870 to 1884. The judge's function was not to satisfy all parties that justice had been done but to interpret and apply an often muddled written text.

[1]So deep-rooted was this conception of the law in old Burmese society that the defeated side had to declare his acceptance of the judgment for it to be valid.

H

Cases were heard in the headquarters town, so perjury was easy. And too many appeal courts led to too many acquittals.

In short, no one could be sure what the decision in any given case ought to have been, but all could see that, in fact, murderers went unhung and moneylenders recovered on deeds all knew to be forged. For a law which worked in such a way, nobody could feel respect, and therefore the explanation of every oddity came to be that the judges were bribed.[1]

In a society where land grabbing was encouraged by the Land Revenue Rules and the law bore no relation to the ordinary man's ideas of what was right and proper, it became increasingly difficult for the individual to retain his moral balance.

He was further freed from any sense of his obligation to his neighbour by the State's clumsiness in breaking down the local self-government which had in the past made of the Burman, as of the Indian or Chinese village, a little State within itself able to live and conduct its affairs however complete the breakdown of authority might be outside its borders.

The old Burmese system had been a personal one in which every man owed loyalty to a circle head, a Myothugyi. Not every man who lived in a circle owed loyalty to the head of that particular circle, however. The system had its administrative awkwardness, and a government whose members were Indian-trained introduced the Indian territorial village. Thus they destroyed at one blow the intricate bonds of loyalty and obligation which the generations had created.[2] The new village and its head could not be expected to enjoy the devotion the people had once given to their Myothugyi.

The administrative village had no organic unity; it might include several different hamlets or only half a residential area. Between 1909 and 1919 two thousand villages and their headmen disappeared by arbitrary amalgamation; after 1919 there began a process of equally arbitrary division; and upon the village and its new head were heaped responsibilities but not power. They were liable for the collection of the land revenue or the surveillance of bad charac-ters; they could be fined for not resisting dacoits or failing to keep up the village fence; but they could not control the way the villagers

[1]G. E. Harvey, *British Rule in Burma,* London, 1946, p. 37, quotes a custom by which the moneylenders of a district would club together to give each incoming judge two years' salary on his assumption of office.

[2]It was like trying to make a Macdonald into a Campbell because he happened to live in Argyll.

kept pigs, and the arbitration decisions of the headman could be set aside in the Chief Court as contrary to "Burmese" Law.[1]

So the village died and where in Upper Burma it had been able to keep up paths and bridges, a monastery and a monastery school, in Lower Burma whose villages often only grew up under the new regime, only one village in four had so much as a monastery and a monk.

The villager in ceasing to fulfil his obligations to his community was also damaging himself. Government's unconscious undermining of the foundations of the old order was extended even to the foundation of moral obligation in any society—religion. A religion loses something when all the formalities of State are conducted by the ritual of another faith. For a hundred years, until the Buddhist ceremony with which the Constituent Assembly was opened and Aung San buried, the religion of the people had no place in the formalities of the State. More important still, the organic unity of the Buddhist Church was destroyed. Its place in the daily life of the people was diminished. The conquest of Lower Burma thirty years before Upper Burma was annexed had already cut off its clerics from the authority of their heads in Mandalay, and after annexation all such authority was simply abolished (1886). The central committee of the church disappeared; the primate was made powerless. All that was left of organisation was the individual monastery and its individual monks. Discipline disappeared as ecclesiastical cases passed from the primate to the civil court;[2] and the monastic schools, which had made of Burma in the old days a country where one man in two was literate, decayed with their monasteries. There was never in Burma the harnessing of the monastic school to the general educational system which occurred in Siam.

The Church declined. But the hold of a cleric does not, however, always diminish with his character. The Pongyi might be unlearned. His yellow robe might be only a cover for a political agitator. His office still entitled him to the reverence of the people. A Protestant government could no more hope for public support for action against the Buddhist monk in Burma than it could in Ireland for action against a Catholic priest. In every revolt there were Pongyis in the lead, in 1886 as in 1931. It was in Young Men's Buddhist Associations that Burmese nationalism found its first expression (1906 onwards). It was a young monk, Vottama, who published the first description of Japan and the war of 1905. The advice of the village clergy decided the course of elections of 1932.

Government's sins, however, were sins of anthropological conquest, not of deliberate exploitation. Religion was damaged, the courts gave their formalistic decisions, in all good faith. In equal good faith were taken the still more damaging decisions which opened Lower Burma to the full forces of enterprise and competition.

Cheap labour was needed, so no restraint was placed on the flooding in of Indians, who came for a season or a lifetime, and then went home with their savings.[1] That this took £5 million a year out of the country in telegraphic transfers alone mattered no more than the remittances sent home by European emigrants in America; but that the Burman was driven from many forms of labour mattered a great deal. In 1931 there were 102,000 Indians against 90,000 Burmans in transport; the Rangoon docks were an Indian preserve till 1930. The reason for the use of Indian labour was not that Burmans could not work, but simply that no man with a wife and family to keep can afford to work for the wages and at the pace of the grass-widower immigrant slaving to make a little to send home. The Indian living in Burma for a few months could exist twenty to a room in coolie barracks; such conditions were intolerable as a permanent way of life for Burmans. This seasonal influx made possible the breaking up of the old comfortable relation between the agricultural worker and his employer. In the 1880s such men were taken on and paid by the year; by the 1930s employers had found that they could divide up their operations into earthwork, ploughing, planting, reaping, threshing and so on and take on a separate gang for each, thus paying wages for six months only. In 1880 a man lived in his employer's family, got board and lodging and 150 baskets of paddy a year; in 1935 he earned board and perhaps 120 baskets of paddy for seven months. For the other five months he was a migrant or out of work. The drop in real wages has been estimated by Furnivall as 20%. The same passion for quick efficiency at the cheapest price affected the professions too. That three-quarters of the railway officers were European or part-European, that the best lawyers were Indian and the oil-drillers Scots or American, at least gave the country better service than it could have got from Burmans, though the failure to train Burmans

[1] 450,000 entered in the peak year 1927.

has left Burma without the middle class which is so necessary to give ballast to independence; but that the vaccinators and the public works contractors were so often Indian was not even efficient, for a vaccinator who cannot speak the language of those he has come to vaccinate, a contractor who cannot recruit local labour because he knows neither language nor custom, are an expensive economy.[1]

Laisser-faire, in Burma as in Europe, failed most when dealing with the land. For the peasant, agriculture was a way of life as well as a way of making a living; and the philosophy of Nassau Senior had no room for such combinations.

The labourers and immigrants who brought Lower Burma under cultivation were as true pioneers as any Middle Western American. They had to clear jungle and drain swamps, to save from their wages or the returns of their land enough money to buy bullocks and seed and to maintain themselves until the land gave a crop. But the very greatness of the effort compared with the meagreness of their resources made their solvency always precarious. Some had to borrow from the very beginning to keep themselves while the land was cleared or to buy the bullocks without which they could not plough. Others were driven into debt by a bad year, by a miller's combine bringing down the price of rice or by litigation over an improperly drawn boundary; others still were tempted by the sirens with which the Eastern moneylender surrounds the men with land to pledge, new clothes and bigger marriages and money to buy more land still. Once in, for whatever reason, few get out; for few businesses produce enough profit to pay interest rates of 20% and 30% and still leave enough to live. The peasant had begun to lose his land already in the 1870s, and the movement had gathered enough way by the 1890s for a Financial Commissioner to say that land had become as transferable as shares on the London Stock Exchange; in the one year 1913-4, 580,000 acres changed hands in Burma. But for long the position was concealed, since no sooner had one man found his position intolerable and let his land go to pay his debts than the moneylender found another to take his place for part of the price cash down and the rest on mortgage, and in due course to lose

[1]The fault was, of course, not the Indian's. It was perfectly justifiable for an Indian vaccinator to go to Burma in order to make a better living or for an Indian contractor to try and do as much business as he could.

The failure lay in the fact that the Indian in Burma, like the Chinese in South East Asia and the European everywhere, was not assimilated into the society in which he lived and worked in the way in which the Irish or the Italians were assimilated into America.

the land in his turn; thus in each generation the thrifty lost their savings and still no independent peasantry was built up.

The crash of 1931 finally brought the position into the open, for now the moneylender, unable for the first time to find anyone with enough savings for the down payment, found himself forced to foreclose; and in 6 years (1931–7) 2 million acres passed into non-agriculturist hands until half the land was held by them while another 10% was held by agriculturists who had gone to live in the town and leased out their land. 59% of Lower Burma was rented in 1939; in 1872 there had been only 35,000 tenants to 534,000 proprietors. There were 1½ million agricultural labourers in 1931 [1] where in 1872 there had been only a handful. In particular districts, and those the richest, the position was worse still. In Insein, Pegu, Pyapon and Hanthawaddy some 70% of the land was in non-agriculturist hands. [2]

The contrast with Upper Burma is striking, for there only one-twelfth of the land had gone to the moneylender, and five-sixths was still in the hands of the villager, though there too the habit of letting was spreading, and one-third of the land was under tenancy; but the letting of a plot by one small farmer to another, who may in his turn be letting some of his own land to someone else, is a less grave social evil than the prevalence of the absentee. It is often only a simple remedy for fragmentation.

In Lower Burma even those who still somehow held on to their land were often in debt. The Provincial Banking Enquiry Committee estimated such debts at £40 million in 1930 apart from seasonal advances. Some of them, perhaps £10–£15 million, were discharged by the foreclosures of the 30s, but other debt was incurred, for it was a decade when prices did not cover costs of production; some, too, was tenants' debt, but even if one assumes peasant owners' debt at only £30 million in 1938—and this is almost certainly an underestimate—it would be nearly as much as their remaining land was then worth. [3]

If the solvency of the peasant owner is thus dubious, the bankruptcy of the tenant is beyond doubt. Every calculation made in the 30s agreed that he could not pay his way. So the landlord, in the perpetual search for men who would pay him half the crop and

---

[1] This is the all Burma figure but the great majority were in Lower Burma.
[2] J. Russell Andrus, *Burmese Economic Life*, Stanford, Calif., 1947, p. 82.
[3] Land has been as low as £4 an acre, but may have been worth £8 or £9 in 1938.

25% on his advance, and still succeed in living with rice at £4 a ton in Rangoon, rang the changes on his tenants year by year. Only in Henzada did more than one half the total number of tenants stay tenants of the same land for over three years; in Insein, nearer Rangoon, only one quarter remained. Those who stayed on the same land only for a year were 40% of the total in Amherst, and nearly one half in Pegu and Insein; in the best districts, Henzada and Pyapen, they were 15% and 18%. Such tenants were not farmers at all, but labourers forced by necessity to run risks their total lack of resources completely unfitted them to bear.

Another typical feature of Victorian development, the disappearance of handicrafts, made the bankruptcy of the countryside hopeless. The English textile industry had grown to the sound of breaking machines and Luddite Riots, and the village paper-making of the Normandy bocages disappeared before the modern paper mill. So in Burma the boatman retreated before the paddle-steamers of the Irrawaddy Flotilla Co., the potter before the import of cheap crockery, the weaver before English, Japanese and Indian piece-goods.[1] Even the fisheries suffered from being auctioned out to the highest bidder on annual leases.

Laisser-faire had thus uprooted the ordinary man from his hold in the traditional community, without giving to the majority the compensation of an improving standard of life. Naturally, ardent crime and extreme nationalism flourished. Where villages consisted of migrant labourers and tenants who were constantly being changed, and where even the village boundaries were fixed by Government fiat and where the village was given responsibilities unmatched by powers, it was impossible that there should be exercised upon the criminal and the undesirable that steady pressure of public opinion and social sanctions which is in every country the main guarantee of decent conduct. So the crime figures went steadily up. (Table 20)

A State which had thus failed to protect either the traditions or the livelihood of the people could not expect to receive any very deep loyalty from them. Some appreciated its peace, others who had not forgotten King Thibaw its freedom from concentration camps and

[1] In the one decade 1901–1910 the numbers engaged in spinning and weaving went down by one half. In 1931 230,000 were still recorded as engaged in cotton spinning and weaving in all Burma, nearly all women and children doing it part time, but how serious was the loss of employment is shown by the fact that they wove only one-tenth of Burma's requirements.

arbitrary execution, yet others the opportunity it gave to the enterprising and hard-working to order their lives in their own way to their own successful ends. The Karen valued his rise in status to full equality with the Burman, and Chin and Kachin and Shan the devotion of a long series of officers who strove to bring them the benefits of Western civilisation without destroying the fabric of their own culture.[1] The Indian valued the opportunity to use his talents unhampered by undue reservations for the more numerous but less advanced Burmese. Men gave the State credit for what it did for them and theirs, and were chary of change for the loss it might cause to themselves or their group, but that was all. It was a poor and negative loyalty, and when the test came in the war, there were many amongst the Karens ready to die for Britain, and some amongst the Burmans ready to desert first the British and then the Japanese for Burma, but in the whole land none were found who would fight for the British Burma in which they had lived for a hundred years. The minorities had never ceased to be minorities, jealous of their separateness, and the majority had never forgotten the destruction of their kingdom, the weakening of their Church, the loss of their land, and the growth around them of a whole nineteenth-century apparatus of government and business in which they had always the lesser part.

The ways in which the Burman found his pre-war society frustrating can be seen most clearly from his actions since he has had control of himself.

Independence has been the first demand, for it was thought that without independence a British government and entrenched minority rights would make impossible the creation of a community whose spirit and loyalties would be specifically Burmese. And with independence has come Burmanisation, of religion, of personnel, of language, of land and industry. Section 21 of the Constitution recognises the special position of Buddhism. In 1938 fully half the senior officers of the Secretariat were non-Burman; in June 1948 there was not a non-Burman officer above the rank of Assistant Secretary. In 1938 English was the universal language; in February 1949 the "Hindu" of Madras reported that Indian clerks were leaving Burma because they did not know the Burmese which had become a necessity. In 1937, $2\frac{1}{2}$ million acres, one quarter of Lower Burma, was in Chettyar hands, and those who still owned their

[1]The work of Scott with the Shans and of Stevenson with the Chins for example.

land owed the Chettyar money. In 1948 the Constitution declared the State the ultimate owner of all lands and forbade large holdings (s.30) and the Land Nationalisation Act was passed to provide for the taking over of all absentee-held land at ten times the land revenue, a reasonable pre-war price but in 1948 less than the value of one year's crop. In 1938 the rice trade was in Indian or British hands, since 1945 it has been a Government monopoly. In 1938 the great industries, oil and mines and teak and navigation, were British; the professional men and industrial workers were Indian. By 1948 the Indian minority had been reduced to 700,000 and British enterprise was of much diminished importance. The oil fields had been destroyed to deny them to the Japanese and the Burma Oil Co. has suspended rehabilitation. The teak leases have not been renewed, but resumed by Government; the Irrawaddy Flotilla Co. has been nationalised and the Constitution provides that all timber and mineral lands, forests, water, fisheries, minerals, coal, oil and sources of natural energy shall be preserved for exploitation by the Union or its nationals (s.219).[1]

The Burman has made clear his determination to be master in his own house. For that he is prepared to pay a high price. The frontier hillmen whose military quality and inaccessible country could make them so dangerous have been conciliated by an autonomy that enables them to rule themselves and to spend on themselves such revenue as their hills produce, while the Burmese carry the burden of Union. Agriculture, police, education, health, roads, justice, irrigation, local government are all State subjects;[2] land revenue, mineral royalties, liquor and opium excises, forest revenues, entertainment and gambling taxes, motor vehicles duties and court fees all go to the State Treasuries.[3]

Unfortunately the desire to run one's own affairs in one's own way is not enough. In the modern world certain very definite skills are also necessary, and the liberalism and *laisser-faire* of the Burmese past have been much less successful than they were in India in creating an adequate supply of these skills in the population.

[1]Recently there have been amendments to the Burmese constitution relaxing some of the provisions which discouraged foreign investment and the Burmese Government has taken a share in the British companies exploiting its oil and its major mines.

[2]Each hill tribe, Shan, Chin, Kachin and Karen, is organised into a separate state within the Union. The dispute with the Karens is over boundaries, not principles.

[3]See the Third and Fourth Schedules to the Constitution Act.

A democracy requires properly functioning political parties and politicians who can lead without aspiring to dictate. Pre-1939 Burma produced no Congress or Muslim League, no Gandhi or Jinnah. The parties were only cliques gathered round particularly dominating individuals. After the war it looked for a time as if Aung San and the Anti Fascist People's Freedom League would give to Burma the firm leadership and coherent aim necessary to transition. Aung San's murder and the break up of the League is the primary cause of the breakdown in law and order which followed. Not only modern democratic politics but the whole of Western style life require a trained professional class to provide the doctors, the engineers, the administrators, the teachers, even the trade union officials, without which no Western style community can survive. Burma suffers severely from the very small number of Burmans who have been trained in these techniques. Burma has had the full apparatus of Western education only for a very short time.[1] It was not possible to take a medical course in Burma till 1931 and as late as 1937 there were only 25 science graduates. The secondary education was long delayed for lack of Burmans or Karens who could teach English mathematics and history. Moreover, of those who did get a higher education, two-fifths were Indian or Anglo-Indian and only one in ten came from the countryside. Since independence Government has been learning the limitations which are placed on its actions by the defects in the skill of its people. Flotilla companies cannot successfully be nationalised if there are no modern engineers. And mining or oil companies cannot be run at all without geologists.

Independence has given back to the Burman his freedom of action and the control over his own destiny which Victorianism had taken away from him, but it has also reversed the process of economic expansion which was the glory of the Victorian era at a time when the world is more in need of Burma's production than ever before. India's food problems would no longer be a menace to the stability of the State in the way they are if Burma's rice exports were once more as large as pre-war. Unfortunately there is no very great urge on the Burman to put the brake on this running-down. Just as he had only a minority share in pre-war prosperity, so he has only a minority share in present losses. The most striking instance is rice. In the worst post-war year 1946

[1]The University of Rangoon was only started in 1920. Before that students from Burma had to go to India and up to 1918 Burma had produced only 400 graduates, many of them non-Burmans (J. S. Furnivall, *op. cit.*, pp. 204-5).

Burma's crop was 4 million tons of paddy against a 1934 average of over 7.[1] Exports of rice were half a million tons against 3⅓ million. So there was perhaps half a million tons more left in Burma; and of what is left in Burma, more now stays in the village, because rent can so often not be collected, because debt instalments and land revenue payments now cost in real terms, even when paid, as they often are not, only a sixth of pre-war and because the frequent difficulty of getting kerosene and imported cloth, the unreliability of train and launch services, have been driving the peasant back on to his own resources, vegetable oil lamps and hand-weaving, bullock carts and country boats. Whatever the cost in law and order, whatever his susceptibility to raiding rebels and the descent of dacoits, economically the peasant may well be better off. Rebel and robber keep off the money-lender and the landlord. And those who have paid nothing since 1941 are much tempted by the Communist doctrine that they should still pay nothing now.

The civil war is the product of migrant, land-hungry Lower Burma. It began in Toungoo and Pyinmana, Thayetmyo and Bassein and it spread to Upper Burma only when the Karen revolt brought to it professional troops and hill sympathy.

Perhaps in the end the Burman will gain both ways. Without Indian capital the ten million acres could not have been brought under rice so quickly, without British tutelage the Burmans could not have learnt to find their way about in the modern world so relatively successfully. When peace comes back to Burma it will be a Burmese, not an Indian or a British peace. But if there is to be peace the State will have to be Burmese not Burman, the equal possession of all its peoples and not just the preserve of a predominant majority.

[1]F.A.O., *Yearbook of Food and Agricultural Statistics*, 1947.

TABLE 17

GROWTH OF ACREAGE UNDER RICE IN LOWER BURMA

		Acres
1830	....	66,000
1845	....	354,000
1860	....	1,333,000
1880	....	3,102,000
1890	....	4,398,000
1900	....	6,578,000
1910	....	7,808,000
1920	....	8,588,000
1930	....	9,911,000
1935	....	9,702,371

Source: J. Russell Andrus, *op. cit.,* p. 43.

TABLE 18

GROWTH OF POPULATION LOWER BURMA AND ALL BURMA

			Lower Burma	All Burma
1856	..	..	1,381,000*	5,000,000*
1872	..	..	2,590,332	—
1881	..	..	3,567,211	—
1891	..	..	4,408,466	7,722,053
1901	..	..	5,405,967	10,490,624
1911	..	..	6,212,412	12,115,217
1921	..	..	6,682,106	13,212,192
1931	..	..	7,765,873	14,647,756
1941	..	..	8,917,533	16,823,798

*The 1856 figures are guesses, those for All Burma my own, those for Lower Burma are the official estimate, which was probably too low.

Source: J. Russell Andrus, *op. cit.,* pp. 22–23.

TABLE 19

GROWTH OF IMPORTS AND EXPORTS

(a) ALL BURMA (in million Rupees)

			Exports	Imports
1868–9	..	..	$32\frac{1}{4}$	$27\frac{1}{2}$
1903–4	..	..	$204\frac{3}{4}$	$145\frac{1}{4}$
1913–4	..	..	$386\frac{1}{4}$	254
1926–7	..	..	$654\frac{3}{4}$	$386\frac{1}{2}$
1936–7	..	..	$555\frac{1}{4}$	218

(b) Commodities of particular interest to Lower Burma (in million Rupees)

			Rice Exports	Clothing Imports	Production goods imports*
1868–9	..	..	$20\frac{1}{2}$	$14\frac{1}{2}$	$3\frac{3}{4}$
1913–4	..	..	$264\frac{3}{4}$	84	$61\frac{1}{2}$
1936–7	..	..	$218\frac{1}{2}$	$56\frac{1}{4}$	73

*Production goods include such items as machinery, lubricants, chemicals, petrol and coal.

Sources: G. E. Harvey, *op. cit.,* p. 40.
J. S. Furnivall, *op. cit.,* pp. 551–3.

(c) Imports and Exports of All Burma at prices of 1898–1901 (in million Rupees)

			Exports	Imports
1868–9	..	..	51	$19\frac{1}{2}$
1898–1901	..		$159\frac{1}{2}$	101
1913–4	..	..	305	$190\frac{1}{2}$
1933–4	..	..	466	163

Source: J. S. Furnivall, *op. cit.,* p. 187.

TABLE 20

MURDER AND DACOITY PER MILLION PEOPLE (ALL BURMA)

		Murder	Dacoity
1896–1900..	..	24.8	9.5
1916–1920..	..	42.9	17.9
1926–1930..	..	59.7	31.9

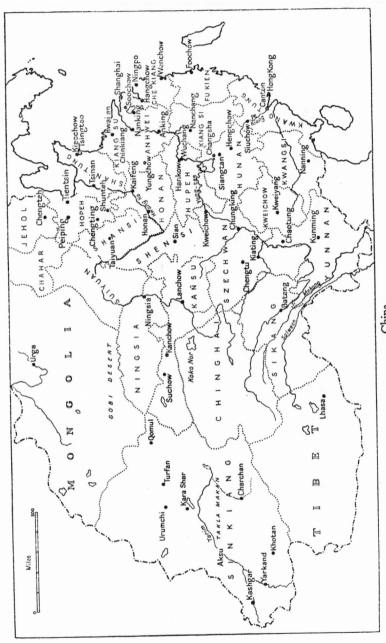

China

Chapter IX

CHINA

Several times in the history of China, over-population and the decay of the dynasty has led to a period of anarchy and revolution ending always with the installation of a new and effective government, and usually with a re-distribution of land. The last hundred years have been another example of this process. This time, however, it has been complicated both by the fact that the over-population has been more extreme than ever before, and by Western interference. The dynasty which was decaying was foreign. Being foreign it had to be so conservative as to be positively obscurantist. Being foreign, too, it was unable to call out from its people the devotion, spirit and sacrifice that would have been required to revolutionise Chinese society and fit it to the new world into which it was being pushed and pulled by the West.

The simple process of revolt and the emergence of a new and more effective dynasty was thus very severely complicated. Western support for the dynasty prevented the first great revolt, that of the T'ai-ping, from succeeding. Subsequent revolts have been increasingly complicated in their motivation. Even the T'ai-ping were not simply peasant rebels. One of the reasons for their failure was that the old-fashioned did not like the Christian element in their doctrine. Both parties in the recent civil war have drawn most of their inspiration from Western ideas. Confucius has often been at the backs of their minds, but their talk has been of parliaments, republics and democracy. Yet the victory of the Communists is not simply a reassertion of an old Chinese pattern. The land is indeed being re-distributed and it is likely enough that the Government will be effective, but the land is being distributed according to Marxian principles, and the Government's effectiveness includes a very Western use of terror.

★   ★   ★

The most bankrupt countryside in Asia is the Chinese. The worst crisis of over-population China has yet had to face has been accompanied by a breakdown of traditional ideas and traditional authority so complete as to lead to a state of near anarchy.

In China, crises of over-population have been recurrent. In the past they have produced anarchy and civil wars which continued until the crisis was solved by a sufficient reduction in numbers. At that stage the rise of a new strong man and a re-distribution of the land always proved enough to restore stability. The present crisis is quite in the tradition but it has been even more severe than its predecessors because the population is so much larger than it has ever been before[1] and because the influence of the West complicated the old simple pattern of decay, revolt and restored authority.

The political theory of Confucian China was well suited to population crises, and the Mandate of Heaven rested with the ruler only so long as all went well. Oppression, banditry, discontent, corruption, each symptom of decay was a separate proof that the Mandate had been withdrawn and revolt was justified to save the State. Confucius himself counselled fighting it out as a remedy for oppression, and said "If a prince's personal conduct is not correct, he may issue orders but they will not be followed." There is in Chinese theory no Divine Right of Kings. Instead there is the view that if men have been pushed into revolt, that in itself showed revolt to be necessary. Every Chinese dynasty was got rid of in its turn, when its sapping by palace vices had caused it to slacken its supervision over the extremities of the land. This slackening let pass unheard the groanings of those squeezed dry by the land-grabbing of the locally mighty, by extortionate usurers and corrupt officials.

The whole theory was that Government rests not on force, or persuasion, or the will of the people, but on the compelling force of moral example. In the 19th century K'ang Yu Wei could still say "When the Great Wang prevailed, the world became a common State. Rulers were elected according to their virtue and ability and good faith and peace were restored". Confucius had similarly said, "He who exercises government by means of his virtue may be compared to the north polar star which keeps its place and all the stars turn towards it". The official, by being good, leads his people

[1]Chinese population figures are never very satisfactory, but it has been estimated that the population in 1600 was 60 million and that it was about the same 1600 years before. In between it has usually been 10 or 15 millions less. The great increase has come since 1600, until today the population is perhaps seven times as large as it was then. (The estimate is Ta Chen's in *Population of Modern China*, University of Chicago, 1944).

to goodness. The Emperor, by proper behaviour, ensures the prosperity of his people.

The theory governs even Chinese law. The idea of a rigid code is abhorrent to the Confucian; the adage that hard cases must not make bad law to him appears intolerably unjust. The function of the just magistrate was to obtain a compromise that would satisfy both the parties and the public. Hence the enormous care for "face", and as for the money the magistrate so often took, that was a court fee rather than a bribe. Magistrates too had families to consider.

The emperor in Peking judged his governors according to the quietness of their jurisdiction. A riot was as bad a blot on their copybook as it was in that of an officer of the Indian Civil Service. The civil servant who was given very few troops or police[1] found it necessary to do nothing which would offend unduly or too often any important class of society, certainly not the village elders or the heads of great clans, preferably not even coolies and small peasants, of whom injustice might make bandits or rebels. A little latitude would be allowed to the landlord, for the official was nearly always of landlord origin himself. So long as the official thus considered everybody's interest, no one objected to his also considering his own. It was estimated that official squeeze in the 1880s amounted to £30 million, three times the Central Revenue.[2] But it was vital to the Government both that the official should not become too extortionate himself and that he should not permit too many extortions by landlord or money-lender, for extortion meant discontent and the ruin of every Chinese régime came when the local gentry had deprived the Centre of power by their malversations and their tax-evasion and had driven the peasants into revolt by their usury and their land-grabbing.

The pattern of events which has brought the Chinese Communists to power is therefore not new. The first Tang nationalised and redistributed the land, the first Ming was a poor monk leading a peasant revolt, the Manchus themselves were let into China by a garrison commander who preferred them to the peasant leader who had taken Peking.

The great increase in population has not been matched by any corresponding increase in available land. The last great rice area, Yunnan, was conquered in the 13th century, and though the

[1] There were only 300 men available to deal with a riot in the Yangtze valley itself in 1883.
[2] E. V. G. Kiernan, *British Diplomacy in China*, Cambridge, 1939, p. 229.

I

Manchus did their best, it was not enough. It is true that between 1650 and 1850 they showed themselves the greatest irrigators in Chinese history with 3,234 irrigation works against 5,240 in the two and a half millenia which had preceded them; in Hunan out of 728 works, 528 were built by the Manchus, in Honan 843 out of 947.[1] It is true also that they stopped nomad invasions by territorialising the nomads and turning their chieftains into feudal princes, too much interested in the titles and the new landownership which divided them from their tribesmen to regret the old days of raiding. The Manchus' achievement was that, being men from the border pale themselves, they understood that the nomad could only be conquered by giving him a village to be taken, a habitation to be sacked; thus they gave to a Chinese society bursting at the seams some more space into which to burst.

This great Manchu system of irrigation and flood control enabled the increase in production to keep pace with the growth of population until well into the 18th century and, combined with the peace which Manchu control of the nomads ensured, made 18th-century China appear to contemporary Europe as a society out of the golden age. Leibnitz could urge that "Chinese missionaries should be sent to us to teach us the aim and practice of natural theology" and Voltaire say that "They have perfected moral science and that is the first of all the sciences".

But this glorious society contained in itself the seeds of its own decay. The very peace and prosperity that Manchu genius had produced led to an increase of population without precedent, and when with the 19th century there came new and less capable emperors no longer able to expand irrigation at the old rate or to look the world in the face with the pride of Ch'ien Lung, not even the opening of nomad land could save the dynasty.

In China proper cultivation had nearly reached its limit by 1800.[2] The Chinese peasant was not familiar with the livestock husbandry by which he might have utilised the hills he so dangerously denuded

[1] Ch'ao-ting Chi, *Key Economic Areas in Chinese History*, London, 1936, p. 36.
[2] The Ordos was first opened up in the 1880s. Chinese settlement in Manchuria was first officially permitted in 1876 and Inner Mongolia was first penetrated on a large scale after the Revolution when the railway was extended to Paotow. Chinese farming in all these areas has expanded steadily ever since and in recent years there has also been a considerable penetration into Ninghsia and Kansu which took some 300,000 people during the years of the Chinese-Japanese war.

for firewood. Between 1766 and 1872 cultivation went up by under 10%, and the increase of one-half since then has been mainly in such outer areas as Manchuria, Ninghsia and Kansu. But between 1766 and 1872 the population nearly doubled. Thus the area of land per head was greatly reduced.

The decline in welfare these growing numbers entailed was in itself sufficient to shake the system. In the mid-19th century there appeared the traditional sign that all was not well. There was peasant revolt, and not as a cloud upon the horizon but as a sudden thunderclap. The Taiping rebellion of 1850–65 shook all the Yangtze valley. The Muslims of Yunnan stayed in rebellion for eighteen years (1855–73). There was trouble in Sinkiang in 1877–8. By all the tests the Mandate of Heaven had departed from the Manchus.

But the decision of who was to govern China was no longer one for the Emperor to settle alone with his people. The Opium War of 1840–2 had at last brought China out into the main stream of the world's life. The attitude *of* the foreigner and the attitude *to* the foreigner began for the first time to matter in Chinese quarrels. Society was sick, but its desperate attempts to cure itself by finding a new and refreshed authority were frustrated. The old cycle of decline, disintegration, restoration, was this time not allowed to work itself out in its own way and according to its own rhythm. The Taipings would have won if not for the foreign semi-Christian zealotry of their leaders and the foreign guns and ships and auxiliaries of the Manchu commander—men like "Chinese" Gordon or the American, Ward.

Their unnatural victory did not help the Manchus. 20 million lost lives and the devastation of half China reminded men of the old saying "When a ruler treats his subjects as grass and dirt, then it is the right of his subjects to treat him as a bandit and an enemy". Revolution from below had been scotched for the moment, yet it was bound to come again if no salve was found for the wounds which had caused it. The revolution from above which took place at the same time in Japan shows what could have been done, and there was no other cure.

The Manchus attempted the impossible feat of making no adjustment to Western culture at all. Westernisation was not open to a conservative régime which had just defeated a revolt whose ideas came, however distortedly, from the West. The support which had saved the régime came from the most conservative class in China, the Confucian scholar-gentry. The Manchu government had no desire for enthusiastic or emotional support from the people. It was enough for its purpose that they should be apathetic. By contrast, in Japan, where the government made a revolution, it needed devotion from the people. This the sacredness of the Emperor attracted. Such devotion could never be given to Manchu Emperors, for both they and their people were beginning to remember that the Manchus were foreigners, whose women were allowed to marry no Chinese but those of the Chinese banners.[1] One of the Manchu Princes said in 1884 "It were better to hand over the Empire to the Foreign Devils than to surrender it at the dictation of these Chinese rebels".[2]

Without the loyalty of the Chinese people the Manchus were powerless. The Bannermen who had once conquered China had so degenerated that in 1911 they were massacred by students and mobs; the Chinese soldier was traditionally the most despised of men. There was no material in China for a Bismarck. So the régime set its face against innovation, though its best servants knew that in innovation lay its only hope. It gave the most ordinary concessions to the foreign trader—the opening of ports or the right to hold land—only when they were extorted by force (e.g. in 1840-2, 1858-60). The Hundred Days of Reform in 1898 ended in a reactionary *coup d'etat*. The Boxers were given covert encouragement to murder foreigners, though the Government must have known its own powerlessness to meet the inevitable reprisals.

The Government was not able even to be consistently old-fashioned. It is true that it rested more and more on the old Confucian ideas under which foreigners were barbarians beyond the pale and railways an invention of the devil. But while such views could be held comfortably enough by the remote gentry of Honan or Szechwan, they were not possible for the Government in Peking, which had to make at least the gestures of adapting itself to an outside world which was no longer tribute-bearing.

The elements of a Diplomatic Service were created under American teaching. The first Chinese took his degree at Yale in 1855. A small arsenal was started near Hankow. The Chinese Foreign Office learnt to play off Americans and English and Japanese

[1]Certain Chinese long resident in Manchuria have been permitted to join special Chinese banners.

[2]Quoted by E. H. Norman, *Japan's Emergence as a Modern State*, New York, 1940, p. 124.

and Russians against one another. These steps, while alienating the traditionalists, were not enough to give China the new vigour which would enable it to look the world in the face or to catch the imagination of the younger generation.

The Manchu dilemma and the fecklessness with which it was faced are shown admirably by the history of taxation. One of the advantages of the lightness of the old Chinese system of government, of payment by squeeze and the neglect of the armed forces, was that central taxation was perhaps one-hundredth of the national income. At the beginning of the 19th century, when population was approaching 300 million, the central revenue was under £10 millions. By the end of the century it had risen to over £30 million and the land tax alone was £10 million.[1] Meanwhile the increase in the population had made the people less rather than more able to pay. This attempt to obtain a revenue of the size required by a modern State was unaccompanied by any attempt to get rid of those burdens on the people which no modern State permits. Squeeze was not abolished; indeed the provincial official increased his cut at the same rate as the Centre increased its demands. Thus to give the State an extra £20 million the people had to pay an extra £80 million. Nor did the State use its new revenues to modernise the country or to reform the armed services. The new transit taxes were so much easier to evade for a foreigner with his Consul behind him than for a Chinese that what Chinese industry there was, was ruined. During their last thirty years, the Manchus lost Tongking, Formosa, their more or less nominal sovereignty over Korea, their freedom of action in Manchuria, and their partial control over Tibet. In the war of 1895, the Chinese had ships bigger than any the Japanese possessed; but the Chinese ships had only one round per gun, for the Dowager Empress had spent the Naval Vote on the building of the Summer Palace.

In 1911 at last the Manchus abdicated, in a Revolution that was more a national vote of censure than a rebellion. But the departure of the Manchus solved nothing. Sun Yat Sen talked of sovereignty and democracy and the people's livelihood, but as yet the country was ready for none of them. The most powerful man in the North, Yuan Shih Kai, was dreaming of Empire. Everywhere local Governors and garrison commanders struck for their own hand. Government of the people, by the people, for the people is possible only where the people, or enough of them, are prepared to

[1] E. V. G. Kiernan, *op. cit.*, pp. 233–236.

fight for their rights. In order to create the modern machinery of commercial law and Central Banks and cotton mills, there must be a class which both has the will to do the actual creating and the belief that to do so will benefit not only themselves but also their country.

Without such classes Sun Yat-sen could only lay down a programme. In doing this, he affected the future profoundly. Some of his slogans were later to be appropriated by the Communists—for example, the doctrine that the soil should be to those who till it. The Chinese have never forgotten his picture of how China could be split, like a melon, in a morning at some conclave of the powers. Every Chinese has hugged to his heart Sun's explanations of how the poverty of China was the result of the millions sucked from her by the foreigner. This was factually a quite false picture. China's merchandise balance of trade has been steadily adverse, but China has always received more money than she paid out. This balance came from foreign investors and from the remittances of the overseas Chinese which the foreign development of South East Asia made possible. But Sun's explanations were none the less believed. They healed China's hurt pride.

Sun had started a movement which was not to stop. As the students returned from America and the Chinese banks and insurance companies and mills grew in Shanghai and Tientsin, there grew up the business and professional class which made possible the railway-building and the arsenals and the Government banks and the admirable diplomacy of the Kuomintang in the 30s.

As the study of the West grew, there grew too the number of those who read Marx and Lenin, who called themselves Communists, who remembered Sun's advocacy of a Russian alliance, and who showed in the strikes of 1925 in Shanghai and their victories over the Japanese and over Chiang Kai-shek that they had learnt without inhibitions all the West had to teach of propaganda and organisation.

Out of the Shanghai bankers and the Communist cadres a modern China is at last beginning to grow. For this China the choice it has made between the Western alternatives of democracy and Communism is of vital importance. But before this choice was made the country had to go through a period of dissolution and chaos, of war lords and civil war and Japanese aggression and civil war again, which disintegrated the countryside and its traditional values. In that disintegration lies the explanation of the Communist success.

Through the years since Manchu authority first weakened, in the 1850's, and especially since 1911, the countryside has fared hardly. The following paragraphs describe this position as it had become in the 1940's, the position which explains the Communist success.

Holdings have got steadily smaller, but families have not diminished. Filial piety demands that ancestral land shall not be sold, but around Canton or Shanghai nine-tenths of the land has gone to townsmen. Dependence on the market has grown, for vegetable oil has given way to kerosene since 1910, and the cloth that was once grown, spun and woven at home is now bought outside.

The subsidiary industries are dying. Paper can no longer compete with the factory-made article. Tea is depressed because there has been a shift of taste in the world market. Junks and shoulder yokes are not in demand. In the silk industry the old hand methods no longer give the evenness of quality which American looms require.

The peasant's income has gone down; the charges bearing upon him have gone up. The State takes more, for it must keep diplomats and planners, students and soldiers. The £50 million in central revenue of 1935 was twice the revenue of 1905, itself two and a half times that of 1850; provincial expenditure went up from 361 to 533 million yuan between 1931 and 1936.[1] The officials take more, for there are more of them—administrative expenditure more than doubled from 104 to 220 million yuan in the five years 1931-6, and they are less controlled; in the ruin of the Kuomintang one has seen how independent have always been such men as General Li Tsung-jen and his Kwangsi troops, how much the authority of the State has been only a reflection of the personal influence of the Generalissimo and the training of his Chekiang divisions. And beyond the legitimate needs of the State there have been the tax-farmer with his 500 and 1000% commissions and the corrupt official with his illegal exactions; men like the chief of marine police at Kin-Tu-Wan who permitted no ship alongside which he had not hired himself and levied for himself ship-bow fee even on them, or like the warlords of Szechwan who collected the land revenue 30 years in advance and put a cess on night soil.

Legal taxes and illegal cesses became inextricably mixed. In Kiangsu there were one hundred different surcharges. In Kwangtung

[1]Too much faith cannot be placed in the exact figures, as inflation and devaluation of the currency have not always kept exact pace but the rough proportions are correct enough.

the land tax went up three and one half times between 1928 and 1933. The position was admirably summed up by the military governor of Kwangtung in May 1933 "All of these taxes have been initiated to meet urgent demands without considering their desirability, their legality or their equity. This simply opens a new avenue for the local gentry to acquire more wealth".[1]

There have been plenty of other avenues. The landlord has been steadily increasing his rent. He has had to do so because his holding also has been reduced by the growth of families. The demands of gentility do not diminish with diminishing acres. They have indeed increased, for now the gentry must send their sons to High School and University if they are to have a future. The comfort of the town, combined with the insecurity of the countryside, lures everyone who can afford it out of the village. Of the landlords of Wusih district in the Lower Yangtze Valley half of those with 16 acres or more had gone to live in a town by the 30s.

The landlord is a more limited phenomenon than the corrupt official. Over one half of Chinese peasants own their own land, though the number varies from 10% or less around Shanghai and Kwangtung to three-quarters or more in some parts of North China. But wherever the landlord exists disintegration of the State has enabled him to take a high toll from the helplessness of his poorer neighbours. A population perpetually outstripping its means of subsistence will pay a terrible price for land; and the landlord's exactions have become the measure of the sickness of society. He can raise his rents until the tenant is left for his work and his capital with less money than an agricultural labourer for an equivalent number of days' work, since the tenants' alternative is unemployment. Sometimes rents are expressed in money; more often they are a share of the crop, and in either case it is exceptional for the payment of them to take less than 45% of the crop. And there are cases where it is as high as 75%. Often the landlord takes more than the rent agreed by sending armed guards to see that at the division of the crop his pile is bigger than was contracted for. In N. Kiangsu, the bigger landlords have been keeping private armies of as many as fifty riflemen. Other devices of the landlord's are to evict tenants and not give them back their rent deposits or to fix an arbitrary rate of conversion between crop and cash. The tenant must pay even though afterwards he may have to borrow so that his family can eat, since if he is unable to find the money he is forced to

[1]Chen Han-seng, *op. cit.*

become a landlord's labourer on a wage which provides only 15/– a year for each member of his family.

None of these exactions would have been possible if the State had been morally or physically in a position to enforce the laws it was quite prepared to pass. The Kuomintang in 1926 decided that the maximum rent should be 37.5% of the crop, and in 1937 that a tenant who had held his land for five years should be entitled to call upon the State to requisition it from the landlord. The Land Law of 1946 provided that rents should not exceed 8% of the land value, and that taxes should increase progressively on large absentee holdings.

Nothing could, however, be done by a State whose own officials were themselves landlords or the hirelings of landlords. Registration officers, for example, have frequently themselves sold to speculators land brought under cultivation by smallholders and have regularly taken bribes from the larger landlords not to register their land at all; in Inner Mongolia the hatred of the Mongol tribesmen for the Chinese has been largely produced by the practice of Chinese military commanders of enclosing Mongol tribal land and auctioning it on their own behalf. The Kuomintang's resolutions have been mere platitudes. They were pious offerings to the memory of Sun Yat-sen's belief in the Government regulation of rent. The real attitude of the State is epitomized by the grant of police powers to the landlords' rent-collecting bureaus in the Lake Tai[1] area of E. China. Modern Chinese history is like that of 15th-century England with its maintenance and champerty and packed juries. When the State is weak, at the mercy of its own great men, then the humble suffer. But so does the State itself. In 1700 one half the land in China was royal or governmental, or temple, or military, and a considerable proportion of the remainder was clan-owned. Since the last days of the Manchus there has been going on a perpetual process of encroachment and sale and usurpation, until today perhaps not more than 10% of China is other than privately owned.[2]

Debt is a more serious burden even than rent, for debt touches almost everybody. It is not only the tenant and the landless who

[1]Fei Hsiao-tung, *op. cit.*, p. 188.
[2]Much temple land, for example, was sold by the Kuomintang in 1927 to provide funds for education, and clan-treasurers and clan-accountants have regularly used their position to misappropriate clan land; for example, the land of the Tsai clan in Wusih was reduced from 1000 to 300 mow between 1930 and 1933.

cannot make ends meet. In a society without margins, it is also the poorer or more improvident owners, or anyone who is suddenly faced with some more than usually crushing military requisition. Where the income of a tenant family was often only £4 a year and where even a family which owned its own land was considered more than comfortable on £20 a year, debt has inevitably been widespread.[1]

In a country where there has been inflation for forty years, where arbitrary exactions and the destruction of war reduce old capital as rapidly as usury and extortionate rents create new,[2] and where the banditry and flight of debtors whose debts have become unendurable makes all lending a gamble, interest rates are bound to be exceedingly high. Government itself does not lend to the farmer at less than 25%. (By contrast the charge in India is 5%.) The Ya pawnshop charges between 120% and 240%. For grain loans rates have run as high as 300%.[3]

No business in the world could maintain such rates. And in China borrowings are for unproductive purposes, maintenance, funerals, food in famines, taxes. The inevitable result is that the peasant has been losing his land.[4] The peasant's independence moreover is lost long before the land itself, since nine-tenths of his debt is the land-lord's or rich peasant's. There is no separate money-lender class like the Marwari of India.

Increasing debt and increasing landlessness are driving the peasant further and further into the labour market. By the thirties about one-quarter of the work of Chinese agriculture was done by hired labourers, most of them tenants and small owners trying to eke out their incomes. This increasing supply to meet a relatively stable demand has naturally resulted in a tendency for wages to fall which in newly settled areas has been extreme. In North Manchuria real wages dropped by two-thirds between 1910 and 1923 as the area began to fill up.

The trouble cannot be solved merely by a change of heart on the part of the landlord or the money-lender. The landlord in China is

[1]Investigators have found two-thirds of the families they have investigated in debt in Kwangtung, one half in Kunming. In the Yangtze valley in tenant villages in some cases every single family has been found to be in debt.
[2]The 80 million dollars deposited each year in the early '30s in Soochow banks came mainly from rents.
[3]The particular instance is taken from Fo-Ping in Hopei.
[4]In Panyu Kwangtung the number of landless families increased by 3.5% between 1929 and 1933 (Chen Han-seng, *op. cit.*).

not necessarily a rascal, or the moneylender always a conscienceless usurer. The rates of the Ya pawnshops are high because the more regular pawnshops which preceded them went bankrupt. The landlord is often himself a small man. Rarely is his holding as big as an English market garden, or bigger than a Provencal peasant's vineyard; his total income may be only a few pounds a year. In a Government survey in 1935, in eleven provinces only 1545 big landlord families were found, and even they averaged less than 350 acres per family.

His rent and his interest do not appear extortionate to the landlord. Rents in the thirties averaged 10% of land values, which is reasonable enough in comparison with the 8% then being paid by banks on time deposits. The 40% or 50% charged on loans by private individuals in the thirties did not seem outrageous when compared with the 18% which co-operative societies felt compelled to charge. Even the landlord's grosser methods are sometimes understandable. If there were no armed guards at the division of the crop, the half-starved tenant might take more than his share; if the officials were not bribed, the landlord himself would be squeezed by the secret police.

It is easy to see the compulsion under which landlord and money-lender have acted. This does not mean that their actions have therefore been the less disastrous. The countryside has been not only ruined, it has been corrupted. Once the peasant regarded it as a duty to himself and to God to pay his dues;[1] now he evades or revolts to the Communists. Once the landlord gave to his people the fruits of his mind in return for his food. "Some work with their minds, others with their bodies. Those who work with their minds rule, while those who work with their bodies are ruled. Those who are ruled produce food; those who rule are fed" quotes Mencius;[2] now the landlord too often thinks only of his rent and his interest.

The last three decades may well have been the worst in all China's long history, for never before have there been so many people to scratch their living from the land, never before has anarchy been organised with quite so many soldiers or nearly so many planners. In a society where without land there is neither food nor independ-

[1]E.g. Fei Hsiao-tung, *op. cit.*, p. 189, "We are good people. We cannot steal even when we are poor. We never refuse to pay our rent".
[2]Arthur Waley, *Three Ways of Thought in Ancient China,* London, 1939, p. 187.

ence, it takes the wages of half a lifetime to buy an acre.[1] So many peasants had been willing to sell their daughters that a good Mui Tsai could be bought before the war for less than £10.[2] It would have cost as much in London to buy an evening dress.

Over-population and collapse of government had brought China's society by 1940 to a state of disintegration and bankruptcy so complete that it is not to be wondered at that millions have seen revolution as the only hope.

The Communist victory was not one over freedom and democracy, for there was no freedom or democracy to conquer. As with the Tudors in England, the Communist strength is that they have given order instead of anarchy, a place in the sun instead of humiliation, the enforcement of a totalitarian law instead of the caprice of the local bully. The price is high. Family loyalties have been undermined, hundreds of thousands have been shot. But most Chinese are prepared to pay it; for the landlord is being abolished, and Chinese troops have won victories against Westerners in Korea.

[1]Chen Han-seng calculates that in Kwangtung an acre cost in the early thirties the whole wages of a labourer for 15 years.

[2]A Mui Tsai is an adopted female child who is expected to be a servant of the family.

Chapter X

JAVA

The steady, increasing, pressure of population on land has characterised most of Asia over the last century. Nowhere can this be seen more clearly than in Java. For in Java the Dutch have long insulated the local people against all the other effects of westernisation. They were not until recently taught Dutch or encouraged to accept such Western political notions as nationalism and representative government. They were protected against losing their lands to money-lenders and against the exploitation of their own aristocracy. They were provided with all the benefits of law and order and a modicum of health, education and communications. Otherwise their society was carefully preserved in its old way. But even the little westernisation that was done—the law and order and the health services—produced a more than ten-fold increase in population which undid all the good the Dutch had done. At first this increase did no harm. There was vacant land to fill up. But for over half a century now, there have been more new mouths than new food, and the standard of living has declined slowly and steadily.

*   *   *

Java is an extremely interesting example of how dangerous European ideas and techniques can be to a non-European society if the government is concerned to preserve the values and the way of life of the society whose balance the very existence of a Western government is all the time subverting. Dutch law and order and Dutch medical services were mostly responsible for the phenomenal increase in the population of Java after 1815. The Dutch concern for the happiness the Javanese found in their traditional culture and the Dutch failure to provide Java with institutions to which the Javanese might have adapted themselves to the new ways of thought and of action of the Western world, are almost equally responsible for the failure of the Javanese community to find new ways of employing the extra people who were so constantly coming into the labour market. The result has been that after 150 years of the most paternal and, in some ways, the most understanding government in Asia, the Javanese have the lowest income per head in Asia, with the possible exception of China.

The lesson which Javanese history has to teach is enforced by a comparison with Japan. The men who governed Japan between 1868 and Pearl Harbour were frequently aggressive and usually ruthless, yet the standard of living of the Japanese common man improved steadily. The men who governed Java in the same period were mostly imbued with the idea that the function of government is the promotion of the welfare of its citizens. Yet the standard of life of the average Javanese declined steadily. It is not enough for a government to be well-intentioned. It has also got to understand that increases in population are bound to mean decreases in well-being unless the new hands can find new jobs to do, and in Asia it has to realise that the jobs will not be created spontaneously by the peasant community itself.

In Europe the necessary increase of resources was brought about by giving the individual economic freedom. The investment of savings by the individual decisions of individual enterprises raised the national incomes. But in an Asian peasant economy, there are no savings spontaneously available for investment. Even if there were, there would be no entrepreneurs to decide which risks should be taken. Therefore, in a situation of increasing population, two alternatives are possible. The Government can force the saving and create the entrepreneurs, as was done in Japan; or outside business men can come in, provide savings made in other countries, and provide also managers and entrepreneurs. This is what happened in Malaya. In Java neither of these methods was followed. Government confined itself to the ordinary activities of the liberal State, for example—education. The foreign capitalist did not come in on a large enough scale to transform the economy, but only in those occasional areas and industries which gave him an opportunity to provide for those specialised needs of his own society which had been the original cause of his deciding to invest at all. The economy as a whole remained substantially unchanged by the efforts of either Government or capitalist, and increasingly outstripped the only resource— land—which it knew how to use.

It has been said that the Javanese were so docile that much could be done in Java that could not be done elsewhere. The quality of native rule in Java bears this out. The nobility was unusually profligate, cruel and useless. The royal families were given to internecine war and recurrently proved unable to enforce order. The demands on the peasantry by those of noble blood were without limit. One in eight of the population was a noble; this compared with one in 40, including the clergy, in pre-Revolutionary France. Yet in all Javanese history there was no peasant revolt, no Jacquerie, for the peasant found his protection in the emptiness of the land. His desa, his village, was his trade union. It decided who should recover what land from the waste. Periodically it reallocated plots as families grew or declined. It elected its own officials and in all ordinary matters provided its own justice and its own police. A tyrannical lord was not murdered; his desas simply moved to a more easy going master. The existence of ample land therefore meant both that the peasant could not for long be intolerably ground down, and that he always had as much land under cultivation as he could comfortably manage; in 1816 there were $3\frac{3}{4}$ million cultivated acres for $4\frac{1}{2}$ million people.

The Dutch, who had taken over virtually all Java by 1743, showed until about 1880 a selfishness as great as that of the native princes. Java existed for the benefit of Holland and few Dutchmen pretended otherwise. Revenues from Java paid for the attempt by Holland to suppress the revolt of Belgium, for the conquest of the outer Provinces, and for the Dutch railways. In the mid 19th century it provided one-third of the Dutch budget, 18 million out of 60 million guilders a year; its total contribution to the home treasury added up to nearly £70 million. On Java, too, was based much of the revival of Dutch trade and commerce. Dutch shipping was favoured by tax exemptions, Dutch textiles by a tariff of 25% against England. The Nederlandsche Handel Maatschappij was given a monopoly in the handling of the products of the "culture" system.

The contributions and the trade revival alone depended upon the Culture System under which each village was compelled to devote a proportion of its land to the growing of commercial crops (notably coffee) for government's use. In theory this system involved no great hardship. The amount of land required was only 3% to 4% of the total and no land tax was supposed to be levied upon it. In practice, hardship was often considerable for the forced labour needed particularly to transport the crop from village to warehouse was very burdensome and the demands made were sometimes excessive —94 million coffee trees were planted between 1833 and 1835.

It became increasingly recognised in the second half of the century that such a system in practice was liable to work very harshly, and the increasing tenderness of the Dutch conscience eventually led to its abolition.

Nevertheless its basic principles were sound. The Javanese peasant would not at that date of his own accord have started growing coffee and sugar. He could not, out of his own unorganised resources, have saved £70 million. The sacrifices demanded of him were no greater than those exacted from Japan in the 1870's and the 1880's. Had the money stayed in Java, had it been used as it was in Japan to build cotton mills and dockyards and research institutes, to send Javanese students overseas and create technical schools, Java might have preceded Japan in giving a lead to Asia.

But the chance was missed. The abuses of the system remained unredeemed by benefits conferred on the Javanese. In consequence when the system was given up there was a revulsion against all government interference in economic development and it was decided to leave it to the private capitalist to develop the country.

The welfare of the peasant, however, continued to decline under the new system also. In 1815 there had been roughly 1 acre for each person in the countryside. In 1880 there was still about three-fifths of an acre. But in 1948 there was only some half acre. In 1815 every man could have land if he wished; in 1903 in one district (Preanger) which was particularly hard hit by the Culture System, nearly half the adult males were landless. In 1939 only 1 in 3 still had land in the crowded district of Kabonongan, though this was exceptional.

Government's failure to arrest this decline was not due to lack of goodwill within the narrow limits set it by its own liberal principles. It tried not only to preserve the old society, but to improve it by endowing it so far as resources allowed with the new social services of the 19th-century West.

The peasant's land was preserved to him both positively and negatively. Alienation to non-Indonesians was prohibited in 1870. Plantations were not allowed to take leases of more than 75 years duration. The Particuliere Landen, areas near Batavia which had been alienated in full ownership at the end of the 18th century, were bought back at a cost of £6 million. The rights of family and desa were fully recognised, so that in the thirties 8.8% of the land was still communally owned, and in 40% of the irrigated plots there was still some restriction on the owner's free right of transfer. The customary law, the Adatrecht, was lovingly studied and carefully applied, without any of the introduction of inappropriate Western concepts which was so fatal in India or Burma. It was therefore impossible for any equivalent of the Indian zemindar to grow up, and in 1925 only 3,387 Indonesians owned more than 17.7 hectares. The development of a money-lender—landowning class like the Burmese Chettyar or the Indian Marwari was made equally impossible by a bold development of government credit from 1900 onwards. There were village banks, State pawnshops, a People's Credit Bank. In 1936 55 million guilders were lent by the pawnshops in loans averaging under 2 guilders each; the People's Credit Bank had 416,000 clients who had borrowed 15½ million guilders; the village banks 856,000 who had borrowed 14 million.

The Government was successful in its primary objective of preserving the basis of the old society by keeping the land in peasant hands. In 1936, 8,431,000 separate owners paid land taxes, but its efforts to go further to introduce such social services as education and public health were limited by the smallness of the surplus over subsistence needs produced by a still predominantly peasant economy. Schools and hospitals cost money; the money has to be raised by taxation, and the taxes have to come out of the surplus. In a society whose basic resource, the land, could pay only some £3 million in land tax, and where the total income subject to income tax was still only some £40 million in 1935, the limits on what could be raised, and therefore on what could be spent, were severe. Nevertheless much was done. In 1840 under half a million guilders was spent on agriculture, religion, arts and sciences together. The State accepted responsibility neither for the teaching of the people nor for their health, neither for the improvement of their agriculture nor for training them in the technical arts. Not till after 1900 did this really change. In 1908 there were only 367 village schools, and no chance of secondary school or University for the ordinary child; the medical services touched virtually nobody outside the towns. After that, change was rapid. In 1936 there were 1,369,306 children in village schools; about a third of the total number of children of school-going age, and 323,000 of them were girls; by 1934 there were some 7100 Indonesian[1] children at secondary school. In 1936 there were 516 Indonesians at the University. By 1934, too, there were over a million vaccinations a year; general hospitals had 15,679 beds; and the death rate was down to 19.2.

The State's recognition of its responsibility for the economic

[1]As distinct from European or foreign Asiatic. The figures include the Outer Provinces for secondary schools and university.

K

well-being of its people was limited not only by its resources, but also and more seriously by its *laisser faire* ideals. It did not accept that it had any obligation to take the initiative in raising the national income as had the leaders of Japan. Yet in Java there was no alternative to the government. There were hardly any native capitalists and most of those who as merchants or shippers, plantation owners or retail dealers did have money were foreign, either European or Chinese. The Javanese people were, therefore, in no position to do for themselves what the State did not do for them.

Such functions as the State did undertake, it carried out successfully. It built harbours and railways and ran excellent forestry and irrigation services.[1] The State's forests, covering 23% of Java, not only provided the peasant with firewood, they also by protecting water-catchment areas and the steeper hill slopes saved him from all the worst effects of erosion. In irrigation the State provided engineering knowledge and materials such as steel and cement which were beyond the scope of the old society, and the increase in the area thus technically irrigated from 450,000 acres in 1895 to $3\frac{1}{2}$ million acres in 1939 yielded an increase in welfare far beyond the 250 million guilders it cost.

Since the State thus limited its functions, the possibility of economic development for Java depended upon the creation of a native capitalist class, such as has grown up in India. Foreign capital can never do the whole job of development since it normally invests in order to satisfy a need in the investing country. The foreign business man knows the markets and profit potentiality of his own country far better than he does those of the country into which he is putting his money, whose tastes and traditional profit margins are usually alike unknown to him. Normally only the native in any country has that intimate knowledge of the market which is required for those thousands of small enterprises without which no great industrial society can be built up.

The truth of this distinction between foreign and native capital is particularly obvious in Java. Native capital is small or non-existent. There is therefore none of that range of small businesses which one finds in Europe or America. But Java is capable of supplying certain of the major needs of the world for tropical products. There has, therefore, been a very large investment of foreign capital,

[1] In the Outer Provinces it took an interest in tin and petroleum and coal mining, but for some reason it never showed so much enterprise in Java itself.

mainly in plantations in order to produce those products. One-seventh
of the cultivated area of Java was under plantation in the 1930s and
in 1939, 13% of the world's tea, 7% of its rubber, 9% of its sugar
came from Java. In addition Java produced 117,000 metric tons of
cinchona bark.

It was a great effort, but it did not mean well-being for the native
Javanese. They provided a few hundred thousand labourers for the
estates and the sugar factories at 6d. a day. They grew most of the
kapok and nearly a quarter of the tea. But that was all. The plantations and oil fields were foreign owned; the engineers and estate
managers who exploited them were aliens. The money for railways
and ports and utilities was borrowed abroad. The wealth which the
new exports created stayed in non-Javanese hands; only one-twentieth
of the property assessed to tax in 1935 (just over £2½ million out of
some £55 million [1]) was Javanese; the rest was European or Chinese.
51,122 Europeans were assessed to income-tax in 1935, that is nearly
5 in 6 of all Europeans who had jobs [2]; but only 20,384 Javanese paid
income-tax out of a population of some 40 million. The smash in
sugar in the thirties took away most even of what benefit the natives
had got; their income from sugar went down from 134 million
guilders in 1928 to 12¾ in 1936.

Such marginal benefits were not enough to prevent a drastic
decline in welfare in a peasant society which knew only one resource
with which to provide for its children, land, and only one form of
saving, the work and waiting involved in bringing the waste under
cultivation. There were too many children to be provided for. The
population was 3½ million in 1795, had become 9,400,000 in 1845,
19½ million in 1880, 34½ million in 1920 and it is now perhaps 50
million. The peasantry were overwhelmed; their efforts to keep up
with the flood were increasingly inadequate. Not even the heavier
use of the land, through double-cropping—15% up in the decade
1929–38—or diversion to such heavy-yielding but inferior crops as
sweet potato, could prevent a decline in average welfare. Between
1913 and 1940 the consumption of rice dropped from 102 to 87 Kg.
per head. There was a counterbalancing increase in the consumption
of cassava, but cassava is only .87% protein against rice's 9.85%.
Thus by 1934 in such crowded areas as Koetowinangoen the average
diet was at a level of 1560 calories; this was below the 1600 of the
starvation period in Germany in 1946. It was considerably below

[1] These figures do not, of course, include land.
[2] 67,000 in 1930.

the 2000 of next door Sumatra. By 1947 the rice available per head was as low as 70 Kg. The average diet for all Java was at a level of 1600–1700 calories. On such a diet men can exist but they have not the energy either for hard work or vigorous play.

In a society so short of necessities nothing has been able to stop men trying to anticipate their future income, however unfavourable to themselves the terms might be. As both the pledging and the alienation of land is rightly difficult, the normal way is to take an advance in return for a share of the crop.[1]

The Javanese economy has thus descended to a stage where one more step in the downward path will mean starvation. For expansion on the old lines there is hope only in sugar.[2] Java's only recourse now is to do what other overcrowded countries, England, Germany and Japan, have done before her, and to apply Western technique and knowledge not only to the Western-owned or Western-run fringe of society, but to its very base, the old peasant-economy itself. It must bring the fruits of Western research to the peasant and provide him with an alternative form of livelihood in factory or cottage workshop.

The most immediate results could be obtained in agriculture. Commercial fertiliser was applied to only 1% of Java before the war, although 1 million hectares had a phosphate deficiency of 15% to 50%. Rice-seed was unimproved; native tobacco was not flue cured and pests took 10% of the crop. Fertilizers, the new insecticide, and weed-killers like Gammexane, immunisation of cattle against rinderpest, hybrid maize, and such like simple measures could quite rapidly produce at very least the increase of 18% in yields which occurred in Korea between 1911–15 and 1931–5. All such measures have the great advantage in a country poor in capital that the waiting period before a return is short. Money laid out will be recouped with a considerable profit in less than a year. In Japan between 1906 and 1922 roughly 2 yen extra of rice was produced for every 1 yen fertiliser applied.[3]

[1]Some such arrangement had been made for all or part of their land by three-quarters of the peasants of Todloengagoeng, E. Java, in 1939. This figure was probably considerably higher than the average (Karl J. Pelzer, *op. cit.*).

[2]Such expansion would have to be considerable to enable Java so much as to balance its payments with the outside world; before the war it had an unfavourable balance of 30 million guilders a year, made up by its export of goods and services to the Outer Provinces.

[3]Shiroshi Nasu, *op. cit.*, p. 122.

What can be achieved by industrialisation was shown by the Dutch themselves when unfavourable terms of trade in the depression and the near approach of war pushed them into action to try and make Java self-sufficient. Table 21 gives some examples of the enormous advance they were able to achieve in the one year 1939–40.

TABLE 21[1]

INCREASE IN INDUSTRIAL PRODUCTION

Industry	Production in 1939	Production in 1940
Starch	187,138 tons	223,742 tons
Rubber articles	858 ,,	2,200 ,,
Tarring	594,000 hides	1,185,000 hides
Weaving	36,618,000 metres	81,823,000 metres
Shoes	610,000 pairs	3,196,000 pairs
Public electricity	325,200,000 Kw.	969,600,000 Kw.
Tinplate works	21,300,000 tons	31,500,000 tons.

Production was still quite small at the end of 1940. Total factory employment for all Indonesia was only 325,000. Yet even this small beginning was absorbing 55,000 workmen a year into factory industry.[2] Assuming that each factory workman requires the work of only one-half another man in transport, building, public administration, food distribution and so on to provide for him—and in England the proportion is fully one to one—and that each workman has dependents, development on this small scale would be adequate to absorb two-thirds of the annual increase in population. The rest could be absorbed by cottage industry where there is great scope in such branches as blacksmithing and batik weaving, as shown, for example by the increase in modern handlooms from 500 to 49,000 between 1930 and 1941.[3] The Outer Provinces with their relatively sparse populations and large native agricultural exports provide a ready-made market. Moreover, since Java already has ports, railways and roads, and housing costs in its tropical climate are comparatively low, the capital required for development, so high for instance in Africa with its lack of communications, or Australia with its immigrants who want houses at once, would in Java be very low.

[1] Peter Sitsen, *Industrial Development of the Netherland Indies*, New York, 1944, p. 40.
[2] Peter Sitsen, *op. cit.*, p. 41.
[3] Peter Sitsen, *op. cit.*, p. 33.

Only a positive policy of emigration[1] and industrialisation can now enable Java to provide for its annual increase. No liberalism, no good intentions, no attempt at creating a welfare State (under all the limitations of poverty) can provide a substitute. But such a policy, vigorously applied and accompanied by an adequate educational programme, could in time give Java the same improvement in its standards of life as Japan attained; at the very least, it would give society a breathing space for the public to be persuaded to stop looking on the maximum of babies as the maximum of bliss. Thus only can the plethora of children be stopped from bringing a famine of all else.

[1]Emigration to the Outer Provinces from Java has been going on for a long time; they had 1,151,000 citizens of Javanese ancestry in 1930, and there is still a fair amount of room for more.

Chapter XI

MANCHUKUO

The outlook of an Asian peasant society is fundamentally dissimilar to that of a Western industrial society. The Asian peasant is concerned primarily with growing enough food for himself and his family and with fitting himself to the traditional pattern of his village and group. European industry is devoted to production for the market, and the model to be followed is that of the man whose originality and force makes him successful in competition.

The change from an Asian peasant to a Western-style business man or industrial worker is profound. There has in consequence been a tendency to avoid the necessity of making this change as far as possible. Western ports, factories and railways, have been set up side by side with the old peasant economy rather than as an integral part of it. The division has not been conscious and it has, in general, certainly not been successful. The influence of the railways and factories, of overseas trade and commercial law, has spread back into the villages and has been one of the major factors in creating the westernising climate of opinion. There is, however, one case in Asia where deliberate action of the imperial power in keeping the whole modern sector of the economy strictly to itself, enables one to see the whole parallelism of the Western and the peasant economies with a quite artificial distinctness. This case is Manchukuo, and this chapter is devoted to a study of it.

★   ★   ★

The 19th-century West brought to the East two great beliefs, the belief in freedom and the belief in the possibility of continuous material progress. It brought two main attitudes, the attitude of the missionary eager to convert the East to a higher way of life and the attitude of the business man, anxious to exploit its resources on the assumption that what was for his own profit could not be to society's loss.

The changes wrought in the East by these Western attitudes could not be rapid. The missionary must convert the individual,

138 ASIA AND THE WEST

soul by soul; the business man cannot increase production faster than he can find capital, technicians, new land and markets.

Of the missionary attitude, the British in India are the best example (see Chapter VII); of the business man's the Japanese in Manchukuo. Manchukuo is a proof of how far the business man can build up his new factories and his new commerce without changing the peasant society beside which he is working.

Manchuria before the Japanese aggression was an Asian peasant economy of a somewhat special type. It was an immigrant country, like lower Burma or Cochin China. It was a Chinese Middle West, not an old settled land like the Shantung or Hopei from which so many of Manchuria's inhabitants came.

When Manchuria was opened in 1876, it contained two quite distinct societies. There were the peasants of Liaoning, Chinese who had been settled there for a millennium, though with a border that advanced and retreated as nomad pressures waxed and waned. There were also the nomads, fishermen and hunters of the other provinces, who had still only rarely taken to agriculture and who lay very light on the land. The influx of Northern Chinese which followed 1876, and which added over 3 million immigrants to Manchuria's population in the seven years 1923-30, 843,000 of them in the one year 1927, raised the population from about 10 million in 1876 to 14 million in 1900, 30 million in 1930,[1] and 41 million in 1947.[2] The empty lands began to fill—cultivation went up from 20 million acres in 1924 to 35 million in 1931,[3] over a million acres a year. As they filled, they became Chinese; the Chinese formed 80% of the population by 1900, 90% or more by 1930. By this time the old lords of the land, the Manchus, had been reduced to perhaps 3%, and were sinified at that. The colonisation moreover took place primarily not in the long Chinese Liaoning, which had a density of 212 per square mile by 1930, and was already providing emigrants of its own in the 1920's, but in the empty nomad provinces. The process is not complete. The Barge area, for example, is still Mongol and nomad, and as late as 1939 the Manchukuo Government could still talk of reclaiming 49 million acres in North Manchuria.[4] But it

[1]F. C. Jones, *Manchuria since 1931*, London, Royal Institute of International Affairs, 1949, p. 4.
[2]United Nations, Economic Commission for Asia and the Far East.
[3]*Japan—Manchukuo Year Book*, 1939, p. 759.
[4]Quoted in speech of Director-General of General Affairs Board of State Council at p. 31. *Economic and Financial Conditions in Japan, Manchukuo and China*. E. Asia Intelligence Series No. 2. Tokyo, 1939.

has gone far enough to give most parts of Manchuria a considerable population. Agriculture is settled and on Chinese lines. The Kirin province had a density of 89 per square mile by 1930.

The immigrants who came were Chinese peasants whose only desire was to find new land on which they could continue to be Chinese peasants. Thus Manchuria in 1930 was still in most ways a typical Asian economy.[1] The majority of the population, 75% of the Chinese and Mongols in 1935, was dependent on agriculture. The agriculture was primarily arable; only 7% of farm income in N. Manchuria came from cattle-raising. Cereals accounted for nearly two-thirds of the area under crops, and it was in cereals that the expansion of production resulting from immigration and growth of population had been most notable—it rose from 185 million bushels to 605 million between 1914 and 1927.[2] Holdings were small; in 1934, for instance, only one payer of land tax in 250 had over 150 acres, but 1,909,000 had 3 acres or less, almost half the total, and of the other half two-thirds had under 15 acres.[3] Tenancy was widespread. Some 30% of farmers were full tenants, and about another 20% part tenants; in the fully occupied areas a certain amount of landless labour also was growing up.[4] Rents as high as 40-60% of the crop were common. Much land in the newer areas was in the hand of officials, urban capitalists, and the remnants of the Manchu aristocracy, who had obtained it by royal gift or tribal right. Debt was widespread and foreclosure frequent. Commercial fertilizer was little used. The farmer was dependent for cash on one crop, the soya bean, exports of which accounted for 60% of all exports in 1930. Handicrafts were declining as in every peasant society in contact with factory industry.[5]

Thus, although two factors, the size of the immigration and the feudal or tribal ownership of so much of the empty land, make Manchurian development somewhat special, by 1930 a society in its broad lines of the usual Asian peasant style had been produced.

Between 1932 and 1945 the Japanese built up beside this old-model peasantry a complete Western style industrial society, which

[1]United Nations, *Economic Survey of Asia and the Far East*, 1947, Shanghai, 1948.
[2]F. C. Jones, *op. cit.*, p. 8.
[3]Karl J. Pelzer, *op. cit.*, p. 100.
[4]Thus in Pulantien prefecture, Kwantung leased territory, one family in eight was completely dependent on labour.
[5]Total imports were £700,000 in 1880. Textile imports alone were £11½ million in 1930.

they provided with all the apparatus of Western economic life, railways, factories, roads, power stations. Yet the basic life of the peasant proceeded unaltered beneath the very chimneys of their mills, for there were no changes which the Japanese wished to make. The first stage of Western influence, the drawing of the peasant into the world market so that he ceased to be completely self-sufficient and became dependent at least in part on the demand for the soya beans he wanted to sell and the price of the kerosene or cloth he wished to buy, had already happened between 1895 and 1920. This had resulted from the building of railways by the Russians and Japanese and the growth in external trade. The next stage has, in other Asian countries, been the growth of a native middle class, which, accepting Western ideas, tries to remake its own society in their image. It sends students abroad to learn to be electrical engineers; it demands control of its own economic life or a democratic Government in which the highest posts would go to its own people and not to foreigners. If Manchukuo had proceeded to this stage, it would have destroyed the whole purpose of the Japanese conquest, for it would have made Japanese capital unsafe, and Japanese technicians welcome only for so long as they were needed to train Manchurians. It would have made Japanese over-lordship anathema.

Under Western systems of government, this development cannot be prevented. Western civilisation is indivisible; the English-man takes Magna Carta with him as naturally as railway engines. But the Japanese had themselves taken from the West only its material achievements; its liberation of the spirit they had deliber-ately rejected. It is for that reason that one can see in Manchukuo, as nowhere else in Asia, what the business man can achieve if he is completely uninhibited by the missionary. One sees also how severe are his limitations unless his mind is influenced by a desire for the welfare of others as well as himself.

The sheer achievement of the Japanese was very considerable. Electrical capacity reached 412,000 k.w. in 1937, 1,768,000 k.w. in 1945. The 3726 miles of railway of 1931[1] had become perhaps 7,500 by 1945.[2] Coal production rose from 9,063,000 metric tons in 1933 to 30 million tons in 1944.[3] Output of magnesite ore went up from 29,000 tons in 1930 to 337,000 in 1936, of gold from 111,000

[1]*China's Struggle for Railroad Development*, Chang Kia-gnav, p. 82.
[2]*Chicago Daily News*, 28th August, 1945.
[3]F. C. Jones, *op. cit.*, pp. 154, 156.

grammes to 3,570,000 grammes in the same period. Production of steel ingots grew from virtually nothing to 1½ million tons, of pig iron from 250,000 tons in 1930 to 3 million tons in 1944, of aluminium from nothing in 1935 to 18,000 tons in 1944. Japanese prospecting permitted lead production to reach 25,000 tons, zinc production 20,000 tons, copper production 4,000 tons in the same year of 1944. An arsenal was created in Mukden employing 20,000 people. From a country without industries Japan took Manchukuo in a short dozen years through the whole course of Western industrialisation, a course which had required half a century in Japan herself, until by 1944 there were plants in Mukden capable of that most difficult of Western achievements, aeroplane manufacture. The population of Mukden itself had grown from 100,000 in 1900 to nearly 3 million.

The strain on Japan is shown by the following table of Japanese investment and of Manchurian imports of construction materials in the years 1932–1939

TABLE 22[1]

Year				Amount in million yen invested in the year	Imports of construction materials in million yen.
1932	..	..	..	97	—
1933	..	..	..	151	—
1934	..	..	..	272	154
1935	..	..	..	379	158
1936	..	..	..	263	152
1937	..	..	..	303	224
1938	..	..	..	484	411
1939	..	..	..	1,103	555

By 1945 total investment may have reached £500 million, 40% of Japan's 1938 national income. It had taken Great Britain, greatest of overseas lenders, a century to lend an amount equal to her 1938 income.

For great effort, great reward. Manchurian magnesite made Japanese magnesium; Manchurian aluminium Japanese aeroplanes; Manchurian gold helped to meet the deficit in Japan's balance of payments with the United States. Manchurian export of metals and ores to Japan went up from £1 million to £3 million in the three years 1936–8. The Manchurian himself gained little. The only

[1]F. C. Jones, *op. cit.*, pp. 137, 136.

consumer goods industry created was some half-million cotton spindles, and textiles continued to have to be imported; imports rose from 62 million yuan in 1934 to 109 million in 1937, and when after that the War forced increasing reductions, the Manchurian simply had to do without. Of all the capital put into Manchukuo only 5% had by 1939 gone into spinning, dyeing, processing of foodstuffs.[1] For such investment, whose only benefit was to the local people, the Japanese had no money.

The Manchurians did not even get the new industrial jobs. The skilled men were Japanese, the unskilled new immigrants from China. Immigration was over a million in each of the years 1942–1944. Immigrants could be got cheaply because of the misery Japan's own campaigns had brought to North China. A Japanese labourer got 31 yuan a day in Mukden in 1938, a Chinese only just over 1 yuan.[2] All the semi-skilled and skilled openings were naturally reserved for Japanese, whom fifty years of factories had given an aptitude it would have taken the Manchurian a generation to acquire.

A native Government, moved by the need to fit their people for the new world they were creating, would have seen to it that the training was given, and written off the cost to experience. That is what the Japanese had done in Japan. In Manchukuo the Japanese had no such motive, and they had their own over-population to think of. So on the South Manchurian Railway every engineer, every higher official down to half the clerks, was Japanese. In 1936 there were 515,000 Japanese in Manchukuo, in 1945 1,327,000; there had been 90,000 in 1930, hardly one in 1910.[3] And they were all in occupations which the new development had created. There were never as many as 25,000 on the land. But as early as 1935 16% were in manufacturing, 30% in trade and commerce, 21% in transport and communications.[4]

There were also 22% in professions and public service. This is a pointer to another aspect of an industrialisation of which special training for the local people forms no part. A peasant society can be run by officials with no training beyond a gift for keeping law and order; an industrial community requires technicians in Govern-

---

[1]E. Asia Intelligence Series, op. cit., p. 47.

[2]F. C. Jones, op. cit., p. 216.

[3]United Nations, Economic Survey of Asia and the Far East, 1947, Shanghai, 1948.

[4]Karl J. Pelzer, op. cit., p. 15.

ment as in every other sphere. Its judges can no longer pronounce simply on the equity of the case, they must be able to interpret elaborate written instruments; the duties of its policemen are no longer confined to catching thieves whose identity the whole village knows, they must be able to detect the elaborate crimes of the forger, to apply all the complicated rules which being close together in a town makes necessary. So the old local official, who sometimes knew the people, but very rarely knew anything else, is displaced, and the foreign expert who knows all there is to know about his subject, but perhaps not very much about the people, gets the post instead. Over 1,000 Japanese judges were taken on by Manchukuo between 1933 and 1939, and by 1937 there were 10,000 Japanese police.[1]

The peasant indeed actually lost by a decade of Japanese development. Production of crops went down from $18\frac{1}{2}$ million metric tons in 1931 to $16\frac{3}{4}$ in 1937. Population went up, yet food went down. The output of the great staple, kaoliang, fell from $4\frac{4}{5}$ million metric tons in 1930 to $4\frac{3}{5}$ million in 1939. Even had there been more to buy, the peasant had less money to buy it with, for the production of his cash crop, the soya bean, fell from $5\frac{1}{3}$ million metric tons in 1930 to 4 million in 1939.[2]

While production thus went down, demands on the peasant went up. The State revenue from monopolies—matches, alcohol, salt—rose from 6 million yuan in 1933/4 to 77 million in 1939, States sales of opium from $5\frac{1}{2}$ million yuan in 1933 to 48 million in 1937, the land tax from $7\frac{3}{4}$ million in 1933/4 to $11\frac{1}{2}$ million in 1936. Against this should be set, however, an unknown reduction in the arbitrary "squeeze" by warlords and officials which had been widely practised under the Chinese regime but which cannot, of course, be traced in any accounts. The Japanese were more efficient tax-collectors, but they were on balance also more efficient controllers of their subordinates.

The defeat of Japan in 1945 afforded a unique opportunity of studying the peasant's own reaction to the whole process of industrialisation. It could not be studied in a similar way elsewhere. In India or Indonesia the peasants were led by a class trained to Western education, ways and ambitions. They ask for independence in order to have more industrialisation, but the Manchurian peasant, left to himself, has shown his total disinterest in the whole industrial

[1]F. C. Jones, *op. cit.*, p. 32.
[2]F. C. Jones, *op. cit.*, p. 180.

apparatus. The Russians removed machinery as war booty; the Chinese Communists blew up railways; only the Kuomintang tried to make the industries work again. But the Communists offered the peasant freedom from his landlord who had collaborated with the Japanese, from the men whose holdings in N. Manchuria sometimes ran to hundreds of thousands of acres, and with whom the Kuomintang was all too willing to deal.

The peasant's support of the Communists is his verdict on an industrialisation which gave no thought to his welfare.

Chapter XII

PLURAL SOCIETIES

As autocracy gives way to democracy, and subjects prepare to accept the duties of citizens, there rises the problem of creating a nation out of a set of disparate groups. The acuteness of the problem varies greatly in different parts of Asia. Japan is as homogeneous as England without Wales. But India had to shed Burma, Aden and Pakistan before it could obtain the spiritual unity necessary to a modern state. China's problem is a very limited one. But in Ceylon and Indo-China and Siam, difficulties between majority and minority, as between one nationality and another, have dominated much of recent history. Indonesia provides an example of the way in which differing economic interests may complicate the integration of different nationalities into a common state. The most notable case of all, Malaya, is studied in the next chapter.

China's losses of territory came immediately after 1911. The allegiance of Mongolia and Tibet and Turkestan was to the Manchu. Their peoples resented the chicanery of Chinese landgrabbers and officials. They were suspicious of Sun Yat-sen's insistence that nation and race in China were identical. Outer Mongolia seceded in 1912, and finally had its independence recognized in 1946. Tibet clung more and more firmly to an autonomy which in practice meant independence until the Communists reabsorbed it by the threat of force; the Muslims of the North West and Sinkiang were prepared to give fealty to the Central Government only on condition that the reality of power was left with their own local leaders; many of the Mongols of Hsingan and Inner Mongolia preferred even the Japanese to the Chinese. By settling more thickly in some of the doubtful areas, the Chinese have won back territory which threatened to secede. But this expansion of the Chinese also intensified the suspicions of the non-Chinese. It remains for the Communists to try to solve the racial problem. Their method will probably be to create local regimes with at least the appearance of extensive autonomy; that is, for example, what they have done with the Mongols of the Hsingan; and in Tibet the Dalai Lama and the Panchen Lama, the people's traditional heads, have been left with at least nominal authority.

Indo-China is an example of an area where each of the constituent states has a real unity of its own, but where the political unity of the whole is an artificial creation of foreign conquest. That would not necessarily of itself have prevented the growth of a common loyalty. But in Indo-China the divisions were too deep. The only unity has remained that given by French conquest, for Indo-China lies on all the watersheds between China and India, between civilisation and primitive tribalism. The Annamite has taken his way of life from China, under whose rule or suzerainty he has been for most of his history, the Cambodian his from India, whose Brahmins and Kshatriyas provided his first teachers and rulers; the Laotian is a Thai tribesman who has taken to rice agriculture; the hill tribes still live in a world of hunting and shifting fields burnt out of the jungle. Over all this world presided the Frenchman, with his missionary belief that truth and civilisation are one, and that their only home is Paris. He is eager to assimilate the peoples culturally. He is lukewarm for economic development.

The problem is made more complicated by the historical role of the Annamites as aggressors against their neighbours. In South Annam they reduced the Cham builders of Po Nagar to a remnant of 130,000 villagers. Cochin-China they conquered from the Cambodian Khmers, first by violence and military colonisation, more lately by the slow seeping forward of settlement and the creation of an alien atmosphere in which the Cambodian villager, of whom there are still about a quarter of a million, finds himself unable to live; since 1945 Viet Minh have hastened Cambodian exodus by an occasional atrocity. Over Laos and Cambodia themselves Annam exercised an intermittent suzerainty in the 18th and 19th centuries, and Annamite immigrants have long begun to penetrate the Cambodian homeland; there are some 200,000 in Eastern Cambodia and the great fisheries of Lake Tonle-Sap are exploited by 30,000 Annamite fishermen. In the hills in Annam and Tongking, wherever there is a valley floor fit for the growing of rice, there the Annamite is to be found, and he is only prevented from encroaching still further into tribal territory by his fear of malaria, mountains and ghosts.

This history has meant that the Annamites, who are three-quarters of the population of Indo-China and occupy most of its rice-land but hold only about a third of its total surface, have taken a quite different attitude to the French from any of the other peoples. The Annamites have always resisted. The original annexation cost three minor campaigns, in 1859–62, in 1873–4, in 1882–5, and intrigue against French rule began immediately; the first plot, scotched in 1867, cost the Annamite Emperor the provinces of Vinh Long, Ha Tien, and An Giang. Time brought, not healing, but further bitterness. The mandarin resented his replacement by a French or French-trained official, the scholar the loss of prestige and of culture which resulted from the substitution of a Romanized alphabet for the Chinese ideographs, which, though never the possession of more than a few, had to these few opened all the learning of China. The people resented the privileges which full citizenship conferred on the "assimilés," who were never more than 10,000 and whom they regarded as deserters.

A further complication was the concentration of French economic interests in Annamite territory. The French owned 250,000 acres of rubber, 250,000 acres of rice plantations, the mines of anthracite and zinc and gold, nearly all the railways. The cities of Saigon and Hanoi and Haiphong, very French in appearance, represented a total investment of perhaps £70,000,000. To the French this sum does not mean very much; in 1952 they have been spending as much on the fighting every two months. But the Annamites saw only the high proportion the interest and dividends bore to the total proceeds of their exports. So every happening which could be interpreted to the discredit of the status quo brought on riots. First there was the victory of Japan over Russia, then the Russian and Chinese Revolutions; then the great depression. Troubles in 1908, 1913, 1920, 1926, 1930–1 preceded the great revolt of 1943. Nationalism and Communism are alike old. We find Phan Cau Trinh saying nearly 40 years ago "The people of Annam wish to be educated, they wish to be respected. They desire to obtain gradually their independence . . . and the adoption of a decent manner towards the natives as a whole"[1] The Comintern addressing Annamite (not Indo-Chinese) Communists in 1927, wrote "The Communist International is especially interested in the fate of the unfortunate peoples living in colonies, such as you Annamites, whose lot has been frightful ever since the day the French barbarian came to loot and destroy".

To the other peoples of Indo-China, the French have been protectors against aggression from the Siamese as well as from the

[1] Thomas Edson Ennis, *French Policy and Developments in Indo-China*, Chicago, 1936, p. 180.

Annamites. The French have not seemed aggressors themselves. It was the understanding and sympathy of the great explorer Auguste Pavie which won over the Laotians; the Moi hill country near Saigon was persuaded into submission by two battalions without the firing of a shot (1932). Cambodia's request for French protection (1863) was justified by centuries in which the once proud Khmer Empire, whose sway had extended from Bangkok to Saigon, had been losing its western provinces to the Siamese and its eastern provinces to the Annamites; as late as in 1946 it was French power which recovered for Cambodia the provinces of Battembang and Siemreap which Japanese patronage had enabled Siam to annex in 1941. For her services France takes but little; her investments are negligible. She owns a little tin in Laos, 27,000 hectares of rubber in Cambodia. Here, therefore, there is no revolt, no fierce passion for independence; the Cambodians for example, have accepted cheerfully enough an agreement (in 1946) which gives them Parliament and ministers and departments at the price only of taking French advisers, of whose advice they stand in grave need in any case.

These differences between the various parts of Indo-China make it impossible to run the country as a unitary state; fortunately the geographical division between the different areas is clear, and a solution of its political problems may be possible by a partition, either partial, as in the French scheme for a federation, or complete, as the Annamites may prefer. In such a solution there would be integration as well as division. The unnatural union between the Annamite and the other peoples would be broken, but the equally unnatural division of Viet Nam into Cochin-China, Annam and Tongking would be ended by the reunion of the three. The new Viet Nam under ex-Emperor Bao Dai, with its separate Army and limited separate foreign service, represents indeed the triumph of this policy; the Annamite country is united into a single State, to which France has granted virtual Dominion status; and the new Annamite State is in effect as separate from Cambodia and Laos as from France.

Ceylon has a society even more plural than that of Indo-China. But she is too small, her minorities too often intermingled, to be administered as other than a unitary state. Her problems are not recent like Malaya's; they go far back into history. There is the original Sinhalese majority, itself divided into Kandyan and Low Country. There is a solid block of Jaffra Tamils in the North and East who came in as a result of the constant streams of invasion from the Indian mainland. There are Europeans and Burghers, who are descendants of Dutch and Portuguese who settled and sometimes intermarried in the island. There are Indian plantation labourers. Centuries of Indian ocean trade conducted by Arabs have left behind them a large population of Moors. Table 23 gives the racial constitution of the Ceylonese population in 1941.

TABLE 23

Low Country Sinhalese	..	..		2,596,479
Kandyan Sinhalese	..	..	..	1,467,429
Jaffra Tamils	..	..	..	697,032
Indian Tamils..	..	..	..	812,113
Moors	..	..	..	383,956
Europeans	..	..	..	10,398
Burghers	..	..	..	39,666

In no other country is there such great variety of race in so small an area. The differences of race are paralleled by differences of economic standing and of religion. There were in 1931 3,731,979 Buddhists, 1,323,225 Hindus, 407,625 Muslims, 597,427 Christians. Of 6000 pensionable posts in the Government 769 were held by the Burghers and 1,164 by the Ceylon Tamils, a proportion much in excess of their percentage of the population; the Moors were mainly shopkeepers or traders; the Indians very largely estate labourers; the Europeans are planters and business men, owning 70% of the tea-growing land and 40% of the rubber-growing land on which Ceylon depends for four-fifths of her exports. The Sinhalese were until recently mainly peasant rice farmers.

There has been ample cause for quarrel between the different groups. The European has feared for his estates; the Indian has been aggrieved because he could only vote if domiciled or given a certificate of permanent settlement. In the 1952 election the number of Indian electors was reduced to a level at which they could not elect a single M.P., by legislation which disfranchised all but Ceylonese citizens, and offered to most Indians the possibility of citizenship only by a registration which no more than a few thousand obtained in time. The Jaffra Tamil and Burgher have been nervous for their Government jobs; the Tamil used also to allege that his areas were discriminated against in irrigation. The Moors saw in the spread of Government-assisted consumers' co-operation during the war a threat to their livelihood. A stiffening of the tests for domicile cut the number of Indian estate workers electors from 225,000 in 1938 to 168,000 in 1943. In the 1952 election, the number of Indian electors was reduced to a level at which they could not elect a single M.P., by legislation which disfranchised all but Ceylonese citizens, and offered to most Indians the possibility of citizenship only by a registration which no more than a few thousand obtained in time.

Yet, with all the difficulties, Ceylon has been able to proceed to its goal of becoming a Dominion without riots or revolt or civil disobedience. There has been no massacre of minorities, nor have any become fiercely disloyal. It is a political achievement without parallel.

How has it been done? One cause of Ceylon's good fortune has been that the minorities were concentrated, not scattered. Thus they have been able to win seats in territorial constituencies without separate electorates or reservation. The Jaffna Tamils number 428,000 out of 455,000 in the Northern Province and 128,000 out of 242,000 in the Eastern Province. Indians number 430,000 out of 1,088,000 in the Central Province. Another cause is the rise of a Sinhalese nationalism which is gradually welding the two branches of the Sinhalese race into one. Another cause is that only one minority, the Indian, can look for outside aid. The problem of the Indian minority also has been eased by the cessation of Indian recruitment to the plantations in the last decade. The number of Indian plantation labourers has dropped from 650,000 to 450,000 while the Sinhalese have recently taken to plantation work and there were 150,000 of them engaged in it in 1948; the Indians who remain will more and more become Ceylonese with a vote obtained by birth or registration,[1] and will turn less and less to an India whose Government, unlike that of China, has always said that Indians overseas must give their first loyalty to their new home. Another cause of the quietness of Ceylon politics is the tolerance of the Sinhalese, who have not been made arrogant by their rise to dominance in an island of which for centuries they have never ruled more than a part. They have always been prepared to ally themselves with non-Sinhalese members, and to take Burgher or Tamil members into their Cabinets; they have recently had three Tamils in a Cabinet of 14. Perhaps the chief cause of Ceylon's good fortune is that the Donoughmore Commission, which drew up the constitution, refused to believe that the

[1]237,000 applications for registration as Ceylonese citizens have been made. Since applications can cover a family, not only an individual, between them virtually the whole Indian community is covered.

best way to protect minorities was to fragment Parliament with racial or economic blocs or to make a statutory minority out of a majority. Their words are worth quoting: "There can be no hope of binding together the diverse elements of the population in a realisation of their common kinship and an acknowledgment of common obligations to the country of which they are all citizens as long as the system of communal representation with all its disintegrating influences remains a distinctive feature of the Constitution".[2]

The most important example of the travail brought on an Asian society as it seeks to create a unitary state is provided by India. In India, the sloughing off of Aden was not so much as noticed. The severance of Burma from India caused little pain, for it was recognised that the connection between India and Burma had always been artificial. Burmese civilisation had indeed once come from India, but in the 1930s men remembered only that the Burmese were Mongoloid and Buddhist. The secession of Burma was a triumphant proof of how partition can sometimes be the best solution.

The secession of the Muslims was a different matter. Hindu and Muslim had been inextricably intermixed for centuries. Though each had a majority in large areas, there was no province which did not have considerable populations of both. Yet the Muslims, with their separate religion, their memories of conquest, their different culture and social structure and even alphabet, were not prepared to give their loyalty to a democracy in which they felt the majority would be permanently Hindu. Out of their reluctance Jinnah made Pakistan.

Partition in the Indian sub-continent can hardly go further. Congress is discouraging the creation of new provinces on linguistic lines for fear they might attract some of the loyalty which should be given to India. The Justice Party in Madras and the cause of Dravidistan are dead. The Muslim in India has awakened to the desolate realisation that now he is only a minority. Therefore, he has followed the Parsi and the Anglo-Indian, the Untouchable and the Christian, and made his peace with Congress, which is prepared to prove its equal acceptance of all who see in India their mother.

The development in Pakistan has been similar. The principles of

[1] As late as 1920 there were only 12 Sinhalese in a House of 37. In 1889 the Sinhalese had had only 2 out of 8 non-official seats.

[2] The Donoughmore Constitution was, of course, open to strong criticism on other grounds—especially because of the curious "committee system" which it provided.

Islam have been proclaimed as the basis of the State in the Constitution. In Pakistan nine-tenths of the population are now Muslim. The garrisons have been withdrawn from the Tribal Areas without any recrudescence of raiding. Provincial particularism has been dealt with with a high hand. On the initiative of the Central Government, two Premiers of Sind have been disqualified from holding office. The Government of the West Punjab has on orders from Karachi been taken over by its Governor. The proponents of a separate Pathanistan have been securely jailed. The problems raised by the division of the two halves of the state by a thousand-mile corridor have not yet been finally solved. But when Mr. Jinnah died while Pakistan was barely on its feet, the machine of Government did not falter in its course. This newest of states had already become a nation and its people citizens.

The circumstances in Indonesia are simpler than in India. Though nationalism has a history of forty years, it became effective only quite recently. Its difficulties are economic rather than spiritual. The inhabitants vary from tribesmen like the Karo and the Batak, the Dayak and the Toba, whose cultivation is still often shifting and whose political organization before the coming of the Dutch half a century ago knew no unit larger than the village or the tribe, to the sophisticated heirs of ancient civilisations in Jogjakarta or Palembang. Full geographical unity dates only from the Dutch conquests of 1880–1910.[1] Past dynasties, Hindu in origin and belief, have however bequeathed to Indonesia a wide common culture, and this has been further reinforced by the conversion of almost the whole area to Islam[2] since 1400. The first Indonesian political party was significantly the Sarikat Islam. Everywhere the blood is Malay. The non-Malays—the Chinese and the Dutch—are only a thirtieth of the whole.

It is the economic divisions which cause trouble. Voting power will belong to the Indonesians. Property is often Dutch or Chinese. The proportion of Dutch and Chinese paying income tax to their total population was in the thirties one hundred and twenty times as great as the Indonesian proportion. Economics alone, however, are not normally a source of revolt, only of friction; a man makes

[1]Between 670 and 1478, either under Sri Vijaya or Madjopahit, most of the Archipelago except for the remoter tribal areas, in the interior of Borneo or the Celebes for example, acknowledged one suzerain if not one ruler.

[2]Bali is Hindu, Amboyna and the Minahassa and the Batak Christian, some of the more primitive tribes still animist.

many more compromises over his income than over his beliefs. Once they govern themselves, the Indonesians are likely to learn, as India and Pakistan are learning already, that it is both painful and slow to raise the standard of living of a peasant society whose savings are only a few million a year. A country which needs outside capital to ease the strain must be prepared to give evidence of its good faith by treating generously the investments foreigners have already made on its territory, investments already much reduced in value and relative importance by the slump in sugar in the 30s, the rise of native smallholder rubber to three-quarters of the total crop, and the devastation and neglect of the Japanese occupation. The Indonesians have not the technicians and the experience to be able to replace foreign shipping and insurance and banking forthwith. No transfer of political power can enable a country to impose such burdensome conditions on foreign investment that the investor cannot hope to make a profit; the money simply goes elsewhere.

It would not yet be true in Indonesia to say that a nation has been born, but at least one is being visibly brought to birth.

The problems of Thailand and Burma are discussed elsewhere (Chapters VIII and XV). Those of the Philippines are not great. The population is heavily Catholic and Tagalog-speaking; the Moros of Mindanao, the pagans of the Mountain Province, are picturesque survivals, not menaces to national unity.

Thus everywhere in Asia the races struggling to adapt themselves to Western ideas of the State have been forced to realize that a nation can exist only if the people have a common tradition and a common loyalty. As Canada and the United States show, neither a common racial origin nor a single dominant religion are necessary. What is vital is that the State should have the capacity to make everyone of its citizens feel equally at home, to find symbols and ideals to which every one of its groups can give equal devotion; the partition of Ireland is a perpetual reminder of the penalty for failing to find a common basis for loyalty. No Asian country except Japan has yet been able to escape from the urgency of the problem of how to create a nation, and the need to find some answer has dominated most of the politics of the years since 1918. It is the most significant fact of the last decade that it is in that period that so many plural societies have at last come near to finding the soul without which the sacrifices progress demands are not possible.

Chapter XIII

MALAYA

Because the unit of Eastern society has always been based on the village, loyalties outside the village, other than those based on blood, have been few and tenuous. The clan, the tribe, the race, have all had a hold on men's devotions, for they are all extensions of the family, and devotion to the family has always been, in Asia, the first moral duty. But in pre-western days, there was always comparatively little loyalty to the State as an institution, and the nation in its modern sense was an unknown concept.

The 19th century, however, did not organise itself on the lines of blood—the importance attached by Germans to blood was a sign of how far they were out of tune with the 19th century spirit. The great 19th century unit was the territorial nation based on a common territory and a common political tradition. Sometimes there was common blood as well, but more often, as in America or Switzerland, there was not. The main-spring of the State was a common set of ideals shared by all its citizens.

The creation of similar nations in the East has been of varying difficulty. In India a political tradition, primarily British, and a long common history, have provided the bond, though the price has had to be paid of losing those Muslim areas which felt themselves to belong to another tradition. In Pakistan the bond is Islam and a sense of difference from India. In China and Japan there have long been a common cultural tradition and a single central government, so that the formation of nation States of the European type presents no great difficulty. In Indonesia the long years of Dutch rule and the wide understanding of Malay in its Indonesian form, have provided the basis on which a nation State is to be built.

If one wants a really clear example of the difficulties involved in creating a nation State in Asia, one must turn to Malaya. There one can see quite starkly all the problems which result when the government is based on a territorial unity which has no reflection in a unity in the minds of its citizens. There have been recent signs that this unity is at last beginning to develop, but until now Malaya has provided an admirable instance of the fact that it is not enough for a country to be rich. It must also be able to acquire the devotion of its people. Without that devotion, all government is discovered in the end to be built on sand.

WEALTH WITHOUT PATRIOTISM

A Western society depends for harmony and happiness on common beliefs and common loyalties more than on wealth. Poverty can be shared, but the worship of false gods is fatal. Malaya is an example in the East of the plight of a wealthy society without spiritual backing.

Malaya has a sickness which is curable, yet which, if left uncured, is fatal. It has acquired wealth without finding a soul. No other country in Asia has grown so much richer so quickly. In no other country has the increase in population been less of a disadvantage. There was little of a pre-existing peasant society to embarrass the general advance by the reactions induced in it by change. But in no other country either has there been so absolute a failure to produce common patriotism, common standards of value, a common willingness to make sacrifices for the common good. Men are still Malays or Chinese, Muslims or Buddhists; they feel themselves neither fellow-citizens nor brothers in God.

The wealth of Malaya is a creation of British rule. Singapore, when Sir Stamford Raffles founded it in 1819, was a village where no town had been since Malacca became a city five centuries before; Penang had a population of only 24,000 in 1812, Malacca of 30,000 in 1834. The Sultanates, when they accepted British protection[1] at the end of the nineteenth century, were but jungle backwaters, with a total cultivated area of perhaps 500,000 acres, and with the smallest of populations; Johore had had 25,000 in 1839, Perak 81,000 in 1879, Pahang 84,000 in 1891, the four states taken over from Siam in 1909 had a population not much over the half-million between them. There was not a mile of railway or made road. The total trade of Perak, Selangor and Sungei Ujong, imports and exports together, was little over £600,000 in 1880. Their annual revenue in 1876 was only £84,000. Of schools and health departments or police or plantations there was nothing; the only major export was tin, and even tin was only just getting under way when the British took over.

[1]The dates are Perak, Selangor, Sungei Ujong 1874, Pahang 1888, Negri Sembilan 1895, Johore 1885 (with a further treaty in 1914), Perlis, Kedah, Kelantan, Trengganu 1909.

In 1870 Cornwall's 10,000 tons of tin per annum was still well ahead of the production of all Malaya.

British rule brought with it the whole power of the West to create rapid material progress, the capital, the order, the means of transport and communication, the commercial law, the care for the welfare of the ordinary man.

Rubber was introduced in 1877, as the result of a typical Western combination of initiative in smuggling the seeds out of Brazil and science in discovering the variety most suitable to acclimatisation in Malaya. Exports had already begun by 1905.[1] In 1920 they reached 196,000 tons, in 1948 nearly a million tons.[2] So with tin. Production was 26,000 tons in 1889, 37,200 in 1920, 85,500 in 1940, 45,000 again in 1941 after all the destruction of the war.

The development of the rubber and tin industries show admirably the capacity of the West to make a society richer. A peasant economy has no use for either commodity. Both need to be marketed in industrial societies which need tyres and tinplate. The peasant himself is unable to provide the capital which is required to develop such industries. Even in the middle ages, tin was mined first for Indian, then for Chinese merchants. With the recent replacement of the Chinese[3] the mining has been carried on to a very considerable extent by European companies. The increasing use of dredges, of engines and gravel pumps both by them and by the still considerable number of Chinese owners, has caused the amount of capital required to increase steadily; non-Chinese companies alone had some £14 million invested in 1936.

Rubber was at first a Western plantation industry, in which some £55 millions of Western money, perhaps three-quarters of it British,[4] had been invested by 1936. The rubber industry required for its expansion the whole apparatus of Western business, ports and banks, insurance companies and brokers. It needed too the whole force of Western science for such improvements as bud-grafting and selected clones. It is true that smallholdings in 1948 produced 294,000 tons of rubber against the production in the estates of 403,000 tons. This is proof of the extent to which Western ways have influenced the Malayan peasant. It does not show that rubber is

[1]When they were 200 tons.

[2]Part was re-exports of Indonesian and Siamese rubber. Production of Malaya was only 698,000 tons.

[3]The share of Chinese mines dropped from 64% to 36% between 1920 and 1936.

[4]Investment figures from Helmut G. Callis, *op. cit.*, p. 49.

South-East Asia

itself a peasant crop; the Malayan smallholder could only take the risk of becoming a rubber producer when facilities had been created and there was a proved market.[1]

The rubber and tin industries led to the expansion of the services without which they could neither be produced nor exported, and only the profits of these industries made possible the financing of the welfare services.

There are some 2600 miles of railway line in Malaya and 5500 miles of all weather road. 10 million tons of shipping were cleared at Singapore in 1948. Employment in collieries and factories in the Malayan Union, negligible in 1900, was 25,000 in 1948. Health is looked after on something approaching a European standard; Singapore's death rate of 14.30[2] per 1000 in 1947—it had been 25.19 in 1931—is lower than anywhere else in Asia except Japan. In the Federated Malay States there was in 1935 one hospital bed for every 300 of the population, and this is up to the standards of Italy or Spain. Education standards have risen steadily; already in 1938 nearly 4/- was spent per head on education as compared with 10d. in Burma, 1/4d. in Indonesia and 1d. in China. Nearly half the children of school-going age, 236,000, were at school, In 1948 there had been a further improvement, and 525,000 children, virtually all those of school age, were attending school. A University has been founded with a large initial grant from the British Treasury. Wages are high; the Indian rubber plantation labourer, making £8 per month (1948), is getting four times what he would earn at home in Madras, where he might be unemployed half the year. The Chinese tin miner, who earned a dollar or more a day before the war, was making certainly five times as much as he could have hoped for in Kwangtung or Fukien.

All this prosperity is summed up in the national income. In 1940 this was £16 per head for the Malayan Union, which was roughly comparable with that of Japan, the only other economy in Asia which had been Westernized. It was three times or more than that of India, China or Java.

The abnormally high income is due almost entirely to Western-style enterprise. In 1940 four-fifths of the cultivated area was under

[1]There is far less risk for the smallholder than for the estates. If the price drops too low, the smallholder ceases to bother about his rubber trees, and concentrates on his food crops. The estates on the contrary may be ruined. Production by the smallholder thus expands more rapidly than by the estates when prices rise.

[2]*Straits Times*, Singapore, 1st April, 1948.

crops introduced from the West (3½ million acres were under rubber, 70,000 acres under oil palms, 50,000 acres under pineapples). Only 14% of the land was under rice, the staple crop of Asia. Squatting during the war and the rice shortage since 1945 has done something to increase the rice area, but it has not added more than some 250—300,000 acres. The biggest single scheme of promoting rice growing affects only 40,000 acres.[1]

Business, not the peasant, pays the cost of the State. (Rubber smallholding itself is a business, not a subsistence activity). The tax structure is, therefore, different from elsewhere in Asia; there is none of the traditional dependence of Asia on land revenue and toddy-excise and such simple consumption taxes as those on salt or matches or textile imports. Instead, the main sources of revenue are of the European kind—taxes on petrol, and tobacco, and income-tax.

In the Federation Budget for 1949, out of a total revenue of Straits dollars 261 million, revenue from tobacco accounts for 59 million, the tin and rubber export duties for 68 million, duties on imported liquor for 14 million. In Singapore in 1949, out of revenue of 103 million dollars, income-tax produced 18 million, and taxes on liquor, tobacco and petrol some 42 million. Taxation in pre-British Malaya was of the poor and the peasant for the benefit of the rich, the Sultan and his nobles; but Malaya to-day is firmly following Western precedents. In Singapore the 30 million dollars spent on housing, education and health come from the business-man's income-tax and taxes on cigarettes and petrol.

The history of Malaya thus shows the West's capacity to bring to a country both wealth and a measure of social justice. It shows also the dangers of riches unaccompanied by any spiritual integration of the community, any growth of a loyalty in which every citizen feels himself to have an equal share. The West's own economic expansion has taken place in countries governed by a common religious tradition and a common patriotism. Employer and employee, merchant bureaucrat and labourer, all feel themselves in some sort brothers. It is significant that to the one exception, Austria—Hungary, the 19th century meant death.

It is true that the brotherhood of the cotton mill owner of the 1840s and the starveling paupers he overworked was not always obvious. But even the mill owner could not deny that his workers were fellow Englishmen and fellow Christians, entitled, if they should one day make money, to marry their grandchildren to his.

[1] At Tanjong Karang in Selangor (*Straits Times*, 22nd November, 1948).

There were none of those barriers which bedevil the East, the difference of language, of colour, of gods. In one Western country the divisions between the people were at first as great as those of Malaya. This was the United States; and American history shows how great is the effort which has to be made if a nation is to be formed out of immigrants who have in common only their discontent with the lands they have left. The United States has swallowed Irishmen, Germans, Bohemians and Italians in turn, and to-day, slowly, it is making the even greater effort of swallowing its negroes. The United States has realised that only a united community, one in which all citizens value the same tradition and all are prepared to die for the same freedom, in which no section feels itself superior and no citizen thinks himself unwanted, can face the stresses of a world in which inflation and slump bring unearned pain and unmerited ruin, and the totalitarian is ever waiting at the gate to turn every rift into a trench. To obtain unity, therefore, America has mustered all the forces, all the symbols of its civilisation from the sanctity of the constitution to "Old Glory", from Lincoln's address at Gettysburg to the pride in the American Way of Life, from the English language to the horror of atheism.

No such effort has been made, no such integration attained, in Malaya. The only possible common language is English, and that is still spoken only by an upper class minority. A common Malayan citizenship has come into being only since the war, and until 1952 was particularly difficult for a Chinese or an Indian to attain.[1] Amongst the men of the different races in Malaya, many still do not think of Malaya as their permanent home. In 1939 25,768 Europeans came in but 24,337 went out. Chinese immigrants were 115,792 and emigrants 106,375. South Indian immigrants were 32,004 and emigrants 46,774. For the very large number of transients who come and go, Malaya is simply a place where they can make enough to retire, or to keep their families at home. Before the war, the Indians sent home half a million pounds each year, the Chinese two million; the Chinese figure rose to nearly £13 million in the prosperous year 1941. There is no common religion. The English are Christians, the Malays Muslims, the Indians Hindus, the Chinese Buddhists or Taoists. There are no symbols arousing common

[1]The 1952 legislation has, however, solved this problem, for it has made a large proportion of the Indian and Chinese Communities citizens immediately, and has made it possible for most of them to become citizens eventually.

reverence in all, no Marseillaise, no Magna Carta. There are no common political parties or common attitude to the outside world. The Malay resents having become in his own country a minority which economically is not very well off. The Chinese resent the favours shown to the Malays, the reservations in which no non-Malay can hold land. They denounce the limitations of the State Civil Services to Malays, and the over-representation of the Malay in the Legislatures (there are 14 Chinese to 22 Malays—including officials in the Federation Legislature). The Malay is passionately interested in what happens to his blood-brothers in Indonesia. Indian organisation is a pale reflection of the Congress. The Chinese are affected by every change in the fortunes of China—in the present Communist rebellion in Malaya the largest number of victims have been Kuomintang Chinese. During the war the attitude of the different peoples differed. The Malays stayed neutral; many Indians followed Subhas Chandra Bose into collaboration; the Chinese followed the lead of their home-country in resistance. The different peoples do not even share the same jobs. The Indians are plantation workers[1] or Public Works labourers; the Malay is a rice or rubber smallholder, a soldier or a policeman; the Chinese is a shopkeeper, a tin miner or business man.

This does not mean that everyday relations between the communities are bad. They are not. It only means that even in peace, so diverse a community cannot easily make the sacrifices which are necessary in a modern society. The man who has left his family at home does not cheerfully pay taxes for the education of the children of others. Thus income-tax could not be introduced till 1940. The voluntary effort in hospital and schools which has so ennobled the last century in England and America is difficult where those with education often cannot so much as understand those without. The Chinese artisan does not like to pay taxes for a vocational education to create Malay competitors to himself. The Malay will not try to improve the country's balance of payments if this means agreeing to Chinese rice-growers being admitted to the reservations. These measures are what is necessary for the country's needs, but it is never possible to make sacrifice fall evenly on everybody. In a society divided by race and in which differences of religion make intermarriage difficult, every sacrifice is looked at with racial eyes; and races make sacrifices less willingly than classes; if only because a man can change his class but not his race.

[1] 200,00 in 1940, three-quarters of all Indians employed.

There are, however, some signs which suggest hope that a common national feeling is at last beginning to grow. Chinese whose sympathies were Kuomintang will have no cause to look with favour on or send remittances to a Communist China. Immigration has been small since 1931, and is at present negligible. The Indian population has actually shown a slight tendency to decline since emigration was banned by the Government of India. The proportion of women amongst the Chinese and Indians, which has been going up for many years, is now approaching normal. The Malays have shown in the fight they conducted against the MacMichael Treaties under the able leadership of Dato Onn bin Jafar that they have at last learned to play the political game themselves, and are no longer prepared to rely on the Government to do their fighting for them. The squatting that took place during the war has taken several hundred thousand Chinese on to the land, and this has caused the country's dependence on imports to decrease, and has lessened the sharpness of racial occupational divisions. The free planting of new rubber which has again been permitted and the abolition of restriction has removed a smallholder's grievance.[1] It is indeed probable that the freedom of the smallholder from the overheads which make up over half of the costs of plantations may one day permit the smallholder to dominate the rubber industry in Malaya as he does in Indonesia. Above all, the division of Malaya into firstly Singapore, which is three-quarters Chinese, and secondly Malaya, where, though the Malays are an overall minority, (2,130,000 out of 4,868,000) they still outnumber the Chinese by a quarter of a million, gives hope that, though one Malayan nationality may be impossible of achievement, two may be within the bounds of possibility. There will be citizens of the Federation and citizens of Singapore, each loyal to his own State and finding expression for his loyalty in his new Constitution, with the opportunity it gives for the non-official to take part in the exercise and the problems of power, the premium it places on party organization and compromise through discussion over the undisciplined passions of the street, the hopes it holds out of the day when Malaya and Singapore can join their Asian sisters as fully self-governing members of the Commonwealth.

[1]How racial everything used to become is shown by the example of rubber restriction. The purpose of the policy was for the general good of Malaya; but what is often most remembered is that in detail it benefited the European planter against the Malay and Chinese smallholders; the smallholder loss has been estimated at £43 million.

Chapter XIV

THE PHILIPPINES:
THE DEFICIENCIES OF ALIEN RULE.

Exploitation has been Asia's excuse for so many of her shortcomings. The Filipino has made his full contribution to charges of exploitation, yet in his case the charges are quite particularly untrue, for the Americans have since 1900 put into the Philippines several hundred millions of pounds more than they have taken out. The Philippines thus provide the best of all examples of complaints which are emotional rather than material. They are directed in reality against Western contempt rather than Western profits, against the inadequacy rather than the superfluity of Western investment.

American rule in the Philippines only began in 1900, when the crude exploitation which had created the old nabob fortunes was long dead. Americans were already so rich that to have taken from the Filipinos every penny they earned would have added little more than a hundredth part to their national income. The Americans came to give benefits, not to receive them. Moved by this sense of mission and the generosity which has been a continuing feature of their history, they at all times put into the Philippines more than they took from them.

They never took a contribution from the Philippine treasury, not even to pay for the Spanish-American war or Philippine defence or the 177 million dollars Aguinaldo's revolt cost them. The Spaniards had allocated half the budget to the Army and Navy, but by paying for defence themselves the Americans not only brought £9 million a year into the islands (average of 1938-40) but also permitted 20% of the budget to go to education which was the highest figure in the world. As a result the Philippines had by 1924 a proportion of children in high school seven times greater than that of their old mistress, Spain. Taxes were always low. Five days hard work made enough money for the average Filipino to pay his dues in 1908. In 1934 taxes still took under 10% of the national income—for comparison, America herself paid 24% of her national income in taxes. The devotion and ability of American scholars and scientists, and the Filipinos they trained reduced the death rate from 27.46 per 1000 in 1905 to 18.8 in 1913.

From 1909 the Philippines enjoyed free trade with the United States. This rapidly changed her from a stagnant backwater to a flourishing tributary to the main stream of international trade. Foreign trade grew from 34 million dollars in 1899 to 256 million in 1926, 297 million in 1941. The following table shows the increase in the United States share from a sixth to four-fifths.

TABLE 24

	Philippine Imports			Philippine Exports		
	1889	1926	1941	1889	1926	1941
United States share of (in per cent).. ..	7	60	80	26	73	80

Much of this growth would not have been possible but for the £40 millions the Americans had put into the islands by 1935. This was invested in telephones, railways, bus services, sugar factories, coconut oil refineries, gold mining, and so on. The benefits went down to the people. In 1900 a labourer made 3d. to 6d. a day, but in 1940 his wage had gone up to 10/- a week.[1]

All that the West had to give, health, education, trade, the productivity of machinery, the growth of cities—Manila increased its population from 285,000 in 1918 to 623,000 in 1938—was thus brought to the Philippines by the Americans in generous measure. Even independence has not lessened their interest. The shock to Philippine exports has been cushioned by a system of diminishing Imperial Preference which will last until 1974. The bases the Americans have leased are expected to involve American expenditure of £20 million a year after 1950. The Philippines at independence were cumbered with a national debt of no more than £6 million and were asked to bear none of the cost of their own liberation. It is estimated that between 1946 and 1950 the Americans spent in the Philippines, in grants, veterans' back pay and so on, £750 million, including a free gift of £114 million for rehabilitation and compensation for war damage. Truly Bataan has not been forgotten.

In spite of all these benefits conferred by America, it may well be that in the end it is the Spaniards who will be found to have left the deeper trace on the Philippines. In an American-style Constitution, Quezon and Roxas behaved like Caudillos. The Spaniards

[1] L. K. Kurihara, *Labor in the Philippine Economy*, Stanford, 1945, p. 39.

made many of the people into hacienda peons, but in return they bound them to themselves in the common beliefs and the common brotherhood of Catholicism, so much so that it took three hundred years for their corruption and oppression to excite opposition. The Americans, to whose individualist tradition colonies are alien and ideas of trusteeship suspect, were already devolving power in 1907 and preparing to go by 1916; and for all the risks involved in American departure for the Filipinos themselves, the whole of Filipino politics for two generations was taken up with speeding the parting guest.

The Philippine experiment was creditable, indeed glorious, to the Americans. But the experiment failed, for reasons both economic and spiritual.

Economically, the experiment failed because the Philippines remained a peasant economy of low productivity. None of the social injustices produced by Spanish rule were corrected. The only remedy used when population increased was to bring more land under cultivation; the farm area increased from 2,828,000 hectares in 1903, to 6,691,000 hectares in 1939, and this almost exactly kept pace with the increase in population. Holdings are small. Out of a total of $1\frac{3}{4}$ million holdings, two-thirds are under $7\frac{1}{2}$ acres; only 20,756 are over 50 acres. There is the deep dependence on a few crops usual in peasant communities. Rice covered 1,829,987 hectares, coconuts 1,051,215 hectares, and maize 816,724 hectares out of a total of 3,953,811 hectares. Yields are low, roughly 1000 lbs. an acre for rice in 1947. Tenancy is widespread. 35% of all farmers are tenants and 15% part tenants. Only one half the land is cultivated by its owners. Rents are high, usually half the crop, and the land-lord often reduces the tenant to virtual slavery by acting as the money-lender as well, so that on some haciendas he even feels able to post guards to see that no outsider gets in to tell his tenants of their rights. Certain overcrowded areas, especially Central Luzon and Cebu, display all the symptoms of economic decline. Thus, in Negros Occidental, nearly three-quarters of the farmers are tenants with no land of their own. In Pampanga only 2,825 farmers out of 23,628 are owners. In contrast more than three-quarters of the farmers own their own land in areas where there is still waste available, in Samar or Surigao, Zamboanga or Davao.

American principles of free enterprise were not suited to the bandit-like habits of cacique-landlords. Governor Early expressed the position in his comment on the Sakdal uprising (1931) "Take away a man's land and he is desperate. The whole of Central Luzon is ready for an uprising. It needs leadership. Only Sandiko has said that land troubles in Central Luzon would not be settled as long as the Americans remain, but will soon be dealt with after they leave. The Americans, General Sandiko says, have too much respect for property rights. Let the United States get out, and the oppressed will soon right things with the bolo".[1]

Governor Early was right. It is one of the difficulties of an imperial Government that its strength permits it to correct only those grievances its own sense of justice considers grievous. A native government, however corrupt, must often from sheer weakness make an attempt to cure such conditions as the people themselves feel to be a burden. Thus the American Government's sole contribution to the tenancy problem was to purchase in the early days some 400,000 acres of church lands for 7 million dollars. It was left to the Commonwealth Government, though it was composed very largely of landlords and caciques, to pass the Rice Share Tenancy Act of 1933, imposing such elementary safeguards as written contracts in the vernacular, a limitation of interest on agricultural advances to 10%, the prohibition of eviction without good reason, and the reservation of 15% of the crop to the tenant regardless of indebtedness.[2] This was later further stiffened by a provision for compulsory arbitration of all disputes, and a requirement that a tenant could only be evicted for specified reasons and with the consent of the Department of Justice.

The main tenancy troubles are in the overcrowded areas of Central Luzon. Not only is the landlord's slice there too big, but also too many people are trying to get a share of too small a cake. In such circumstances legislation can only be a palliative, particularly where the landlord is so often also the political boss and the cousin of the Constabulary captain. There was sporadic bloodshed in these areas all through the 30s, and there has been steady Hukbalahap guerilla revolt ever since 1945.

The best solution of overcrowding is to provide other less oppressive ways of making a living, for those for whom there is no longer room on the land. This the Americans did by investing capital and by creating conditions in which others would invest. But the very responsiveness of America to the demands of Philippine

[1]Quoted by J. P. Hayden, *The Philippines*, London, 1942, p. 400.
[2]The Act had been applied by 1941 throughout Central Luzon. Karl J. Pelzer, *op. cit.*, pp. 98–9.

nationalism prevented their doing it very effectively. For only the few would risk their money in a land where nationalist excess made their future returns so uncertain. Modern industry therefore remained small, accounting for only 5% of the national income. In its three main branches, mining, sugar and saw mills, it employed only some 90,000. The export crops covered a quite limited area, sugar 230,000 hectares and abaca 292,000, or roughly one-eighth of the cultivated area between them. Even for this the Philippines paid the price that a quarter of their national wealth was in the hands of foreigners before the war. Spaniards and Americans monopolised sugar and cordage. Americans owned half the public utilities, the biggest coconut oil refineries, and most of the mines of gold, iron, chromite and manganese. Spaniards controlled most of the tobacco industry, Chinese the lumber industry, and three-quarters of the rice mills, Chinese and Japanese between them operated two-thirds of the retail trade. Foreigners handled 80% of the exports and imports. The Filipino had neither the capital nor the technical knowledge for effective competition; his only hope was in State studentships and State bounties and State discrimination in his favour. That was how Japan built up her industry, and that is what the Philippines Government has been doing since independence. No foreigner except an American can now own land. Filipino bids can be up to 15% higher and still be accepted on Government contracts. 60% of the permanent employees of any business must be Filipino citizens. The right to sell at retail has been limited to natural and juristic Filipinos. The Government has gone into lines of business as unrelated as Central banking and making milk with mechanical cows, textile mills and tobacco, credit for peasants and hydro-electric development; future plans include State steel and chemicals, plywood and rice distribution. Outside the field of Government's direct operations, investment has been made so much more attractive for the Filipino than for the foreigner that two-thirds of the capital raised in 1947 came from Filipinos. But the smallness of the total amount raised, just over £3 million, shows why the Americans had to rely on foreign enterprise, and why the new Government of the Philippines for all its conservatism is having to rely on development by the State. The development cannot be by Filipino private enterprise because the Filipino economy simply does not save enough to produce the capital.[1]

[1]For the facts given, see "Nationalisation in the Philippines", by Claude A. Buss, at p. 80 of the February, 1949, issue of *Fortune*.

Economically the Americans had made the Filipino richer than anyone else in Asia except the Japanese. But that was not enough, for at the end the average Filipino had little more sense of owning his own country than had the Harlem Negro. His income, even in real terms, was no higher than that of the poorest American class, the Negro share-croppers of the South. The rise in average worker's income from 3d. a day to 10/- a week was a considerable achievement. But it rankled a dependent people to know that in the imperial homeland men earn twenty times as much. They found it hard not to think that some of that wealth must have been sucked from the fruits of their labours.

Had the Americans made Americans out of the Filipinos, as the Spaniards had made Catholics, the resentment might have been less. The labourer might have seen in the riches of his rulers a spur to effort rather than a source of curdled envy; and his rulers might have been prepared to share with him as in their own land they share with their own poor.

This indeed is the key. The static Filipino peasant economy could only have been turned into a dynamic American free-enterprise economy, the local loyalties of the Filipino could only have been merged into a wider American loyalty, by turning the Filipino into an American, with an American willingness to save and to invest, to take risks and to buy the mass-produced, an American loyalty to the Flag and an American capacity to parade on "I am an American Day" without feeling embarrassed.

This the Americans' own attitudes and the Filipino reaction to them made impossible. The little brown brother could not be an equal. Filipino immigration into the Continental United States was made more and more difficult. Business men of no particular standing would ask Filipino immigration doctors with U.S. Navy Reserve commissions if there was no white doctor available; Americans in lifts would fail to extend to Filipino ladies the natural courtesy of taking off their hats; American visitors to the homes of Filipinos of culture and education would express surprise at seeing a good picture.[1]

It was no worse in the Philippines than elsewhere. This racial arrogance, which is often more a fear of the unknown, a discomfort at the strangeness of a strange people, has bedevilled all European

[1]The particular instances are taken from Carlos Romulo's *Mother America*; these attitudes are of course not confined to Americans in the Philippines. They have been typical of the more ignorant white everywhere in Asia.

relations with Asia. It has caused Asians to look askance at Europeans however great the material blessings they might bring. To-day it induces in many a certain sympathy for a Russia in which they have been told a Kazak is the equal of a Russian. In Asia the memory is still strong of the notices "Indians not allowed" at the clubs in India, the "No dogs or Chinese" notices in the parks of the treaty-ports, the ruling out by President Wilson of a Japanese clause prescribing racial-equality at the League of Nations. Thus Asia does not always see the West immediately as the champions of freedom. Nothing outrages self-respect like racial discrimination. The foreigner may be accepted at his own valuation when, like the English originally in India, he brings rescue from a century of anarchy; but once the people have become accustomed to law and order, they begin to question his claims to superiority. The questioning takes an indirect form, for directly to assert equality is either too insulting to a pride which insists it cannot be in doubt, or useless, since the power which permits the enforcement of inequality, the exclusion of the "native" from the clubs authority attends, is safely in the foreigners' hands. So they complain that the foreigner exploits them and point out that despite foreign rule they are still poor and illiterate and backward. The foreigner answers with irrelevances and statistics, proving that he spends more on defence than he gets in trade, pointing to his new schools and hospitals and laws. But never until recently did he meet the real point. The pattern is always the same, whether the ruler be Dutch or French, American or English; Madariaga finds it underlying the revolt of the Creoles of Spanish America.

The democratic nations are under a particular difficulty in meeting the grievances of their subject peoples. They rightly think their most valuable gift to their colonial subjects to be their own tradition and culture. These include Burke and the Declaration of Independence, Magna Carta and the Gettysburg Address. The subject peoples begin to ask why they too are not entitled to these, to Government of the people, by the people, for the people, and all the freedoms of the American constitution. The American, shot at with his own ideals, was helpless. The American on the spot might say the Filipinos were not fit for self-government, as so many Englishmen did in the old days in India. But what mattered was not the American on the spot, but the great tide of public opinion at home. The American at home, like the Englishman at home, was uncomfortable once he had lost the sense of mission. In his lexicon, nations were

entitled to govern themselves; had not Wilson put it in the 14
points, had not Lord John Russell asserted it in Italy? Men were
entitled to elect their government and refuse to pay taxation unless
they were represented. Would it not be denying the whole of his
history to deny it? So American policy in the Philippines, like
England's in India from the days of Macaulay, was necessarily one
long retreat, one long preparation for the day when self-government
and democracy could be installed and the trauma in the American
conscience cured. [1]

In the process of retreat, imperialism increasingly disables itself
from conferring even economic benefits. The home capitalist,
frightened by nationalism, has to charge too high a risk-premium
for investment to be possible in any but the most profitable enterprises, while the Government, always in retreat, can neither make
the reforms nor ask for the sacrifices which are necessary to release
the springs of energy hidden in the native society itself. So in the
interval between the arousing of a local Western-style nationalism
and the attainment of full independence the society is necessarily
spiritually distorted and economically slowed down; it has been the
West's dilemma that if anarchy was to be avoided the interval had
none the less sometimes to be a long one.

[1] There was a legislature from 1907, a Filipino majority in the Philippine
Commission from 1913, virtually complete Home Rule from 1935.

Chapter XV

THAILAND

Thailand has been one of Asia's most fortunate areas. Rapidly though the population has increased, it has, as yet, not reached the stage where all the vacant land is filled up. The Thai peasantry, therefore, is still in a position to live the life of its fathers, somewhat improved by the amenities of health, Western education, and law and order. But even in happy Thailand one can see the disintegrating effect of Western influence. Everywhere in the East, the classes which matter have realised that in order to count in the modern world, one must have wealth and power, and in order to have wealth and power, one must have industries, technical education, and the whole apparatus of Western life. But the creation of these in societies without a Western environment of savings, business enterprise and the habit of free scientific enquiry, involves carrying a very great strain. The Thais have so far very wisely confined themselves to a moderate pace in their westernisation. But because their problem has been uncomplicated by over-population, what they have tried to do, how far they have succeeded, and what it has cost them, show very clearly what Asia admires materially in the West and how impossible it is to adopt the material side of western life without having in the end to transform Eastern society spiritually as well.

★   ★   ★

The way in which the intrusion of Western ideas and Western techniques upsets the balance of an Asian peasant society can be studied most simply in a country where the whole process is not complicated by over-population, rural bankruptcy and the decay of the old native civil authority. Such a country is Thailand. In Thailand the population was originally so sparse that the increases which have occurred in the last century have still left ample land for all. The old peasant life, therefore, still goes on undisturbed and still gives happiness to the majority. But even in Thailand the need to make an effort to keep up with the West in such affairs as law, defence and commerce has led to the growth of a Western-oriented middle class, and this middle class has shown all the interest in modelling the whole of society to its own image and to attain its own ideals which has been so typical of such classes everywhere.

Admittedly the changes of the last fifty years have done no more than create a quite small whirlpool in the river of peasant contentment. Thailand is still a country of happy peasants. Outside the commercialised area round Bangkok, where 84% of farmers are tenants, debt and tenancy are still the exception. There is enough land to go round not only for this generation but for the next. Tables 25, 26 and 27 show the position.

TABLE 25

Section	% tenants	% landless	Average holding in acres
North East	5	18	2½
North	5	27	4
Centre	30	36	10
South	5	14	2½

TABLE 26

Section	% in debt to nearest half %	Average debt	Average Income (a baht was just under 2/-)	Average Expenditure	Expenditure on food	Expenditure on clothing
North East	19½	6.77	37.07	52.77	8.72	3.73
North ..	17½	17.16	78.75	79.64	16.10	5.46
Centre ..	61½	233.82	292.29	288.67	49.80	12.65
South ..	18½	9.59	91.54	82.50	23.92	5.82

The excess of expenditure in this case is due to capital items.

TABLE 27

Section	% of debt owed to relatives (to nearest 9%)	Amusement and social items approximately, assuming 4 baht per adult male head.
North East	73	4
North ..	20	10
Centre ..	48	25
South ..	84	11

The figures come from Andrews, *Siam in 1934–5*. They show that even in the early 30s, a time bad for farmers all over the world, the Siamese peasantry had good cause for content. Debt was low; generally it averaged only two or three months' income. Even in the Menam delta it was under a year's income. Much of it was owed to relatives. Taxes were low in 1938. The field tax, the capitation tax and miscellaneous land taxes together only came to just over a million, or perhaps 7/– a family, which was certainly under 5% of the average family income. Even these taxes were abolished in 1939, and replaced by such taxes as income-tax and amusement tax, which mainly hit the townsman. Thus all the peasant then had to pay was the tax for primary education and the local improvement contribution, and the proceeds of these were spent for his own direct benefit. Happily, the peasant can look forward to this ease of existence continuing. No more than 10% of the country is cultivated. Although there has been no survey, it seems likely that as much more must be available for cultivation, though it will need clearing or draining. Even in the great central plain only 15% of the land is cultivated. There is still considerable scope for the extension of technical irrigation—in the Mae Nam Suphan plain for example where at present only 20% of the rice fields are cultivated.

Thus at first inspection Thailand is a truly halcyon picture. If happiness lies in living an accustomed life in the accustomed way, in having a wife and children and enough to eat, time for a cock-fight or a regatta, money and devotion to keep going the local temple, the Thai peasant is happy indeed.

Thailand has not only been fortunate in the happiness of its countryside. It has also had the good luck to conduct its relations with the West with great ability. The Thais have never provoked the West by treating its envoys as tribute-bearers as did the Chinese or by refusing trade as did the Japanese. They have never tempted the West by internal anarchy as did India or by the possession of spices as was the case in Indonesia. They have been trading with the West since 1603 and in the 19th century they accepted Western demands for extra-territoriality and fixed tariffs without resistance. They have been fortunate too in their strategic position. Lying between an area of British expansion and one of French expansion it was convenient for both to retain Thailand as the buffer State. Thailand, therefore, lost only border areas to Western annexations[1]

[1]Siam lost to France, Laos (1889–1895), Battembang and Siemreap (1907), but Siam had never held more than suzerainty over Laos and had only acquired

and of those border areas only Laos was a province of Thai population.

In a slightly desultory way the Thais positively welcomed the new techniques the West brought with it. They let British capital develop their teak and their tin.[1] They built 2,000 miles of railway and paid two-thirds of the cost from their own resources. They created a reasonable Army and Navy and welcomed British financial advisers and Danish officers for the gendarmerie. But they avoided the foreign debt which in Victorian times so often provided an excuse for foreign interference. They never owed abroad more than £12½ million and their foreign debt had been reduced to £4,800,000 by 1941.

The new Westernised middle class thus created, which has dominated Thai politics since it destroyed the absolute power of the King in the revolution of 1932 is, however, unbalanced. There are too many officers, not enough business men. That is why there have been so many *coups d'état*. The reason is that since there is still enough land to go round, since until yesterday there was always a Government job for every educated boy, the Thai has always avoided the more exacting routine of business. In business the hours are longer; the intervals for leisure are less; the emphasis on making money is greater; the contacts with one's neighbours are more through the cash nexus than is common in the traditional occupations. In business there is neither the mutual help nor the leisure of agriculture. There is neither the power nor the capacity to do good which belongs to the bureaucracy. So business and the harder professions have been left to foreigners or the Chinese.[2] In 1931, 95% of Thailand's industry and commerce were in foreign or Chinese hands, and in 1939 the Financial Adviser estimated that 90% of all commerce and trade was in Chinese hands. In the early 30s foreigners controlled tin, shipping, half the teak and much of the import and export business, the public utilities of Bangkok, banking and insurance. The Chinese owned five-sixths of the rice mills, provided most of the merchants and 70% of the non-agricultural labour, including most of the retailers[3] and all the professional

Battembang in 1778 and Siemreap in 1831. Britain obtained a protectorate of the Malay Sultanates of Kelantan, Trengganu, Kedah and Perlis in 1909 but real Siamese control in this area dated only from 1892.

[1] £13 million had been invested by 1938.

[2] For the business man to be a member of a minority or a foreigner is frequent in Asia, e.g. the role of the Chinese in Indonesia or of the Hindus in Sind and the West Punjab before 1947.

[3] Except the dealing in local produce which is done by Thai women.

carpenters and pedlars and rice-boatmen, and did nearly all of the duck-raising and pig-breeding.

This dominance of the military in Thailand brings out with especial clarity two features which are universal in peasant societies in the process of modernising themselves. First, there is a desire for the profits of business without any understanding of the risks or losses which have to be incurred to make those profits, or of the importance of competition in keeping costs low, or even of the fact that high costs and tax-free profits are in effect a tax upon the consumer. Second, there is the importance attached to power; the primary objective of Westernisation, and particularly industrialisation, is power, and wealth as a source of power rather than the raising of the standard of life of the people.

In Thailand after 1932 the will to power is the key to all events—just as it has been in Japan, or in the Russia of the third Five-Year Plan. The European soldier or administrator retired from the West has been accustomed to argue that among the universal corruption, he had found truth, goodness and happiness only among the peasants. Thus he recognizes the admirable adjustment to life of the independent peasant, free from debt or not yet conscious of the danger to him of his debt. No opinion causes a deeper sense of outrage in the Eastern nationalist. This is not merely because the nationalist has usually been represented as the Satan in this Paradise. It is also because he realises, perhaps quite obscurely, that this happiness and self-respect of the individual peasant are not accompanied by any corresponding happiness in the nation or self-respect in the State. He feels that, to be listened to, countries must be as powerful as the Russians or as rich as the Americans.

The conclusion is drawn that only power gives a place in the sun. Of the leaders of 1932 Luang Pradit drew up a draft Act[1] giving the Government power to buy all land and administer the whole economic system, Pibul Songgram called the party he founded in 1947 "Right is Might" and has twice made himself dictator. Real power lies with the tanks of the Bangkok garrison and the guns of the Fleet. These made a second coup in 1933, suppressed conservative, princely revolts in 1933 and 1934, forced the King into abdication in 1935, and put Pibul back in power in 1947.

For power, not only wealth is needed, but wealth expressed

[1]The Economic Administration Act. It was never passed, but reveals the mind behind many of the actions especially of 1939–40.

through certain social forms. There must be infantrymen who can read, Air Force mechanics with an adequate technical education, armies which are not decimated by malaria and which have behind them proper ordnance factories and adequate research. So the power-seekers (who in the East are often really no more than seekers of self-respect) demand education, public health, industrialisation. At once the idealists chime in in agreement. They have taken from the West, and indeed learned from their own religions, not an admiration for force but a belief in the brotherhood of man, and in the equal importance under God of every individual soul. They too want public health, to save lives and reduce pain; they too want education, to fulfil in every man his highest potentialities and to enable him to contribute of his best to the community; they too want industrialisation, to raise the standard of life and to make available to everyone the simplest Western amenities, soap and electric light.

The difference between democrat and dictator is thus one of values, not of policies. Nehru expands his navy, Pibul his schools; the difficulty which all face is that these new attainments are all so expensive. Thailand's revenue in 1948 was well under one-hundredth of the United Kingdom's. The £1½ million it spent on education was only a twentieth of that spent in the United Kingdom as long ago as 1913. If the percentage of literacy in the country, 30-40%, compares favourably with South America's 30%, or India's 12.2%,[1] this is only because the monastic schools, the product of the endowment of centuries, are still in good enough order to provide two-thirds of the total primary education. Thailand spent £200,000 on public health in 1938, but France spent £10 million a year in the thirties, quite apart from social security expenditure or that of local authorities; the British 1949-50 budget provides £120 million for hospitals alone. Still more expensive are armed forces—in 1952 £1,700 million in Great Britain, £1,300 million in France, £20 billion in the U.S., £150 million even in India. On a £30 million[2] budget Thailand can hardly hope to carry much weight amidst the clash of arms.

Most expensive of all is industrialisation and economic modernisation. Great Britain invests some £2000 million a year; the Greek programme for 1949-50 is nearly £90 million; even the Norwegians with a population less than one-fifth Thailand's expect to average

[1] UN Economic and Social Council E/Conf/6/26, dated March 9th, 1948.
[2] At the official rate. At the free market rate it is only £20 million.

over £110 million a year between 1949–50 and 1952–3.[1] Of course not all England's or Norway's capital expenditure goes on machinery and factories. But housing for the workers, new port facilities and new locomotives are as much a part of any industrialisation programme as lathes and presses. Such expenditure is quite impossible for Thailand, whose national income, though never precisely estimated, must be considerably lower than the Philippines' £340 million (in 1946)[2] and whose savings are so low that it took the Post Office Savings Bank a quarter of a century to raise £1½ million.

There is indeed the rub. The old economy's yields may be adequate for its simple wants. But they yield a very small surplus for investment.

The Thai revolutionaries did not lose heart. They may perhaps have remembered that income per head in Europe before industrialisation, in the England of 1800 or the Norway of 1850, was no higher than that of Thailand in 1930. Only around 1880 did the U.K., the U.S.A. and Germany reach a steel production of one million tons a year. Certainly the Thais had the advantage that they could take their time. They have not got the over-population problem of India or China or Japan. They, therefore, decided on the slow and sure, though limited method, of developing as they could out of their own resources, without either foreign loans or the pressure on their people of a five-year plan.

Such a policy has to face two dilemmas. The first is that the heavy industries, which give the power and independence which come from being able to make one's munitions, are also the most expensive in their demand for capital, and need the most foreign technicians for the longest time. On the other hand, the light industries, which require comparatively little specialised skill or capital and which give great employment and have an immediate mass market waiting for them, make no contribution beyond uniforms to the nation's armed forces. The other dilemma is that there is often a choice between increasing the income of the country as a whole and increasing the income of the majority group. The Thai has the choice with his savings of creating new industries, or buying out the foreigner, or carrying the immediate losses involved in substituting Thais for Chinese.

[1] O.E.E.C., *Interim Report on the European Recovery Programme*, Vol. II, Paris, 30th December, 1948.

[2] United Nations, *National Income Statistics of Various Countries*, 1938/47, New York, 1948. Prices in the Philippines were very high in 1946.

In the thirties, the Thais chose to develop light industry and to get rid of the Chinese. By 1941 the Government had built factories for paper, sugar, silk, leather, cigarettes and tobacco, distilleries for soya bean oil and wine, a cannery, and an oil refinery, and had taken over eleven rice mills and a British coastal shipping company. Their private enterprise had constructed a brewery and a cement factory. The factories were not very big; the cigarette factory only cost £8,000, the sugar mill £100,000; all industry still only employs a few thousands; but it has nevertheless been enough of a beginning to make Thailand self-sufficient in sugar. The next step is to build cotton mills, though here there is the problem that Thailand has so far failed to grow cotton successfully.

Industrialisation is not yet a necessity in Thailand. There is more enthusiasm for the replacement of the Chinese. As nationalism grows, the majority wish to assert their independence and solidarity not only against the outside world but also against their own minorities. It tends to consider their success as the unfair result of circumstance or Governmental favouritism. In Thailand in the 19th century the Chinese immigrant was looked on with favour by kings who admired his capacity to work and his ingenuity; he was neither taxed, for the basis of taxation was the land revenue and the head tax which he did not pay, nor called up for military service. Not until 1928 was the first attempt made to limit immigration with a head tax of £1; this became £9 in 1933, £18 in 1938, and in 1939 there was added a levy of £3.7 a year. After the revolution, discrimination began even against those already settled in the country. The salt monopoly cut at the Chinese salt farmer; the Vehicles Act did away with the Chinese taxi-driver; the Fisheries Act prohibited the Chinese from taking part in in-shore fishing; Thais were encouraged in every business, from butchery to food hawking, by preferences, by propaganda and by vocational education. Just before the war, the Government started the Thai Rice Co. to break the monopoly of the Chinese rice dealer and rice miller. Since the war, this has been enlarged into a Government monopoly of rice procurement. (The Chinese, who have gone into the smuggling trade to Malaya, probably still make the larger profits). Since the war, too, immigration has been still further limited. At the end of 1948 the quota allowed was only 200 a year.

Behind this policy, lies not only Thai resentment at Chinese wealth and Thai determination to open the lucrative possibilities of commerce to their children on terms sufficiently weighted in their favour to make up for the age-old experience of the Chinese. There is also a very real fear that the Chinese have no loyalty to Thailand, that they accept the thesis of all Chinese Governments that, whatever nationality a Chinese may have by birth or adoption, his race keeps him always a Chinese. When the Communists took Peking, the circulation of the Chinese Communist paper in Bangkok promptly doubled. So parallel with the economic measures go cultural ones. The importation of teachers from China was stopped in 1928, officially at least by enforcing a Thai language qualification, and here again, after the revolution, the Western-style middle-class nationalism of the new rulers quickened the pace. In 1933 it was found that few Chinese children could read the simplest Thai text; the Government therefore insisted on 21 hours of Thai out of a 28-hour school week; in 1939 they reduced Chinese to 2 hours a week for the under 14's and closed 25 schools in four months.

It is not by such methods that a modern economy is created. As long as Thailand has enough land and her peasants stay out of debt, they are not likely to ask for more (at least so long as the price of A1 ordinary rice stays in the neighbourhood of £30 per ton at Bangkok). But it is not the way to produce the industrialisation of Japan or Bombay. It does not provide the surpluses to pay for jet-fighters and hospitals.

Chapter XVI

JAPAN

If they are not to be dangerous, the material achievements of the West have to be part of a civilisation which does not regard the power they give as the final end of life. The brotherhood of man and humility before God are necessary beliefs if the capacity to split the atom is not to prove totally destructive. The dangers of accepting the material power which Western science offers, untempered by the meekness and consideration of the traditional faith of the West, has been shown most clearly by the Nazis.

There is also an admirable Asian example in Japan. Everywhere in Asia, except in India, the West's material achievement has tended to be more obvious than the spiritual qualities of its civilisation. Railways and guns make an immediate impact; liberty and democracy are concepts which require time for their appreciation. The Japanese realised that if they were to hold their own in the modern world, they must make themselves as materially powerful as any Western nation. Their very considerable success in the attempt to do so is one of the great *tours de force* of history. But the Japanese were totally uninterested in any other side of the West. They very much preferred their own tradition to anything the West might offer. They, therefore, failed absolutely, for what made the West great was as much the willingness to die for freedom as the capacity to build battleships. Their misunderstanding brought its own Nemesis when they calculated that by attacking Pearl Harbour they could bring America to terms.

This chapter is a study of their material success.

THE THINGS OF THE BODY

The Japanese who made the great revolution of 1868 wanted no part of Western civilisation beyond its techniques of gaining wealth and power. Their attitude was simple. They had revolted against the Shogun in order to go back to all that was oldest, and to their minds, purest in the Japanese spirit. The divine right of the Emperor, the sacredness of the Japanese race, Shinto, Bushido, and the Taika Reform of A.D. 646—these were their ideals. They were in reaction against centuries of influence from overseas. They opposed Chinese Confucianism and Indian Buddhism—except in their own very Japanese form of Zen. They wished to re-assert their old values. They did not wish to substitute for them weak Western admonitions of democracy and humility, loving one's neighbour and the brother-hood of man.

Thus the Japanese leaders were fundamentally different from the Indian. In India over the last hundred years every standard has been re-assayed in the crucible of Western values. The Japanese differed also from the Indians in their immediate appreciation of the possibilities of power and national self-assertion which lay behind the new Western techniques. They understood instinctively all the more discreditable motives and intrigues of Western expansion. Pure science, to judge by the paucity of the results they achieved in this sphere, left them quite unexcited, but they immediately appreciated the quality of Western cannon and Western tactics. Already in the 1840s and 1850s Japanese theorists were studying the British campaigns in the Opium War and producing complete mercantilist theories of economics. Japanese samurai were learning Dutch and translating treatises on electricity. Japanese clans were making guns and building reverberatory furnaces. Mito built their furnace in 1855 straight from the instructions in a Dutch text-book. The lesson of Chinese defeats and their own weakness in front of Perry's frigates were taken well to heart.

They learnt effectively. Takasugi's Kiheitai, trained on Western lines and equipped with Western style artillery, were of decisive importance in the battles with the Shogun. Choshu and Satsuma, most anti-foreign of the clans, swung round at once to admiration of the West's power and to eagerness for the West's friendships when their excesses brought on the bombardment of Kagoshima and Simonoseki (1863 and 1864). This change-over was of crucial importance, for these two clans provided the basis of the Royalist opposition to the Shogun, and after the Restoration dominated the Army and Navy until 1920.

The reactionaries who made the revolution of 1868—the so-called Restoration—were young men. The Emperor was only 15. Ito was to live another forty years, nearly all in office. They were also men of great enterprise, who had fought in the Civil War and engaged in the murder plots which already disfigured Japanese politics. Ito and Inouye had smuggled themselves to Europe to study the West at close quarters. They had the courage to plan, and they could look forward to being long enough in office to see their plans come to fruition.

The basis of their planning was summed up by a later Prime Minister, Baron Hayashi, when he said in 1895:

"We must continue to study according to Western methods, for the application of science is the most important item of warlike preparations that civilised nations regard. If new ships of war are considered necessary, we must build them at any cost. If the organisation of our army is found to be wrong, it must at once be renovated".[1]

The Japanese victories over China in 1895 and Russia in 1905, the Twenty One Demands of 1915, the attacks on the West of December 1941, were surprises only to the West. For the Japanese they provided the fears and the hopes which drove them down their planned roads.

To judge by their actions, the Japanese grasped at once the triple base of Western power. These were firstly the direct effectiveness of its instruments of war. Secondly the use of the surplus over the needs of subsistence which had been made possible by science and industry to provide the taxation and the education without which these instruments could not have been created, or, if created, could not have been used. The third was the drawing of the whole population into a war effort which was made possible by giving every man all the rights of a citizen, and thus at the same time all a citizen's obligations. Every Japanese reform over three generations was directed in the end at one or other of these objects, however unconscious the ordinary Japanese may have been of what was intended. To create wealth, to turn subjects into citizens—these were thought desirable in Japan, as in Germany, because they increased the power of the State, not because they augmented the happiness of the individual.

The Japanese leaders followed three lines of attack. First was the deliberate creation of strategic industries however high the cost might be. The second was a general industrialisation on the ordinary economic principle of selecting first those activities in which Japan's advantages were greatest. The third was the destruction of those attitudes, regulations, and ignorances derived from feudalism

[1]Quoted by G. F. Hudson, *op. cit.*, p. 130.

which might make it difficult to use the peasant as a soldier, or impair his quality when so used.

The society with which the men of Meiji began in 1868 was not merely utterly peasant. It was also more deeply in decay than any other in Asia. In Japan, as nowhere else except in parts of India, there was a feudal system in which the lord, not the State, held jurisdiction, the lord, not the peasant, owned the land. For two and a half centuries the Shogun had enforced peace. Nevertheless the peasant was compelled to surrender one-half his crop, and sometimes more—in the Matsudaira fief it was 80%—to keep in factious idleness a fighting class of 1,500,000 samurai, some 5% of the population. 78% of the population were dependent on agriculture. Holdings were tiny, averaging 2⅓ acres. Over-population had lasted so long that for two hundred years the peasant had been resorting to infanticide to keep numbers roughly stable. The cultivator had no reserves. Every famine brought deaths by the thousand, as in 1837, and every disaster and every unforeseen demand of his lord took him to the usurer. By 1870, despite a formal prohibition of land alienation, 30% of the land had in this way passed into the hands of landlords. The wretched tenants could keep but one-third of their crop for themselves. A proverb said that the peasant should be so taxed that he "neither lived nor died".

The peasant was the foundation of the State, but he had in it no rights. A samurai who felt his honour or dignity affronted by a peasant could cut him down at discretion. The peasant was prohibited from leaving his land or carrying arms. He could not carry on any but specified occupations. He could not wear any but specified clothes. He could not grow any but specified crops. On everything he paid a tax, on his doors and his beans, his windows and his daughters, and at all times he was liable to forced labour of man and beast. These were conditions quite unparalleled in Asia.

The Meiji reformers had therefore none of the room to manoeuvre that was given to, say, the Siamese Government by the circumstance in Siam of ample land and a contented peasantry. In many prefectures cultivation was approaching its limit. An increase in taxation was impossible. Peasant discontent had produced eighty-four revolts between 1860-7.

There was only one set of incomes in society from which the new masters of Japan could hope to get the increased taxes and savings they required for their plans. It is a sign of the singleness of purpose of the reformers that, though they were themselves samurai, it was the samurai incomes they picked on. The samurai and daimyos, whose political functions had been ended at the Restoration, were expropriated of their tribute from the peasantry for some £40 million (mostly paid in bonds at 7%) plus the payment of some £8 million of old debts. That worked out at only about 3 years' purchase of the peasant's rice tribute which was now taken over by the State as land tax. The real burden on the State was further diminished by the depreciation of the yen, which by 1900 had become worth only half of its 1870 value. By this one action the State attained a series of ends. It provided itself with an income of which it stood in desperate need. Between January 1868 and November 1869 revenue had amounted to only 8,300,000 yen against expenditure of 51 million. Paper money could not be issued indefinitely. But by the late 70s the State was paying its way and the land tax was providing 80% of its revenues. A reduction of the tax burden was even possible. Under feudalism the peasant had surrendered 50% of the crop. In the 1880s he surrendered only 10% to the State. By this reform the State also secured a host of eager officials. The samurai could not live on their bonds. The best of them became soldiers, policemen, and bureaucrats. Their experience in clan government and clan armies enabled the State quickly to reach a high efficiency. But this was at the price of having its whole new machinery steeped in the military spirit, a price which has recently proved expensive. Finally, by these reforms, the State provided itself with an investing class. The bonds could be turned into ready money, and those who had had their incomes severely cut naturally looked for ways of employing their money by which they could earn more than 7%. By 1880, forty one million yen had been put into banking. This represented three-quarters of the national banks' total shareholding; and the banks have always been the primary financiers of Japanese industry.

The State had thus at one stroke obtained civil servants, investors and an income. It proceeded to get itself citizens. All the restrictions on peasant migration, occupations, dress, crops, and land alienation were abolished in the early seventies. Even the curious Japanese caste of untouchables called the Eta was given formal equality. Duties followed hard on rights. Takasugi's Kiheitai had already shown what peasant soldiers could do. Conscription was enforced in 1873. Thus was started that connection between the countryside and the Army which was to produce the anti-capitalism of the officers' corps in the 1930s.

There were still wanting the industries and the techniques of science and production which give wealth and power. Japan set about securing them just as methodically. The key of the whole process—the creation of direct war potential—the State kept to itself or gave to those families which, because of their past functions as financiers of the Restoration and of the Government's early days of penury, it felt it could trust. The foundries, furnaces, shipyards, which the clans and the Bakufu[1] had built up, were taken over, and foreign experts were employed to improve them. Dutchmen, for instance, were employed at Nagasaki, Frenchmen at Yokosuka. By the 1880s Japan was building her own torpedo-boats. By the early 1890s she built her own light cruisers. In 1892 she constructed her first locomotive. In 1905 she was perhaps less dependent on Western munitions than her Russian enemy.

The Government was equally quick in providing itself with those instruments without which no war can be fought, even though they are not in themselves munitions. War needs technicians. By the end of the 80s schools had been set up for gun manufacture, engineering and the navy. War requires the rapid movement of large bodies of troops. Railway building was subsidised, and in 1906 the main railways were nationalised. War implies the rapid transmission of information. The Government pressed forward with telegraph and telephone buildings.[2]

The way in which the Government employed its favourite firms to build up that part of production for war which it did not itself wish to undertake is shown by the history of the Mitsubishi Company and its shipping enterprise. In 1874 the Government gave thirteen ships to Iwasaki Yataro, founder of the firm, for the transport of troops in the Formosan campaign. This enabled him to make £2 million. The Government then sold to the firm its Yubin Jokisen Kaisha fleet for £50,000. This was well below cost. It gave the firm an annual subsidy of 250,000 yen. Later, after the State had made a short excursion into competition, Mitsubishi was allowed to buy the competitive fleet also, and was given an annual subsidy of

[1]The Shogun's Government.

[2]All these have also their peace-time uses, and had in the West been invented with these uses in mind; but the Japanese concentration on war potential is made clear by the appointment of a distinguished General as the first president of the railway supervisory board (in 1892), the decision not to leave the telegraphs to private enterprise because the resultant lack of secrecy might be embarrassing to Government, and the immediate use of the telephone to connect all branch police stations to headquarters.

880,000 yen for the amalgamation. A few years later, the Nagasaki shipyards were also sold to Mitsubishi. From 1896 Mitsubishi received shipbuilding subsidies. The initiative of Government is thus clear at every stage. Equally clear is the Government's deep-rooted preference for acting through the "chosen instrument". It felt distaste for—or perhaps merely failed to comprehend—the idea of free competition as a good in itself, the force which lies behind so much American legislation.

Even in the development of ordinary civilian industry, it was still the Government which took the initiative.

The Government had indeed no option. Japan had no entrepreneurs. Traditionally her merchants were the lowest section of the population, ranking below the much-squeezed peasant himself. They enjoyed a position only because daimyo and samurai were dependent on them for their functions as money-lenders, rice-brokers, and the agents of clan monopolies. Their profits came from usury and went back into usury or foreclosed land. They had no tradition of industrial production, for what little there was of this was monopolised by the clans, as paper manufacture was by the Tosa or porcelain by the Owari. They had no experience of overseas trade, for whatever foreign trade had not been successfully forbidden was controlled by the Choshu and Satsuma clans. They were accustomed to obtain a safe 20% or more on loans to embarrassed peasants and feudal nobles; in the early days of the Restoration they were able to lend even to the Government at $1\frac{1}{2}\%$ per month; thus they saw no great attraction in investment in industry with its very considerable risks of losing not merely interest but also capital. From a class with these characteristics it was impossible to expect capitalist adventurers, the Henry Fords and the Lord Leverhulmes, who built up the Western economy.

The Japanese saver and investor preferred to deposit his money in a bank or trust company or to take out an insurance policy; deposits alone multiplied some hundred and twenty times between 1892 and 1926; with a Bank rate rarely below 7% before 1909, and still $5\frac{1}{2}\%$ in 1932, such deposits provided a very reasonable return as well as absolute safety. This phenomenon explains the domination of the Zaibatsu. The business men and the handicraftsmen could raise money only by applying to the bank, so that advances went up 150 times between 1892 and 1926. Bank deposits were nearly two-thirds controlled by Zaibatsu institutions (and it was the same with trust and insurance companies as they became important investing media) and short-term interest rates were high, $11\frac{1}{4}\%$ in 1892, 13% in 1901, 10% in 1909, 11% in 1922, $8\frac{1}{2}\%$ in 1934; since few businesses, taking good years with bad, make sufficient profits to permit the repayment of loans taken on such terms, the hold of finance capital tightened from decade to decade, with all that means in concentration of control, unadventurousness—for the banker is using his depositors' money, not his own—and the influence of accountants.

Because there were no entrepreneurs, Government incentive was necessary at every stage. The first cotton mill, the first modern silk filature, the first sugar factory, the first cement or glass works, were all built by Government; the early gold, silver, iron and coal mines, some of which had already been developed by the clans, were mostly Government-run. The Government had, however, neither the resources nor the managerial ability to do everything itself. Therefore, just as in the development of war material, it started to bring in the great merchant houses. It indicated to them a particular line it wished them to take up. It sold them its own mines and factories at less than cost.[1] It even imported machinery and sold it to them on instalments. This was done with cotton spindles. Even in a peasant industry such as silk, it was the Government which, by producing disease-free strains of eggs and providing conditioning houses, made possible the capture and increase of a market which China had held for 2,000 years.

In those spheres where the capital required was specially high, or the skills particularly new (as in exchange banking and colonial development) the Government continued to participate actively. The Yokohama Specie Bank had one-third Government capital. The Bank of Chosen, the Bank of Taiwan, the Industrial Bank (constituted in order to tempt the overseas investor), the Oriental Development Co., the South Manchuria Railway Co. all had the Government as a large shareholder. The culmination of this tradition was the large mixed companies of the late thirties and early forties. Government took up half the capital of artificial petrol and light metal manufacturing companies. It formed coal and steel monopolies with a large Government interest. It greatly increased its overseas investment, and gave the most direct of incentives to its war industries, as by guaranteeing 1000 million yen of bond issues for munition companies.

Japan is thus a successful instance of Government planning and

[1] As the cement works which had cost 468,000 yen was sold to Asano for 250,000.

Government encouragement in a country where capital was scarce and shy, scientific discovery and mechanical skill unknown. The West has never had to build strategic industries ahead of the time when they were economically appropriate; for in the race for competitive strength the West has always been ahead. It has been able to proceed steadily from those forms of production which require less capital, skilled labour and scientific technique to those which require more. Cotton textiles came before steel because they can use rawer labour and because the same capital investment permits a turnover three times as great, and because their requirements of elaborately-treated raw materials and scientific research are so much lower. To this rule there has been in the West but one major exception, the railways, whose demands on capital, skill, and invention are of the largest, but which are a necessity at the very earliest stages of any industrial revolution because without them raw materials cannot reach the factories, or finished goods their markets, sufficiently regularly or cheaply. Russia, on the other hand, has been an example of a country where the plan of development was governed by strategic considerations. Precedence was given to the factories and the educational institutions which were of importance for war, at the expense of those which produce consumer goods; hence the very large percentage of savings which has characterised Russian planning and the need for propaganda and terror to make the population accept a policy in which a higher standard of life for themselves was always postponed to an undefined future.

The Japanese model shows that Asian industry is likely to grow according to an amalgam of these two techniques.

Works with immediate value in war have been regularly built well before their turn. Japan was constructing locomotives and cruisers before she made steel, battleships before she made buses. Similarly China had an iron works before she had a cotton mill, and India's first ordnance factory was contemporary with its first jute mill. More recently Japan has built up its aeroplane and its motor industries together, while in America they were separated by a generation.

Side by side with this fostering of the industries without which no war could be fought, there has also been a growth of the normal Western type. A short sketch of the rise of Japanese non-governmental industry may be illuminating.

First came the industries requiring little capital and low mechanical skill, cotton, silk, food processing. All of these had an immediate mass market.[1] Tables 28, 29, 30 and 31 show the development; beer has been taken as the example of food-processing, for every drinking nation with which the West has come into contact has copied the brewing of beer immediately and gratefully. One of the first factories the Japanese Government built was a brewery in Hokkaido.

TABLE 28

				Silk Production	Silk Exports
1868	..	..	..	268,000 Kwan	175,000 Kwan
1929	..	..	..	11,292,000 ,,	9,140,000 ,,
1936	..	..	..	11,287,000 ,,	8,054,000 ,,

TABLE 29

			Value of Silk Exports (in million yen)
1868	..	..	6
1870–4 (Av.)	..	..	6
1900–4 (Av.)	..	..	72
1914	..	..	161
1919	..	..	624
1929	..	..	784
1936	..	..	392

TABLE 30 '

	The growth of the cotton industry			
	1887	1900	1920	1936
Spindles	100,000	1,100,000	3,800,000	10,500,000
Production of Cotton yarn (in bales)	25,000	766,000	1,800,000	3,750,000

[1]Cotton's market was in replacement both of an old Japanese handicraft which had been universal and of an extensive new import, which ran around one-third of Japan's total imports in the 1870s. Silk production satisfied a large overseas demand which grew steadily as wider and wider classes of women, particularly in America, took to silk stockings and silk underwear. (As late as 1933–7 silk provided 60% of Japan's exports to America, where Japanese silk was favoured, because the improved methods of reeling of Japanese filatures produced an even, strong thread suitable for fully mechanical weaving.) Food processing found a market because the rapidly growing towns required their food in more ready-made form than the peasant whose wife could husk or parch her grain at home.

The growth of the cotton industry—*contd.*

	1887	1900	1920	1936
Exports of cotton tissues, yarn, and materials (in million yen)	*	39†	510	534
% of value of total exports	—	14†	26	25

*Net import equal to one quarter of Japan's total imports. Cotton textiles were only 2% of exports as late as 1899.
†1903.

TABLE 31

	Beer Production in Hectolitres
1892	17,460
1900	156,000
1927–8.. ..	1,435,000
1937–8.. ..	2,300,000

Next in order came those industries which provide the power, the communications and the constructional materials, without which no growth of industry is possible. First and basic to all the others, were coal and railways. In a maritime and trading nation like Japan, these included shipping and shipbuilding. Next came steel, electric power and cement. The steel and electricity industries had to wait for the society to learn the necessarily rather difficult techniques. The cement industry could not be started until there was a sufficient urban demand. Simultaneously, there was an expansion of industries making consumer goods, such as glass, paper and canned food, without which the towns could neither conduct their business, build their houses, not feed their workers. Tables 32–38 give figures illustrating the addition of this second sector to the economy.

TABLE 32

	Coal Production (in million metric tons)
1880	1
1905	13
1921	26
1936	42
1940	52½

TABLE 33A

					Railway mileage
1880	..	..	..	..	300
1904	..	..	..	..	4,700
1924	..	..	..	..	10,400
1934	..	..	..	..	14,500

N.B.—Freight carried went up from 2.7 million tons in 1892–3 to 90.4 million tons in 1925–6.

TABLE 33B

			Shipping		Ship-building
1880	..	..	66,000 tons	1904–8 (Av.)	41,000 tons
1903	..	..	3,657,000 ,,	1922	71,000 ,,
1925	..	..	3,496,000 ,,	1936	295,000 ,,
1939	..	..	5,729,000 ,,		

TABLE 34

				Finished steel production (In metric tons)
1896	..	..	..	1,000
1906	..	..	..	69,000
1922	..	..	..	627,000
1936	..	..	..	4,352,000

TABLE 35

				Cement Production (In metric tons)
1890	..	..	..	Small
1920	..	..	..	1,353,000
1937	..	..	..	5,769,000
1940	..	..	..	6,852,000

TABLE 36

				Glass production (in cases of 1000 sq. ft. per month)
1890	..	..	..	Small
1930	..	..	..	188,000
1937	..	..	..	339,000

TABLE 37

				Production of Paper (In metric tons)
1880	..	..	..	Small
1902	..	..	..	51,000
1913	..	..	..	170,000
1930	..	..	..	802,000
1939	..	..	..	1,400,000

TABLE 38

				Canned foods production (in cases)
1900	..	..	..	125,000
1930	..	..	..	4,937,000
1938	..	..	..	15,191,000

The next real advance in Japanese industry came with the increase in productivity which accompanied the weeding out of weak firms in the deflation of the late thirties (see Table 39). This was followed by the growth of the industries using large supplies of capital and intricate techniques. The Manchurian Affair, the China Incident, and the preparations for Pearl Harbour, speeded up this development. Chemicals and engineering manufacture leapt up. A few figures will illustrate what happened:-

Machinery and tools production	1931	443 million yen	1938	3,801 million yen
Aluminium	1931	Nothing	1938	20,000 metric tons

Japan and Korea

Sulphate of
  ammonia   1930 226,000 metric tons   1936   880,000 metric tons
Sulphuric acid 1913 188,000   ,,   ,,   1936 2,432,000   ,,   ,,
Caustic Soda 1920   4,100   ,,   ,,   1937 356,000   ,,   ,,

In 1930 Japan produced 458 cars, in 1936 9,633; but while in 1936 she still had to import 31,000, in 1939 she actually exported 5,684.

It was not just a coincidence that by 1936 Japan had become self-sufficient or nearly so, in machinery, vehicles, scientific instruments, and aircraft; and that the China Incident broke out in 1937.

That all this development was accomplished, at least until 1936, without any undue strain is shown both by the increase in cotton textile exports already cited, and by such examples as the increase in the production of woollen yarn from 64 million lbs. in 1929 to 123 million in 1936, of rayon yarn from 5,5000 tons in 1928 to 123,000 in 1936, and of Japan's share in world trade from 2.9% in 1929 to 3.59% in 1936.

Japan did not of course become an industrial power on the scale of Great Britain or Germany. The time was too short, her inventiveness too little. But she did draw level with France, overcoming a handicap of half a century in time. The comparability of France's 6,200,000 metric tons of steel, 48 million metric tons of coal and 1,270,000 metric tons of sulphuric acid in 1938 with the figures for Japan previously given is therefore a fair measure of the greatness of the Japanese achievement. Real income per head in Japan was, however, still only about a quarter that of France.[1] How much had been achieved in comparison with Japan's own past is, however, clearly shown in Tables 40 and 41.

TABLE 39
TYPICAL INCREASES IN PRODUCTIVITY

Output per operative in cotton spinning per year.	1926	5,700 lbs.	1936	9,300 lbs.
Salt required for one ton of ammonium sulphate	1929	1.7 metric tons	1936	1.2 metric tons
Barrels of cement produced per operative per year.	1929	2,201	1933	3,081
Coal hewn per miner per year.	1927	140 metric tons	1933	266 metric tons

[1]There were nearly twice as many people in Japan as in France, and advance in other sectors had not kept up with that of manufacturing.

TABLE 40

			Real wages	Bank deposits 1900=100	Real national income
1883 ..	..	..	82	—	—
1892 ..	..	..	59	19	—
1913 ..	..	..	114	337	172
1919 ..	..	..	105	2,036	206
1929 ..	..	..	178	2,008	351
1932 ..	..	..	248	1,850	382
1938 ..	..	..	151	2,390*	396*

* 1934

TABLE 41A

			Factories using power	% of total no. of factories	Workers
1900 ..	..	..	2,388	33	422,019
1914 ..	..	..	14,578	47	948,265
1929 ..	....	..	48,822	82	1,825,022

TABLE 41B

			Value of factory production (in million yen)	Rent of buildings
1900	..	..	780	46
1914	..	..	1,372	135
1929	..	..	7,717	650
1937	..	..	16,716	800*

* 1934

Real wages doubled between 1883 and 1938. Thus the increase in wealth benefited all. This is an excellent proof that what is of primary importance to national well-being is the size of the cake which has to be distributed. The Japanese Government's interest, however, unlike that of Western Governments, was confined to increasing the size of the cake; the size of the slices which different individual citizens got was to it a matter of almost complete indifference. Protection for labour was quite inadequate; no effective trade union could function, because its leaders necessarily fell foul of the secret police. Only in 1939 was work limited to 12 hours per day for males over 16, and this at a time when France already had a

o

40 hour week. In Osaka in 1925 two-thirds of the businesses gave only two rest days per month to their employees. Business and income taxes were very light. They yielded under a million a year or 4% of the budget, in the early 80s, £6½ million, under one-tenth of the total, in 1914–15 and £28 million, about one–seventh of the total, in 1937–8. This may have been a reflection of the high propensity of the Japanese business man to save. On the average in the years 1923–31, a third of earnings were invested. But this financial policy became a definite economic error when in the late thirties, with the rise in military expenditure, the Government took to borrowing to meet its deficit instead of raising taxes. Thus, in 1936, national taxes were only 6% of the national income, but the Government borrowed another 6%. Germany had pursued the same policy in World War I.

Another example of the Government's lack of concern for social justice was the repeated use of inflation as a means of securing for the entrepreneur the profits which were necessary if there was to be high saving. Another was the way in which industry was allowed to batten on the countryside.

A few figures will make clear the extent of the inflation. Wholesale prices increased four times between 1883 and 1938; monetary circulation eight times between 1892 and 1934; bank deposits six times between 1914 and 1920. The yen dropped from 4/- in 1877 to 1/2 in 1938. The battening of industry on the countryside is not so immediately obvious. It was negative rather than positive. Industry was able to deny the worker the benefit of a provident fund, and the State to deny him health insurance, or unemployment insurance, or old age pension, because the ultimate responsibility for the worker was shifted from industry and the State to the land. Because of the deep Japanese sense of family obligation, a man with no other source of income would always be supported by his relations, and since so many Japanese workers were recent immigrants from the countryside, the relations were more often than not peasants. Moreover the Japanese farmer was perennially short of money; it was his regular practice to send his daughter into a city factory to earn her own dowry, and to enable him to pay his debts with her wages. Hence the very high percentage of women workers in Japanese industry. It was 60% in the 1890s, 70% in 1910–14, over 50% still in 1924; in cotton textiles at the end of the twenties 83% of the workers were women, and 60% were girls under 19. There was a rapid turnover of labour. One-half the girls in combined spinning-weaving mills worked for under four years. There is no cheaper way of staffing a factory than with a succession of adolescent girls, but this can only be done when there is some other sector of the economy from which the girls can be recruited and to which they can be sent back.

The Government's lack of interest in social justice goes right back to the Restoration itself. The Meiji Government accepted the tenancy relations which had been created by illegal alienations of 30% of the land. It increased rural borrowing and increased the tendency for the peasant's land to pass to the usurer by its actions in making alienation legal and in fixing the land tax in money. The fact that the peasant now had a title to give as well as a crop-share to pledge, increased his credit—and the curse of all peasant societies has been the tendency to borrow up to the limit of credit. The fixing of the tax in money, even though it was lower than the rice tribute had been, meant that the peasant was exposed to all the hazards of the market and the weather; with the tax (including local tax) set at 30% of the gross proceeds it was no help to him in a bad year that the tax had borne lightly on him in a previous one. By 1881 mortgage debt was 141 million yen compared with an assessed value of only 123 million yen. By 1892 another 10% of the land had passed to landlords. Between 1881 and 1904 the number paying land tax of 5 yen or more dropped from 1,809,610 to 1,083,697.

Thereafter, the decline of the peasant-owner was slower, but it continued steadily.

Tables 42A and B show the progressive deterioration.

TABLE 42A

			Tenant cultivated land	Owner cultivated land
			(in million cho to the nearest tenth of a million)	
1887	..	..	$1\frac{8}{10}$	$2\frac{8}{10}$
1903	..	..	$2\frac{1}{2}$	$3\frac{1}{10}$
1938	..	..	$2\frac{8}{10}$	$3\frac{1}{4}$

N.B.—This overstates the case in favour of the owner, as more of the less valuable upland was owner cultivated than of the rice fields. In 1934, 53% of the rice was tenant-cultivated. Even so, it will be noticed how much greater the increase in tenant cultivated land has been than that in owner cultivated land.

TABLE 42B

GROWTH OF DEBT AND RENT					
	Debt in millions of yen				Rent in Koku per tan on rice fields
1881	..	..	141	1873	..	..	.75
1911	..	..	711	1913	..	..	1.12
1929	..	..	4,000	1938	..	..	1.05
1938	..	..	6,000			

N.B.—It was estimated that 80% were in debt, and that 40% of the debt was unproductive. Rents were fully half the crop.

The Japanese countryside was thus as deeply in decline by the 1930s as the Indian. The Japanese Government could not plead that there had been, as in India, an increasing pressure on the land, and an increasing exhaustion of soil fertility. On the contrary, industrialisation with its drawing off of surplus population into the towns, its artificial fertilisers, and its scientific research, had increased both acreage per head and yields. Where 15 million people had cultivated 11 million acres in 1870, 14.1 million cultivated 15 million acres in 1930; where production of rice per hectare had been $11\frac{1}{2}$ koku in 1880 it was $19\frac{1}{2}$ in 1885–7. Western research, Western industry, Western trade, had brought higher productivity to agriculture as to all other sectors of Japanese life. In the late thirties 2 million tons of sulphate of ammonia and 100,000 tons of phosphate were used on the land. Japanese rice yields were the highest in the world. The silk industry which had grown in response to American demand gave a supplementary income to 2 million farm families, and employed 600,000 people, mostly farmers' daughters, in reeling and weaving.

The Japanese had successfully proved the truth of the *laisser faire* argument, so unpopular in Europe between the wars, that the first necessity in national economy is to increase the size of the cake. A Japanese agricultural day labourer in 1934 received 11d. a day. This was about twice the Indian wage. A Japanese tenant cultivator made some £34 a year. This was between two and three times the income of an Indian tenant. Since central revenues from other sources was increasing, the State needed to collect no more in land tax in the late 1930's than in the late 1880's. Thus the real burden of land taxation went down by perhaps 85%, because the same tax in terms of yen was collected in spite of the severe drop in the value of the yen.

But for a society to be just and stable, it is necessary that the slices into which the cake is divided should not be too outrageously unequal. To secure this, the Japanese Government took no steps at all. In this it contrasted with the Governments of the Indian provinces or of Java. When the land tax was reduced in the seventies, nothing was done to see that the benefit was passed on to the tenant; the tenant's share stayed at the same third it had been in feudal times, while the landlord's went up from one-fifth to over half. At no time was anything effective done to reduce or control rent or debt or its fragmentation of holdings.

To sum up. The Japanese Government had shown that, by the use of Western technique, there was an almost limitless possibility of increasing the national income. But the object of the Japanese governing class in adopting these foreign techniques was only to conserve. They wished to sacrifice no more of their old society than was required to preserve its fundamental values. They had not wanted to come out of their seclusion, and they decided to Westernize their economy only in order to prevent anyone ever again being able to compel them to act so vitally against their wills by a display of force as minimum as Perry's. Admiral Togo's victory at Tsushima, the growth of the Yokohama Specie Bank and the success of the Japanese textile exports in driving Lancashire out of all the poorer markets of the world, were the measure of their success.

The revolution in Japan was a purely technical revolution. Japanese students went abroad to learn to design ships or make oil engines. They did not, like the Indians and Chinese at Cambridge or Harvard, learn a civilisation as well as a technique. Their constitution was copied, not from the liberalism of England or America, but from the absolutism under parliamentary form with which Bismarck had endowed the Germans. They raised their educational expenditure from 11 million yen in 1914-15 to 146 million in 1937-8; but they used the new education to inculcate the old values, so that teachers committed suicide if the Emperor's portrait got burnt. They abolished privilege to ensure efficient services, not to give equal opportunity to all; the best civil service jobs always went to Imperial University graduates. For the Japanese leaders the new English ideal of a property-owning democracy would have been an abomination, for democracy was a dangerous thought, and property but a State instrument for the increase of power. In business as a way of life, offering to the small man all the satisfaction of controlling his own destiny and taking his own risks, they took no interest; their economy was dominated by monopolies and oligarchies. English wartime concentrations of business took great care to preserve the rights of the individual, despite the great administrative inconvenience, whereas in Japan the small business man was simply concentrated out of existence.[1] It is typical of Japan that nationalisation was the policy of the reactionaries of the Kwantung Army, who thought the State could increase its war potential quickest by dispensing with cautious and profit-minded intermediaries; nationalisation for the purposes which have made it popular in the British Labour Party, increased workers' control or the possibility of taking into account social as well as economic costs, would have seemed sentimental to any Japanese Government.

Japan is therefore a warning as well as a model, a reminder that in the contact of civilisations it is the effect on men's souls which is vital in the end. The things of the West, its locomotives, its cotton mills, its guns, turned the Japanese into aggressors, but the Western spirit has made free men and democrats of the Indians. Sixty years of material planning brought to Japan General Tojo, a hundred years of English education produced in India Pandit Nehru.

[1]John R. Stewart, *Japan's Textile Industry*, New York, 1949, p. 22. So that the 82 spinning companies of 1937, for example, had been reduced by the end of the war to the "Big Ten". (Large integrated organisations controlling spinning, weaving, dyeing and finishing.)

Chapter XVII

RELIGION

The impact of the West caused not only economic and social changes. It caused changes in the texture of men's minds. It changed, in varying degrees in the different countries, their instinctive ways of behaviour, their judgments of value, their ideas about how society should be organised, and their religion.

In a settled civilisation, the institutions of a country are the outward expression of its people's ideas and habits of mind. For example, the American economic system reflects the willingness of its people to take risks, combined with their ability to reconcile law and freedom; the natural resources of North America are no greater than those of South America, but the South has had a different history because the minds of its peoples were different. In Asia, when western institutions were first copied, these often wilted because the ideas of the people on whom they were imposed were not in harmony with them. But gradually, in many of the Eastern lands, the nature of men's minds underwent a change. They grew more like western minds. When this happened, the Eastern lands could be regarded as undergoing true revolution. Until it happened all the imported new institutions had a precarious life. They were artificial and unrelated to the spirit of the people.

The following are a few examples of attitudes or assumptions in the West in modern times which were unknown in Asia before the western ascendency.

(a) Traders feel that it is proper or incumbent on them to take a part in the political life of their country. This concept was formerly unknown to Asia. No merchant in India or China or Japan had ever aspired to the political power of, say, the Lord Mayor of London.

(b) Traders feel that their business is honourable. It is work approved by God. (This attitude is found especially in Protestant countries). By contrast, in traditional India the merchant ranked below the teacher and soldier. In China he ranked below the peasant and artisan.

(c) Truth is something to be arrived at by induction and experiment. It is not something to be deduced *a priori* or to be received by revelation. This is the famous scientific attitude of the West which has prevailed since the 17th century. Without it the West could have had neither the spinning jenny nor the steam engine.

(d) The actions of the state are to be judged by utilitarian tests.

These attitudes of mind, which were not innate in Europe but were evolved at definite moments of time, were as much a part of the history of progress in Europe as the invention of the steamship or the telegraph.

It was not easy for the East to appreciate this. Its first reaction, when assailed by the West, was to suppose that the success of the West lay in its technical apparatus and its tangible goods. It tried to copy these. The Japanese for example tried to copy the externals of western life to the minutest detail, and believed at one time that it was as important to dress like Europeans and to play games like Europeans as it was to import Western railway engines or western cannons. Only gradually did Asia discover that the starting point, if it wished to put itself on even terms with the West, was to make a revolution in its mind. It had to adopt a whole series of new ideas. The individual citizen had to become convinced that his world was not bounded by the interests of his family, that he had duties to all men simply by virtue of their being men, that it was wrong to bear false witness even in his family's interest, and that countless other new maxims suggested by the West were valid.

The inner connections between the ideas of a people and its external institutions can only be appreciated through intimacy. A man must live in a civilisation if he is to understand the spiritual attitude which lies behind it. The Asiatics who first learned to understand the deeper meaning of Western civilisation were those who went to live for some years abroad. In China the influence of this class was enough to start the Chinese revolution, but the size of this class was too small for it to be able to turn China into a Western state. Only in India has contact with the West been so close and so prolonged that a large class has been created with a genuine understanding of democracy and of the rule of law.

Thus the impact of the West changed much in the Asian mind. Traditionally, the grand interest of Asia had been religion. What, during the past century, has happened to the great Asian religions? The fact of chief consequence was that Christianity made little progress. The Western governments made little effort to impose it on their colonial territories by using political power. (If they had conquered the East two or three centuries earlier they would certainly have made this attempt). Asia was, however, subjected to an active bombardment by Christian missionaries. As has been pointed out by Professor Latourette, the conversions made by Christianity in Asia during the half century had important consequences for the Christian churches. But for Asia they had less consequence. The percentage of converts was too small.

Though the Asian peoples did not become Christian, their religions felt the influence of Christianity. The Christian missionaries brought two new sets of ideas: Christian metaphysics and Christian ethics. Their metaphysics did not leave a deep print on Asia: it was otherwise with their ethics. In nearly all the Asian religions, the ethical system underwent changes during the last century, and these changes took usually the form of a synthesis (usually unacknowledged) with ethical ideas which were specifically Christian. This happened in Hinduism, Islam and Buddhism.

It is hard to summarise briefly the effects of this change. But, speaking very broadly, it may be said that the traditional impulse in the Asian religions (except Islam) is to save the soul by renouncing the world and withdrawing into meditation or asceticism. The attitude of the 19th-century Christian missionary in Asia was that the soul could be saved by a man loving his neighbour as himself, and serving society. The instinct of the religious man in Asia had previously been to abandon the world; under western influence, it became, at least partly, the typical western instinct of the 19th century to engage in a crusade for social justice and the improvement of man.

Such a change of mind has had profound consequences. It has impelled to political action the type of man, forceful, emotional and self-sacrificing, who in the past separated himself from society and held aloof, at least spiritually.

The traditional religions went through other changes in addition to changes in their ethical ideas. In China, Buddhism entered on a decline, measured by the number and quality of its adherents and its impact on thought and action. Confucianism enjoyed a certain measure of revival. Its ethical ideas seemed to offer a workable basis for a modernised Chinese society. In Japan the government performed a *tour de force* in creating State Shinto, which was an elaborate form of State worship. State Shinto was proscribed by the victors in 1945. Whether is has a future it is too early to say.

In India, Hinduism, challenged by Western scientists and moralists, re-stated its metaphysics in such a way that they harmonised with modern western science. It began to purge itself of the taboos and social institutions which had brought it into such bad repute. A number of Mohamedan thinkers tried to do the same for Islam, but they had on the whole smaller success.

Religion still exercises a greater fascination on the Asian mind than it at present does on the European. Every visitor to the East to-day is conscious of this. Yet he is also conscious that among the Western educated classes there is a general scepticism. As in the West, religion in the East has been shaken. Rationalism and criticism have forced men to give up many of their religious beliefs. Thus a void has been created in many minds. The traditional religion is rejected, but the hunger for religion remains. Herein lies the attraction of Marxism for much of the Eastern intelligentsia. In the guise of secularism, it is really, in its Eastern form, often a religion of a very heady type.

PART THREE

Chapter XVIII

THE NEW ASIA

The picture of the new Asia is now becoming clearer.

Unless their governments disappoint all present expectation, China and India will be the two dominating political structures. Between them they contain seven or eight hundred million peoples of Asia's 1200 millions. Their capitals, Peking and Delhi, will be among the dozen chief political centres of the world. Their leaders will be the leaders courted by the other continents. Their ideas will give the tone to Asian civilisation. Their economic systems will be the models for the rest of Asia. Their armies and air-force, though not perhaps dominating the continent, will be the strongest of the Asian countries.

History appears often as a blind muddle, without any national theme. But as the stage is being set in Asia to-day, it seems possible that the history of the next period may show clearly as a battle of ideas, and to some extent as a moral conflict. For the new China and Modern India, both of them the products of the nationalist revolution in Asia, stand clearly for different systems and different philosophies.

India is an extraordinary example of an ancient society which has adopted, with singular completeness, the political ideas of alien peoples. It is true that much in modern India comes from India's most ancient past; there are few educated men of Hindu origin who do not accept one form or another of the Hindu philosophy as their guiding light. Yet India, in spite of the peculiarities of its social system, has evolved as the result of more than a century of British rule a political civilisation which can be called genuinely liberal. It is the only state in Asia (Ceylon excepted) which has done so. It has not mechanically copied western institutions: if its westernisation meant only this, it would not survive. The dominant classes in Indian society have taken over, in their spirit and in their very bones, the basic ideas on which modern liberal civilisation rests, and the institutions of modern India reflect this psychological revolution.

The West European or American may feel thoroughly at home in modern India. Its system of government, modes of thought and ideals of political conduct are democratic and parliamentary. It guarantees liberal freedom to the individual citizen, even while accepting, as in England, collectivist ideas in its economic policy. Though its government has been compelled, in the disturbed times since independence, to use powers of arbitrary arrest, it has done so with restraint, and has not exceeded the action which the most liberal state in the West might well permit itself in time of so great crisis.

The new China, on the other hand, is a Communist State, though the dependence of its revolution on the peasantry instead of the proletariat has given its Communism a few distinctive features. The fall of the Kuomintang meant that China had rejected the possibility of evolving the liberal state. To set up a liberal society, on American rather than British lines, had been the ideal of the respectable early members of the Kuomintang. They failed partly because of the shortcomings of their party, partly because in the conditions of China it was impossible to foster a liberal system. India had been able to grow into liberalism because it possessed a middle class which over two or three generations had been trained in liberal ideas (often in British universities), a professional civil service, and an efficient and non-political army. China had none of these. It had not, like India, through long association with a western country, grown so western in its structure that it could operate a western system of government.

The Communism of China is increasingly following the Russian pattern. Mao has written extensively on "New Democracy". He is anti-Trotskyist, and believes in the evolutionary development of Chinese society. Communist government in the first stage is to rest on an alliance of peasants, workers, and "patriotic capitalists" or "national bourgeoisie". Chinese Communism has remembered that Marxism requires a bourgeois revolution before there can be a proletarian one, however much the two may have been telescoped in Russia.

Though it may not be quite the dictatorship of one class, it has the following characteristics which mark it off from the liberal state in India.

(a) The state will not guarantee universally the rights and individual freedoms of its subjects. In a major statement of policy as late as July 1st, 1949, Mao Tse-tung wrote: "We are really dictatorial. The experiences of several decades amassed by the

Chinese people tell us that the right of reactionaries to voice their opinion must be deprived, and only the people are allowed to have the right of voicing their opinions".

(b) The institutions of the state will not be parliamentary. The government will not be elected.

(c) Though the government may in the first instance be a coalition, the Communist party will hold supreme power, and will never relinquish it—except by force. In India, on the contrary, while Congress to-day holds supreme power, it is liable periodically to be turned out by ballot if public opinion moves sufficiently against it.

(d) It is not based on the rule of law. The Communist Government will not let its power be circumscribed as is the power of government in a liberal state.

A form of government and a form of society are not adopted for their intrinsic merit. They are acceptable at any one time because the individual living under them finds life tolerable, and because under them society is able to deal fairly effectively with the problems facing it. India will not defend Liberalism and China will not defend Communism because these systems have become fetishes, but because they seem to be the most suited to these countries in their needs at the present time.

The supreme interest of both India and China to-day is to end, or at least reduce, their terrible poverty. Poverty is the outstanding fact in their lives. Their intelligentsia have come to believe that with modern technical knowledge this poverty can be overcome. India maintains that its own liberal system will prove the most efficient as the means for raising the standard of living. The new China maintains that under a liberal system it is only a section of society which will advance its living standards; only under Communism can the poverty of the whole society be relieved.

The rest of Asia will watch to see which system in fact is able most rapidly to build up wealth, strength and prestige. It will probably imitate whichever country is the victor in this competitive struggle. If China should begin to prove conspicuously the more successful, it might even happen that India would abandon its own Liberalism and go Communist, though Communist China is hardly likely to become liberal if the contest should go the other way.

In the contest, India, by the very fact of having a more or less liberal economic system, starts with one great advantage. An increase of national wealth such as is needed in Asia can be brought about only by the investment of very large sums of capital. India, with its relatively good credit and its western connections, should be able to obtain much of what it needs from abroad, especially from America. India has already modified the regulations which might have deterred the foreign investor. It is true that capital no longer goes round begging to be invested as in the years between the two wars. That period, when capital was abundant, is now recognised to have been peculiar; the world has now returned to the more normal state when capital is scarce and hard to get. Yet if India plays its hand properly, it should be able to raise abroad, at reasonable rates of interest, much of the capital which it needs.

The Communist programme in China will need no less capital than the semi-capitalist programme in India. But it is unlikely that it will be able to raise much of this capital abroad. Why should America lend to it? What guarantee would it have that the capital would not be confiscated? Russia cannot in the immediate future become a substantial exporter of capital. The funds for the development of China must therefore come from the country itself, already impoverished by nearly forty years of upheaval. Savings will have to be forced. Nobody need doubt the high intentions of many of the present leaders of Communist China. But they will have to perform miracles of ingenuity if, in organising economic development, they are not obliged to set up the apparatus of compulsion, concentration camps, forced labour and the police state which is the curse of the modern world. They will be driven to it the sooner because China lacks the machinery of government, the civil service, and the public tradition, which are necessary to any government starting on such a great venture.

China will therefore be handicapped. Communist economic development is likely to be accompanied by what, to the Western world, seem to be political enormities. These may act as a deterrent to other countries to follow suit. Will this be decisive? It depends on what is the speed of economic advance in China, and what is the degree of the enormities committed. The youth of Asia is willing to pay a high price for economic transformation, and is willing to sacrifice many of the amenities and freedoms of the liberal system if poverty can really be turned into modest plenty. It does not mind being driven by the pistol and the whip if the results are really spectacular.

If India is to demonstrate that the liberal system gives the best return, it must cause rapidly an upward movement in the whole

Indian economy. It must accompany this by measures of social justice which relieve the worst grievances of the discontented classes. Already it has struck out at the landlord and the money-lender. The class which has created modern India as a liberal state, and which now upholds it, is a comparatively small and westernised upper middle class. The rest of India, the great majority of the people, are open-minded. Some, out of poverty and frustration, are inclined to revolution; but not many; the Communist vote in 1952 was only 5% of the total. They can be won to support the liberal state by one thing only: by economic prosperity.

If the west, especially America, is interested in the fate of Asia, if it wishes to check the spread of Communism over the continent, it should clearly put all possible aid behind the Indian Government in carrying through its plans of economic transformation.

The following chapters suggest, tentatively, the details of an economic policy for Asian countries.

Chapter XIX

CAPITAL AND SKILL

The three categories of the classical economist were land, labour and capital. To these the advance of scientific knowledge and mechanical complexity has now added a fourth, skill.

Asia's economy has been traditionally based on two of these factors. It has applied more and more labour to more and more land in order to provide sustenance for its growing numbers. Now that land is at last running out, Asia will have increasingly to combine labour, the supply of which grows ever more ample, with capital and skill. For Asia this is a novel combination.

That is the hard economic fact behind the stridency with which all the new nationalisms call for industry, and heavier industry, factories and more factories, for it is by industrialisation that they hope to employ the extra millions who are born yearly and to find the resources to arrest the decline in well-being which is making of their countryside tinder for every revolutionary spark.

This solution has, however, an old-fashioned incompleteness. 19th-century science, 19th-century capital had little to offer Asian agriculture beyond irrigation, and advice that was usually bad. In consequence it did not change fundamentally the peasant's life. The advice was not taken, and though irrigation was carried out on a grand scale, this fitted easily enough into a tradition where the state had always irrigated and the peasant's crop had long been helped by well and canal. But 20th-century science and 20th-century capital offer to the Asian peasant a technical revolution which involves a transformation of his whole way of life. Artificial fertilisers, insecticide, weed-killers, new varieties of seed, can double the production of the peasant's pest-ridden and exhausted land; but in return they will exact from him a high price in change. They must be paid for; he will therefore have to sell more of his crop, and his dependence on the market will be increased. They must be properly used; the peasant will therefore have to go to school until he can read a manufacturer's instructions and has learnt enough science to make an intelligent choice of the variety most suitable to his own land.

and to make an intelligent calculation of the balance of advantage between extra cost and extra yield. In so far as he does this successfully, he will cease to be a subsistence smallholder and become a business man. His farming will be a means of making money as well as a way of life.

The application of capital and the acquisition of skill therefore face Asia with a double revolution. The first is the more obvious. It is the growth of Western industry, an urban proletariat, and a managerial middle class, with all their demands for social change and all their power of concerted political action. The other, however, is the more important. It is the final commercialisation of the countryside, the transformation of the peasant into an active participant in the market, instead of its passive instrument.

The risks in forwarding this revolution are heavy, the tensions may well be great. Yet the present descending spiral of poverty leaves no option but to embark on it. Japan's example shows that only by this revolution can the spiral be reversed.

The effort and strain involved by this remedy will be great, for Asia at present, with the partial exception of Japan, is grossly under-capitalised and terribly lacking in every modern skill. At the beginning of 1949, all the shares quoted on Indian stock exchanges had a value of under £500 million; total property assessed to tax in Java and Madura in 1935 was under £40 million; the value of all the implements of a Chinese farmer was rarely as much as £5; many an Annamite peasant could not even keep a buffalo because he needed for his own food the land on which he would have grown fodder for the beast. Skill also is deficient, at least in its modern sense. Behind the Asian peasant there is the accumulated experience of centuries, but it is experience directed to one object only, small subsistence farming. Not only does it not equip him to be a steel worker or an engine-driver, it does not even fit him to be a modern business-farmer in the American style, able to mend a tractor, read an agricultural journal or shift his crops about according to the best market forecasts. The lore of weather and beast, the wise saws of a grandfather, and a lifetime of absorbing the practice of the village, are of little help in writing Co-operative society minutes or mending a tube-well pump.

If production is to be increased so that the new mouths can be fed and the old hands given work, the peasant must be given new skills which will make of him an adequate factory worker and a properly commercial farmer. That means an extensive, and therefore

P

expensive, educational system, for the universal inculcation of literacy is but the beginning. Changes have to be made in the peasant's way of thought which are harder to learn than reading. He has to acquire the sense of time, of regularity, so unimportant to the subsistence smallholder, so vital in a factory where lateness and absenteeism mean an impossible rise in costs; above all he has to acquire that handiness about a machine so unheard of in a society of wooden implements, so necessary if factory lathes and village diesel-engines are not to be perpetually out of action through breakages.

More important even than skill is capital, for without capital there can be neither the machines on which to practise thè skill nor the taxable capacity from which to pay those who are to teach it.

Capital can still work its miracles, in Asia as in Europe, in India or China as in Japan. In agriculture high level dams and tube-wells can still bring water to millions of fresh acres. Fertilisers and all the rest of the panoply of Western science can still augment the yield of millions of old ones. Now that these discoveries of recent years have made it possible to obtain great increases in production by the intelligent and large scale application of capital to agriculture, agriculture ought to get the major share of any savings that may be available for investment. Less training is needed, and there is less risk of social disturbance, when all that is required is to teach the peasant how to farm his own land in a businesslike way, than when he is moved into a town to become a factory hand. The emphasis by the nationalist parties in the East on industrialisation as a more interesting aim than the improvement of agriculture is an accident of history. It reflects agriculture's poor terms of trade in the 1930s. It is a reflection too of the fact that science and the machine were applied to industry so much earlier than to Asian farming; cotton mills are a century older than synthetic nitrogen, steel works preceded D.D.T. by seventy years.

The total capital needs of industry will, nevertheless, be greater than those of agriculture, for Asia not only requires large industrial development, it is also now ready for it. The land has a large labour surplus, which no increase in agricultural efficiency can possibly absorb; some improvements may indeed reduce the need for labour. Fortunately, in many industrial lines a domestic market large enough to carry local plants has now developed. Indonesia can now find a market for locally-manufactured cotton textiles, India for locally-manufactured locomotives. In addition, the requirements of a reformed agriculture for such items as fertiliser will have to be met from local production if the balance of payments is not to be impossibly burdened. And now that many of the Asian countries are independent, and that wars begin with such suddenness, the Asian countries will no longer be able to rely on armaments supplied from European sources thousands of miles away which have to be carried over a line of communication all too easy to cut. They will have perforce to set up their own war potential.

There is thus scope for a large immediate increase in industrialisation, and, once started, industrialisation breeds industrialisation. The demands for machinery, raw materials and transport which every new industry makes, tend inevitably to create other industries to supply them. The increase in education, the Westernisation of thought and the urbanisation of habits which are the concomitant both of industrialisation and of the modernisation of the countryside, themselves help to create that complex of demands, from shoes to refrigerators, from books to cinemas, which industry exists to serve. The taxation, which industrial profits make possible, pays for the education and health which gives the peasant the ability to work harder. The knowledge that there are better explanations for his cow's sickness than witchcraft, better ways of keeping up with the Joneses than going hopelessly into debt for a marriage, his increased surplus, his saving beforehand for his social expenditure which releases for productive investment not only his money but also the moneylender's, all these in turn increase industry's supplies, industry's capital resources and industry's market. Capital starts an ascending spiral quite as definite as the descending spiral induced by overpopulation.

Chapter XX

THE ROLE OF THE STATE

In the industrialisation of Asia, the State will have to play the same leading part as it did in Japan.

There is in Asia less mental resistance to State intervention than in the West, for Asia has a long history of effective and helpful State action. For the Westerner, state intervention is apt to mean the red tape of mercantilism, state monopolies, the labour camps of Russia. For the Easterner, it means the dykes of Tongking, the tanks of South India, the controlling of the Yellow River, the relief works of the Famine Code. Much of Asian agriculture depends on water control. Much of Asian water control involves areas so large, labour so immense, insurance so extensive, that only the State can organize it. Thus for two thousand years Asian Kings have been judged by their engineers rather than their generals. The State has thus come to be looked on as the father and mother of its subjects, to which it is natural for them to turn for help and comfort; the villager indeed thinks of Government so personally that he is even willing to do it favours, to subscribe for instance to a war fund to help prosecute a war of whose purposes he has but the dimmest understanding. To the Asian peasant, government, for all its occasional cruelty and its frequent incompetence, is not a malign body inventing forms to plague him, but a philanthropist who feeds him in famine, lends him money for a well, protects him from oppressors; when Government fails to live up to his expectations, as in Kuomintang China, withdrawal of support gives him a sure revenge.

In Asia, moreover, there are no ready-made nuclei of opposition, for government is by local officers appointed by and responsible to the Central Government, but with powers wide enough to enable them to give real assistance and protection to their people. There has not for centuries, except in feudal Japan, been at any level above the village any of that local self-government which is embedded so deep in England or America. Police and justice, education and grants from the waste, all are organised by government. The bad official peculates and takes bribes, but though bad men may create revolutions it is the good men by whom a system is judged. The good official protects the widow and the orphan and gives land to the landless, spares the lowly and humbles the oppressor.

There have never grown up in Asia those associations of free men coming together for a common purpose which so often make State action unnecessary for a Westerner. Trade union and provident society, joint stock company and city corporation are all found to-day in Asia, but they are European innovations. The Churches in Asia offer the State no such competition as they do in Europe. This is partly because Eastern religions have no hierarchical organisation of any strength, partly because of the Islamic tradition of combining secular and spiritual authority, partly because Buddhism looks on the need for secular rule as a sign of man's sin, partly because the Confucian scholar was the guardian of the right path as well as a State official. In Asia the freedom of conscience has not been enough attacked to have had to be defended. The King was always too much himself God's vicegerent ever to be brought in God's name to Canossa.

The vast majority of Asian peasants are therefore content to accept Government's wisdom so long as their rice-bowls are not emptied. Their passive acceptance frees Government from the fear of opposition. Its spur to positive action is the lack of a business class capable of discharging economic tasks for society. It is no accident that the most *laisser-faire* of the great Eastern States, Indonesia, was also industrially the most backward. Everywhere in Asia local capital is scarce, because for centuries too solid a show of wealth brought confiscation, and because the illiteracy and subordination of women caused them to attach a quite inordinate value to jewellery. So savings went unproductively into hoards or on to women's bodies instead of into the productive investment which increases capital like a rolling snowball. In 1924-5 India still imported £70 million of treasure, but as late as 1929 the Indian Government had to pay 6% on Treasury Bills. Capital is, moreover, even more expensive than its scarcity would warrant, for most borrowing is unproductive and the rate of interest therefore depends on the urgency of a man's need to eat or marry, not on the profits he can make on what he borrows. Industry, which does not normally hope to make an average of more than 10% on the money it borrows and which often has to be content with considerably less, holds few temptations for money-lenders who can get 25% by lending to neighbours every detail of whose affairs they know.[1] In all Asia, only the Parsis have shown imagination, and the courage to risk their all upon a dream and wait for fortune.[2]

In Asia, therefore, if savings are to be mobilised, it is the Government which has to go to the market. This is not surprising. Even in Europe before 1914, the French peasant had preferred Russian Government bonds to the equities of his own industrialists, and English maiden ladies could be tempted more successfully with Central American 7% than with a good cotton mill ordinary. In Asia, if waiting is to be done and the sound risks taken, it is the Government which has to act. If foreign technicians are to be recruited, the Government is often the most suitable agent to employ them. Many a man will go out to Asia as Director of, say, Aerodromes with the hope of a decoration at the end of his career, but will not trust himself as a bania's manager though the pay and conditions may be better.

A great deal of the development so far accomplished in Asia has, therefore, depended directly or indirectly on the Governments. We saw this at length in the case of Japan. Some of the early Indian railways were indeed privately built, but normally only under Government guarantee, and to-day in India the railways, the irrigation, the hydro-electricity and the telegraphs and telephones and ordnance factories, which represent the largest concentrations and the greatest achievements of capital in the country, are Government owned. The great canals which opened up Cochin China, the dam in the Yalu River bigger than Boulder, were government enterprise. Private enterprise has nothing to show on the same scale. The Japanese Government in 1925, at the height of its short burst of economic liberalism, still employed one-fifth of all Japanese who were engaged in mining, manufacture, and transport. The Victorian Dutch Government in Indonesia mined the coal of Sumatra and Borneo, took shares in the nickel of Celebes, the tin of Billiton and Singkep, the oil of Djambi, and owned plantations, salt works, teak forests, railways and the Bangka tin. Even before Communism the Chinese Government owned all the heavy industry of China,

[1] Investors in such companies as Unilevers or I.C.I. or Dorman Long get only 10% on their equity. The original shareholders of the Assam Co., the great Indian tea company, waited 13 years for their first dividend of 2½%.
[2] The Zoroastrianism of the Parsis made it easier for them to Westernise than it was for Hindus or Moslems.

over half of its cotton textiles, and the four biggest banks.[1] The Siamese Government owns paper, sugar and tobacco factories, an oil refinery, a shipping company and rice mills, the Ceylon Government manufactures plywood, glass, paper, rolled steel, acetic acid, ceramics and leather, and is planning to go into cotton textiles. The Philippine Government is following suit. Indian Governments had spent on irrigation alone by 1942–3 an amount equal to half the paid-up capital of all private companies put together, and their total investments on railways, telegraphs, irrigation, ordnance factories, their quarter share in colliery production, and so on were perhaps three times as great. The activities of the Indian Government are still expanding. It is building a fertiliser factory, has made agreements for factories to manufacture telephones and prefabricate buildings; it is producing trainer aircraft and has a half share in an international civil aviation company. It has nationalised the Reserve Bank, proposes to build a steelworks and to take a half share in three shipping corporations. It has started a series of multi-purpose river schemes to provide irrigation, flood control and hydro-electricity whose total cost runs into hundreds of millions. So vast are Government's schemes, that they considerably exceed the whole of India's savings. Even more striking is the extent of state enterprise in Pakistan. Its railways, its barrages, its Port Trusts, its provincialised motor transport, its carriage shops and its ordnance factories represent a Government investment of nearly as many millions as there are thousands in private investment in cotton mills and jute baling presses.

These examples have all been taken from countries with Right Wing Governments, all of them passionately anti-Communist, most of them quite unsocialist, who have acted not on theory, but in unconscious response to the traditional belief of Asia that innovations are for the State to make, enterprise a quality the State should show. The capitalist wanted safety and high interest. In India or China he did not take a chance on new processes, as did Brunner and Mond in Europe. He did not over generations combine service to the public with the building up of a great business, as did the Cadburys or the Crosfields. The typical capitalist fortune in Asia was made in opium contracting, or cloth wholesaling, or money-lending, or broking, or even, as with the Soongs, in speculation overseas. When it was found that money was to be made in cotton spinning

[1]Nationalisation under the Kuomintang was, of course, rather different from what is understood in the West.

or engineering, the capitalist bought machinery, technicians and buildings; even then he tried to persuade the public to find the money, and he made his own profits out of acting as the mill's cotton buyer or cloth seller. From such merchant and finance capital there could be expected no ideas on improved production and little enterprise.

The desire that the State should interfere is, therefore, in the East a result of the lack of enterprise by the capitalist rather than of Socialist thinking. It rises from the need for more production rather than from the desire for more just distribution. The fear öf standing still, not the immorality of profits, worries the Asian.

Chapter XXI

THE SHORT TERM

Everywhere, except in Siam, the war has brought freedom to the people of Monsoon Asia. But everywhere, except in Ceylon, it destroyed capital and brought a lowered standard of life. The masses in whom sovereignty now resides can get per head only 87% as much to eat, only two-thirds as much to wear, as they did before the war.[1]

One country alone is better off than before the war, Ceylon. Her national income was in 1947 nearly half as much again as in 1938, while her population had gone up by only one-sixth.[2] Rice production doubled; the fish catch was nearly trebled; Government expenditure multiplied four times and still the Budget was balanced; exports increased by 30%; cotton piece-goods imports were some 40% higher in 1948 than in 1938; wheat, flour and rice imports were 30,000 tons higher. In spite of this all-round rise in standards, there are shadows in the picture. The killing of a quarter of the rubber trees during the war by slaughter-tapping, the turning of the terms of trade against Ceylon (in 1948 she paid six times as much as before for her food and five times for her piece-goods but only got two and a quarter times as much for her tea and one and three-quarters times as much for her rubber[3]), these are formidable adverse features. These disadvantages may, however, not be permanent. In the boom which followed the outbreak of the Korean War, Ceylonese terms of trade improved enormously, to one-fifth better than pre-war; in 1952 they swung back again, to about one-fifth worse, but that is the result quite considerably of the very high price

[1] In 1947–8. And even that was made possible by Western aid of over £250 millions, through American grants to Korea, Japan and China, and British, French and Dutch loans or grants to fill the balance of payments deficits of Burma, Indo-China and Indonesia respectively. In addition, the drawing down of their sterling balances by India, Pakistan, Ceylon in part represent drafts on capital—India took nearly £50 millions in the last six months of 1948, in addition to borrowing £23 millions from the International Fund over the year.

[2] At 1947 prices, 1938 national income 1242 million rupees, 1947 national income 1736 million. Population 1939, 5,810,000; 1947, 6,879,000.

[3] Coconut products in 1948 were selling for 4¼ times the 1934–8 price. The overall export price index (1934–8 = 100) was 253 in 1948.

of rice, and Ceylon has a six-year plan for making herself self-sufficient in rice.[1] Her industrial programme, which will, for example, make her self-sufficient in cement by 1950, and enable her to manufacture half her cloth requirements by 1953, should greatly relieve the strain on her balance of payments. Now that she has some £50 million of sterling balances savings, bank deposits approaching £70 million, and dollar exports of nearly £13 million in 1948, she should have no difficulty in financing the expansion of production to keep pace with her rapidly rising population.

No other country has been so fortunate. India and Pakistan, though equally undamaged, suffered severely from war-strain. Machinery had been worked to death, land had to be diverted from cotton to food, capital goods and transport equipment have been hard to get, food has had to be bought abroad at ruinous cost. Population in the two Dominions in 1948 was perhaps an eighth larger than in 1938, but there has been no corresponding increase in production. Indeed there was a slight decline, for though the factories turned out slightly more, the fields brought forth slightly less.[2] The great commercial crop, jute, the golden fibre on which so much of the economies of both countries depends, dropped from $12\frac{1}{2}$ million bales in 1940–1 to $6\frac{3}{4}$ million in 1947–8.

In consequence of this, there might have been expected a decline in welfare of the order of one-eighth, and for this estimate there is some confirmation. In India real earnings per year in organised industry dropped from Rs. $287\frac{1}{2}$ in 1939–40 to Rs. 249 $\frac{1}{2}$ in 1947–8[3] though real earnings rose again to roughly the pre-war level by 1952.[4]

Within this overall drop, however, there is concealed a very considerable change in the terms of trade between one section of the population and another. When the price of the peasant's produce was halved in the early thirties, the rest of the population benefited, for salaries, wages, debts, land revenue, were not cut by anything like corresponding percentages. Peasant debt doubled in eight years,

[1]Rice from Burma cost £13 million in 1948.

[2]Indices from *Eastern Economist*, New Delhi. Industrial production (year to August 1938 = 100), 105. Agricultural production (av. of 36–37 to 38–9 100), 97 (good grains 98, cotton 52). This is for India. Pakistan's industry is unimportant, agriculturally 1947–8 was so bad that Pakistan has imported wheat from Russia, though Sind and the W. Punjab have a good grain surplus of over half a million tons.

[3]*Eastern Economist*, New Delhi, December 17th, 1948, p. 1050.

[4]The best firms did better. Levers' real wages, for example, rose by 40% between 1936 and 1952.

but the civil servant and the factory workman were better off than they had ever been. The war has reversed the process. The share of tertiary production (which includes transport, commerce, the professions and government services) in the national income has gone down from 31% to 21%[1]; the senior civil servant or Army officer gets the same rate of pay as before; the factory or agricultural labourer's wage has lagged behind the rise in prices; but the peasant's produce is fetching four, six, sometimes eight times what it did before the war.[2] There has been no corresponding rise for a peasant-proprietor in his land revenue, or for an occupancy tenant in his rent; and since Indian debts are normally in money terms, many a man who in 1938 was hopelessly insolvent has been able to pay off his money-lender. There was a reduction of nearly £40 million in the money value of the Madras peasantry's debt during the war, and all over India co-operative societies which have been classed as beyond hope ((c) and (d) in the official classification) have had their outstanding debts paid on such a scale that they have occasionally been embarrassed to know how to reinvest the money.

Not every peasant has benefited. Only the man with a surplus has prospered. The millions who have an acre or half an acre, who grow not quite enough for the food of the family and have to supplement their crops by their labour, have suffered in the same way as the town work-man. Similarly the landless harvester of the countryside has suffered, for wages have lagged behind prices, though to a lesser extent.[3]

The other great beneficiary of these changes has, of course, been the ubiquitous black marketeer, whose depredations on society have recently been estimated, or rather guessed, to have cost £400 million in profits which have paid no tax. This is still much smaller than peasant gains, but its social consequences are much more severe. Even to-day it is only the very big peasant who could make £500

[1]*Eastern Economist*, New Delhi, December 31st, 1948, p. 1123.

[2]The official procurement price of wheat in the U.P. for example, is over 4 times pre-war, and the open market price has been around eight times.

[3]Some illuminating figures for Madras are given in the *Eastern Economist*, January 28th, 1949, p. 145. The bigger landholders (gross income in 1945 some £300) cleared or partially cleared debt in 38.4% of cases, as against 20% of increases; the medium landholders (gross income just under £100) reduced debt in 40.4% of cases, increased it in 28.8% but the small landholders (gross income just under £60) increased debt in 37.2% of cases, against reductions in 33%. These are money values; in real terms the picture would be much more favourable. How the change in prices has benefited the bigger man and hit the small man is also shown by the figures for surpluses (+) and deficits (−) after taking expenses from gross income.

a year, while the flaunting of black market wealth is a perpetual invitation to revolution.

The social advantages of the changes have been greater in Pakistan than in India, because in Pakistan the proportion of peasants with a surplus to sell to the total agricultural population is considerably higher, because the towns are still relatively few, and because Pakistan is a large exporter of cotton and jute, both of which fetch very much higher prices than pre-war. India has suffered because its imports of cotton, jute and food, account together for nearly half her total imports.

In other countries the tale is one of universal disaster mitigated or unmitigated. The best-off is Siam. The rice crop of this country has increased enough to make it probable that exports will again in 1949 be almost as great as before the war, while still leaving for its own increased population slightly more per person than before the war. Its rubber exports also are now perhaps twice their pre-war rate. But on the other side has to be set the destruction during the war of Siam's tin industry, the bombing of its only cement works, and damage to its railways, which the Government estimates will cost £40 million to repair.

The country worst off is China. Its countryside has been devastated by 11 years of bitter war. Its industry ground in 1947 to a virtual standstill (Table 45).

Japan is absolutely better-off than China. Its industry is still Asia's largest, and the Americans spend £100 million a year in seeing it does not starve. But relatively to pre-war conditions, Japan's descent has been steeper than China's. Over 6 million Japanese have been repatriated from overseas; shipping and investments which brought in £27 million in 1936 have nearly all gone[1];

	1939 In Rs.	1945 In Rs.
Big landholders	+ Rs. 652	+ Rs. 1,118
Medium ,, ...	+ ,, 121	+ ,, 117
Small ,, ...	+ ,, 8	− ,, 1
Tenants	− ,, 2	− ,, 44
Labourers	− ,, 9	− ,, 11

The scale should be remembered; 30 acres would bring a man into the big landholder class. In 1945, moreover, Madras prices had still not quite doubled; in other provinces, where increases have been greater and in Madras itself since 1945, the advantage both to the better-off peasant as against his neighbours and to the peasantry as a whole against the towns has been clearer still. Before the war almost all the debt was held by landholders.

11,300,000 tons of shipping were left, but a large proportion is needed for coastal traffic.

it has lost 30% of its industry and perhaps 3 million houses by bombing; two-thirds of its cotton spindles were melted down as scrap during the war; and its traditional silk exports to the United States have been decimated by nylon.[1] Even in 1948 industrial production was still only one-third of 1938; the textile production on which Japan has in the past depended for exports was only one-fifth. Tables 50A, B and C show what the decline has meant for the Japanese people in lower consumption, production, imports and exports.

Indo-China and Indonesia suffered very much less damage during the war than China or Burma, though the oil wells were scorched, though there were large falls in agricultural production through Japanese oppression and lack of markets, and though there were some specific instances of Japanese destruction such as the rooting-up of tea-bushes in Java. Since the war, while Cambodia and Laos and most of the Outer Provinces have recovered normally and quickly, the three Annamite Ky, Java and most of Sumatra have been subjected to a prolonged guerilla war, with all which that means in destroyed machinery, dynamited bridges, blown-up railways, and danger for cultivator and trade alike. Tables 43A, B, D and 46A and B provide a few figures to illustrate how economically disastrous have been the results.

Burma has suffered even more gravely. Burma suffered first the scorching which blew up all its oil wells, then a Japanese rule so oppressive that its rice area decreased by a third while Allied bombing destroyed its communications and damaged the cities—at the end of the war she had lost nine-tenths of her locomotives—then a long and severely fought campaign which left most of the towns and many of the villages in ruins, and finally a continuing civil war, which does not do a great deal of extra damage but does effectively stop the recovery which would come quickly enough if the oil could be drilled again, the rice acreage extended without fear of robbers, the minerals moved to the sea. (see Tables 43A and B and 44).

By contrast, the Philippines have been enabled by American generosity[2] to recover quickly, though they finished the war with

[1]The development of substitutes for the staple exports of the East has to be kept in mind. Synthetic rubber is being substituted for natural rubber; paper for jute.

[2]Though the trouble in Burma is not the result of any lack of British generosity. £80 million were granted her as gifts or loans between liberation and independence. In the Philippines there was an immediate influx of U.S. dollars, and a corresponding consumption of consumer goods.

their capital half-destroyed, their main hydro-electric works sabotaged, and most of their carabaos eaten by the Japanese.

In Malaya, conditions have been still better. Though all the tin dredges were destroyed, 60% of the locomotives lost, and the plantations allowed to run down, only 5% of the rubber trees on which Malaya primarily depends were cut down. The enforced rest from tapping helped to produce a rubber output higher in 1948 even than in the record year 1941. Capital, too, has been available quickly enough and in sufficient quantity to bring tin production back to 45,000 tons in 1948 as compared with 60,000 in 1941. Malaya's chief economic worry now, like Ceylon's, is the high price and inadequate supply of rice.

The decline in the standard of life in the area taken as a whole has now reached a stage where subsistence economies cease to be able to bring forth even subsistence. At present the consumption of cotton cloth per head in India is $11\frac{1}{2}$ yards, in China 11 yards, in Japan 2 lbs. of cloth of every sort. This is near-nakedness. Even in the tropical Gold Coast cloth consumption averaged $14\frac{1}{2}$ yards per person in 1947. The food consumption of much of India, China or Java is 1600–1800 calories per head, of Tokyo 1950 calories. The next stage is famine, the famine which reminded us in Bengal in 1943 as in China year after year that it is not yet in Asia a dead memory from a forgotten past.

A few selected figures to illustrate the results of the war are given in Tables 43–50.

TABLE 43A
FOOD

A. Rice production.

Country			1934–8	1946–7	1947–8
Burma	..	..	6.971	3.836	5.429
China	..	..	50.064('31–'37 av.)		
India	..	..	29.204('36–'37 to	46.006	46.507
			'38–39 av.)	29.239	—
Indo-China	..	..	6.498	4.286	4.797
Java and Madura	..	6.081	4.338	5.145
Japan	..	..	11.500	11.453	11.194
S. Korea	..	..	2.520('30, '34,	2.236	2.570
			'36 av.)		
Philippines	..	..	2.179	2.198	2.335
Malaya ..	..	..	513	421	548
Siam	..	..	4.357	4.642	5.174

N.B.—Rice may be taken as typical of the food supply position. Some
other crops e.g. wheat in Japan or maize in Java would show worse
figures, but on the other hand, fish, the main source of protein, gives
better ones—roughly back to pre-war by 1948 except in China.
Source: E.C.A.F.E. Food and Agricultural Conditions in Asia and the Far
East 1948 E/CN/11/144 dated November 27th. 1948.

TABLE 43B

B. Rice exports.

	THOUSAND METRIC TONS		
	1934–38 Average	1946	Jan.–July 1948
Burma	3.070	431	976
Siam	1.388	446	480
Indo-China	1.290	99	76
Korea	1.272	—	62 (imports)
Formosa	612	—	Nil

C. Rice imports.

	THOUSAND METRIC TONS AS MILLED RICE		
India	1.879	368	544
Japan	1.791	16	—
China	833	67	242
Malaya	548	277	301

D. Sugar exports.

	THOUSAND METRIC TONS.	
	1934–38	1948
Taiwan	833.2	150
Indonesia	1.045	75
Philippines	861.2	256

TABLE 44

A. Transport.

Loss of locomotives in percentages in liberation.

China	50%
Siam	30%
Burma	90%
Indo-China	50%
Indonesia	36% (very doubtful figure, as records incomplete)
Malaya	60%

A. Transport.—*contd.*

Loss of shipping (including rivercraft)

China	50%
Burma	90%
Philippines	100%
Indonesia	50%

Source: *The Economic Background of Social Policy including Problems of Industrialisation:* I.L.O. 1947.

N.B.—Transport has recovered quickly where there has been peace. Malay now has 225 locomotives against 173 pre-war, Siam has been supplied locomotives by both India and Great Britain to bring her back to her pre-war strength, the Burmese railways were back at a third of pre-war capacity as early as mid 1946. The Philippine, Indonesian and Chinese loss of shipping has been virtually made good. In Burma, Ceylon, China or the Philippines, there were substantially more lorries in 1947 than in 1938, in Malaya, Siam and Indonesia as many.

In Indonesia, Indo-China, and China, however, continued civil disturbances have prevented a full restoration of the railway system, which have even in certain areas, notably in Indo-China, deteriorated further.

TABLE 45

DECLINE IN INDUSTRIAL PRODUCTION

A. China (including Manchuria)

Max. pre-war production		1947 production
In million metric tons		
Coal	41	16
Pig iron	3½	Nil
Steel	1½	Negligible
Yarn	5—	2½
In thousands of metric tons		
Tin	13	1¾
Zinc	15	Negligible

Electrical capacity. July 1945, 2,749,735 KW. 1947, 1,324,440 (largely due to Russian removals.)

August 1947. Out of 25.914 kilometres of railway only 10.229 in operation.

B. Miscellaneous examples of total destruction.

(a) All oil wells and refineries in Burma and Indonesia.

(b) All Malayan dredges.

(c) All Philippine coconut-oil mills.

TABLE 46A
DECLINE IN PLANTATION EXPORTS

Indonesia

	Av. 1936–40	Jan.–May 1947
	In thousands of tons	
Pepper	54	1
Tea	80	2
Coffee	75	1
Sugar	1.000	Negligible
Tobacco	43	Negligible
Palm oil	200	—

Source: E.C.A.F.E., Survey of Reconstruction Problems and Needs, E/CN 11/39 dated November 3rd, 1947.

TABLE 46B
INDONESIAN BALANCE OF PAYMENTS

In million guilders

1939..	..	..	..	..	..	+ 24
1946..	..	..	..	..	..	− 426
1947..	..	..	..	..	..	− 711
1948..	..	..	..	..	..	− 378

Source: Unilever Research Dept. calculations.

TABLE 47
RUBBER PRODUCTION

In thousands of long tons.

				1941	1948
Malaya	..	..	..	600	698
Indonesia	..	..	..	650	432
Indo-China	..	..	..	40	43
Siam ..	..	..	..	45	95
Sarawak	..	..	..	35	40

Source: Figures for 1948 from Rubber Statistical Bulletin, for 1941 from E.C.A.F.E., Food and Agric. Conditions in Asia and the Far East, E/CN 11/144, p. 37.

TABLE 48
COTTON PRODUCTION

	1934–8 1	1947–8
		In thousands of metric tons
China	682.5	466.2
India and Pakistan	1.145	748.0 (of which Pakistan 200)

Source: E/CN. 11/144 dated November 27th 1948 p. 34

TABLE 49

SERIOUS DAMAGE TO THE REST OF THE WORLD THROUGH REDUCTION IN TRADE

Fats and oils exports (oil equivalent)
In thousands of metric tons

	1934–8	1948
China (inc.) Manchuria) ..	660	85
Philippines	355	517
India	515	170
Indonesia and Malaya ..	736	357
Ceylon	98	90

The good Ceylon and Philippine figures and most of the Indonesia and Malayan figures are accounted for by copra or coconut oil. Coconut trees were neglected during the war but not otherwise damaged. For all other oilseeds the decline has been catastrophic.

TABLE 50

JAPANESE ECONOMY

Japan

A. Consumption

	Pre-war	1947
Charcoal ..	36 bales per family	24 bales
Clothing ..	10 lbs per person	2 lbs
Paper	30 lbs per person	7½ lbs
Soap	2000 grammes per person	100 gr. per person
Rice	1½ quintals per person per year.	1 quintal

B. Production (Monthly average)

	1938	1946	1948
Coal (in thousand metric tons)	4,057	1,698	2,810
Crude Steel (do.)	539	46	142
Silk (Bales of 132 lbs) ..	59,933	7,452	11,248
Cotton piece goods (sq. yds.)	274,750,000	20,142,000	76,990,000
Rayon (spun and filament (sq. yds.)	130,443,000	6,089,000	7,475,000
Electric light bulbs ..	25,896,667	4,401,275	14,961,665
Ammonium sulphate (metric tons)	92,333	38,902	78,847
Cement (do.)	454,000	77,000	153,000

B. Production (Monthly average)—*contd.*

Electrical energy (Millions	1938	1946	1948
of KW H)	2,571	2,386	2,900 (approx.)
Industrial Production Index			
(1930=4=100) ..	177	32	55 (Dec. 48, 64)
Textiles	124	14	23 (Dec. 48, 26)
Machinery	350	38	72 (Dec. 48, 94)

C. Foreign Trade

(a) Exports

Monthly averages (metric tons)

	1938	1946	1947
Silk	2,388	438	88
Cotton Piece Goods (thousands of sq.			
metres)	158,419	68	26,444
Rayon piece goods (thousands of sq.			
metres)	36,017	0	233

Source: S.C.A.P. Japanese Economic Statistics January 1949.

(b) Imports.

	1938	1946	1948
Rice	169,230	1,364	3,528
Wheat	5,866	36,234	62,472
Raw cotton	47,606	13,235	6,779
Pig iron	89,366	167	915
Coal and cokes	423,472	0	97,492

In all these countries, great political changes have taken place.

Korea has been liberated, Malaya has a new Federation, China has gone Communist, America has given the Philippines their independence, Indonesia has been emancipated. The French in Indo-China, have conceded freedom and are fighting only to protect it from Communism. Japan was for six years governed by a combination of General MacArthur and democracy for which there is no precedent in her pre-war constitution. Only in Siam, which took the war so lightly, and whose peasantry have been so untouched, have two revolutions left Marshal Pibul Songgram dictating precisely as he did in 1940, with over against him that same Pridi Panomyong who has been his leading collaborator or his leading enemy ever since the original revolution of 1932.

Power has passed to the people. The people support Nehru. They have ousted Chiang Kai-shek. With the people, the French hold Cambodia without a fight; without them they cannot move in Annam without escort.

It is not only, perhaps it is not even mainly, that the foreigner is departing. It is also, and perhaps mostly, that within each country those classes which for generations, sometimes millenia, have traditionally held authority, are losing it, to be replaced by new men, Westernized in mind and dependent for their support upon that stratum whose traditional function has been obedience alone. In Japan the Sun-Goddess's descendant is being turned into a constitutional monarch, the officers' corps has been disbanded, trade unions are permitted, the Zaibatsu are being broken up, the peasant freed of his traditional burden of landlord, money-lender, and centrally appointed official. It is a long way from the serfdom of 1860 to the voter whose votes choose the Diet which governs unrestrained by Imperial prerogative or House of Peers.

In China the monopoly of the Confucian scholar has been finally broken; it is the peasant and the Westernized student whose support is now essential to Government.

In India, a hundred years of emancipation have culminated in the abolition of Untouchability in the Constitution, while adult suffrage, the disappearance of princely autocracy, the coming abolition of the zemindar, the new restrictions on the money-lender, and the steady spread of education are continuing to take away from Brahmin and Rajput and Bania the privileges their caste has given them over aeons. In a democratic world the votes and the majorities are with the Sudras; and the country's Hindu majority can again govern the whole of it as they have not for 700 years.

The Ceylonese have achieved freedom after a thousand years and more of Tamil invasion, Portuguese and Dutch and English conquest. Within Ceylon, the Sinhalese majority can again set their country's course after centuries in which wealth and power and knowledge went mainly to others.

The Pakistani's emancipation is twofold. Before the British the rulers of Sind were Baluch; of the West Punjab they were Sikh; of East Bengal Persians and up-country Mussulmans; under the British much of the power went to the largely Hindu middle classes who filled the professions and the clerkships, and did the broking, exporting and money-lending which came with communications and a money economy. Now for the first time it is the local Muslim who holds power; the Bengali Muslim who a generation ago was rarely so much as a clerk, now insists that his half share in the population of the State entitles him also to a half share in the seat of power.

The Burman has freed himself from the Indian and from his own money-lenders far more than from the British. The Karen has been enabled to assert himself against the Burman by revolt or equality unimaginable to that Burmese King of the 1850s who threatened to decapitate any Karen he found reading.[1] It is nearly as new in Indonesia to have leaders who are not Sultans as it is to have Prime Ministers who are not Dutch. Ho Chi Minh's Communism is directed against the great Annamite landlords of Cochin-China quite as much as against the French.

The upsurge of the people has thus been even more against privilege in their own society than against alien rule. While the foreigner has usually given full value, and more than full value, in capital and knowledge, peace and justice, for the profits and the salaries he has taken, their own rich have been parasites without function; exploiters without mercy.

It is therefore a particularly difficult time for new Governments, often not yet certain of themselves, always short of skilled administrators, of capable Ministers, of qualified technicians, of sufficient police. Capital has been destroyed, savings are hard to make, skill is everywhere in short supply. Merely to get back to the position of 1938 will in most places require very great efforts. Of the £55 million which is to be the very partial Governmental contribution to the rehabilitation of Malayan business, £35 million is coming from the Malayan Government. Everywhere in Malaya and Indonesia private business-men have been exhausting their credit in an attempt to rebuild to their pre-war position; the oil companies alone in Indonesia are spending £60 millions.

Yet Governments whose policies need to have a more than Crippsian austerity, who can offer their people only toil and sweat if the future is to be free from blood, are faced with populations whose new interest in politics leads them to expect the millennium now they are free. They have been told so long that all their troubles are due to exploitation. Foreigner, money-lender, landlord, official, all have been cast, separately or in conjunction, as the villains of the piece. Now that the people have the vote, they expect an immediate increase in well-being, the solid well-being of more to eat and more to wear, not just the spiritual satisfaction of feeling themselves every man's equal. Such new-found dignity does not survive an empty stomach and a shivering body. No longer can Asian Governments rely on the age-old apathy, the fatalism which saw in aggres-

[1] J. S. Furnivall, "Twilight in Burma", in *Pacific Affairs*, New York, March 1949.

sion the hand of God, in benevolence an unexpected and personal goodness. In future, governing is going to be harder. Farmer and factory-hand have seen their governments go down in a few weeks before a people still as Asiatic, and once as poor, as themselves. Defeat has prevented the substitution of a Japanese invincibility myth for that of the European; it has not restored the prestige of the old order, everywhere revealed as vulnerable, even in countries like India or Ceylon where it held its own, if only because everywhere in the crisis Governments very properly appealed to their people for support. The people were thus made, as never before, partners in their own salvation. They will not forget of their own free will, and their Governments are too poor, too weak, often too squeamish, to be able to make them forget by force; permanently effective terror requires good communications and an expensive secret police.

This transference of power to the masses is a revolution from which there is no going back, not only because the masses themselves have become conscious of their rights and their power, but because the two great systems which to-day compete for the world's loyalty, the American and the Russian, both emphasize the mass. The Americans are egalitarian as well as democratic; Russian theories of the dictatorship of the proletariat require at least a proportion of worker and peasant support. And in a world which is more and more becoming one, neutrality gets ever more difficult; so also does the preservation of those types of privilege which are hostile to both American and Russian ideas. For the people are always being excited from outside, and a Government which does not want to lose its elections or have its soldiers desert must make wide its base.

This means that the standard of life of the masses must be raised, and that can be done only by Westernization. Neither the Vedas nor Confucius can teach a man how to make two blades of grass grow where one grew before. That can be done only by saving and investment, research and the application of research. The future is with factories and fertilisers, technological institutes and budget surpluses to cover capital expenditure. To that path every model, Britain, Russia, the U.S., points; and the old society no longer has the strength to resist for there is no longer the free land available on which the new generation could find the contentment of their fathers. Peasant agriculture cannot provide the surplus, the guns and the schools, without which any nation feels inferior in the modern world. Even the scholars of non-Western learning have lost their prestige. In Radhakrishnan's own Benares Hindu University only half a dozen students can be found to take Indian philosophy.

Westernisation, therefore, is bound to dominate the next generation, but a far deeper Westernisation than any the West itself could impose. Revolutions, if they are to be truly effective, must always come from inside; men and classes and ideas which to the Westerner are picturesque because they are anachronisms, are to the Asian traitors, stumbling-blocks, sinners against the new light of progress. Outside a limited class, the West had neither the strength to insist upon its ideas nor the manpower to propagandize them. But as wider and wider ranges of Asians themselves learn Western ways, so their influence ripples out through bigger and bigger classes. The returned student, as he grows older, changes his village as no outsider can.

Now, too, Asia has to hurry. If standards are not to be caught in a vicious descending spiral of poverty and population, babies and debt, Western technique must go out into the land on a mission, transforming agriculture and creating industry in a generation or two. Otherwise Asia will subside into the miseries of 1600–calories existence. The peasant has to be changed not only economically by bringing him fully into the money economy, but spiritually. A man who has learnt by his own experience that there are better ways of growing crops than those he learnt from his father soon comes to believe, by a not always accurate analogy, that there may be better ways of worshipping God or governing his country. A man who has found sulphaguanadine a better cure for dysentery than any charm has his whole faith in magic seriously upset. A man who learns to read, and whose son goes to work in a city factory, has brought to bear upon him the full confusion of the realisation that it is possible to live otherwise than he has always done. Such realisations do not always make for happiness, for men are happiest when they can enjoy their pleasures as the reward of their own effort and write off their misfortunes as the wrath of God. To suspect that one's misfortunes may be the result of wrong choices by oneself, one's village, or one's society is very disconcerting. To many indeed it will be no more, creating only that vague and purposeless discontent which so often degenerates into the jealousy and envy which make ears so ready for the agitator. But to some it will be a spur, a reminder that men have been able in the past, and therefore will be able in the future, by their own efforts, to make life easier and more satisfying for themselves, their families, and their neighbours.

The transformation that is coming will thus be profound; but it will also be slow. Technicians take years to train, fertiliser factories years to build, students years to grow to an age when society listens to their words. It will be a generation or two or three before Asia's transformation reaches the stage where it is giving an appreciably better life to the ordinary man—it took certainly 40 years in a Japan which was confining itself to material change and not diverting any energy into a simultaneous spiritual revolution.

The Governments have therefore got to find reforms and measures to satisfy the immediate demands of their people, and to keep them happy until the longer-term programme can show results.

Such reforms are bound to be of a Left-wing cast, for in Asia there are no Conservatives.[1] Some of the classes which in Europe compose the Right are small, like the shopkeepers; others are foreign, like the Chinese or European business man in South-East Asia; others still are tainted with collaboration, like the North Chinese landlord with the Japanese; some, like the Indian princes, are simply dismissed as out-of-date, that most destructive of all political criticisms; some have destroyed their own influence by a refusal to adjust themselves to the facts of the modern world, like the Confucian scholar or the Brahmin priest. So the stage is left free for intellectuals who are on the Left originally because it was on the European Left that they found sympathy and a doctrine, and now increasingly because the official, landlord and professional classes from which come the University students, have no connection with business, and in countries where business is in the hands of a minority community, or of Europeans, or of exclusive families, can only get the jobs, the wealth, and the influence business has to offer through nationalisation. As elsewhere, too, the persons who are the most violently Left-wing are the sons of the most reactionarily Right. The undergraduate who knows that his education is being paid for by the grinding of the faces of his father's tenants, or out of the proceeds of his father's bribes, is better material, in his shame and schizophrenia, for Communist talk of exploitation, than the son of an English or American industrialist, so largely protected by his knowledge of his father's ability and hard work.

The Left, however, as we have discovered in Europe, is far from monolithic. The real division in Asia is between the Liberal-socialist, who finds his inspiration in M. Blum and Mr. Attlee, and the

[1]On the Right are only the reactionary and the discredited.

Communist who looks to Lenin for his doctrine even when he does not also look to Moscow for his orders. This is clear in the Indonesian Republic; it is clear in Burma and India. If the Communist wins, society will be turned upside down. But there will still be changes if he loses.

Japan and China are in an exceptional position. In Japan there will be strong votes cast for the Conversatives out of nostalgia for the old world which SCAP is so determined to destroy. In China the Liberal-socialist has been ground out of existence between the reactionary and the Communist.

Nationalisation of certain enterprises, such as inland navigation in Burma or new steelworks in India or hydro-electricity in Pakistan, are inevitable; even a right wing Government like that of the Republic of (South) Korea, provides in its otherwise very American constitution that mines, marine resources and waterpower shall be owned by the State, foreign trade shall be under the control of the Government, and any enterprises having public character shall be managed by the Government or juridical persons of public law (Arts. 85, 87). Certain social services, like health insurance for Indian factory workers, will be insisted on. Certain taxation changes, to make the rich pay more and the poor less, like the abolition of the salt duty in India or the introduction of income-tax in Malaya, are inevitable.

Much of this is only the small change of Western Liberalism. Certainly little of it will touch the Western business man. He will have to pay more tax, but he will get it back in double income-tax relief at home. He will have to employ more local technicians, but they will cost him less than Westerners. Countries whose need for capital far exceeds their own savings, whose immediate requirements of skill far outrun their own technicians, can now see their need of foreign aid as they never could when there was a foreign government or an unequal treaty to blame for their ills, and free land to provide for their population. By enormous sacrifice and much waste they can manage without. But democratic governments do not find it easy to ask for any but the most obviously necessary sacrifices, for their people tire in time of the promise of "jam tomorrow". They are therefore tempted to make terms with foreign enterprise which will enable foreign savings and skill to supplement their own, and it is probable that they will choose reasonable agreement, protecting their countries from domination by foreign interests, and the foreigner from the fear of confiscation or of being unable to earn or remit profits. To-day in India, Pakistan or Ceylon the foreign investor meets with a real welcome, especially if he brings with him new technical skills and if he shows himself willing to help in building up the management class these countries so badly need; even in Burma the Government has slowly swung round towards co-operation. Everywhere agreement is now possible because the negotiation is now between equals, where both have something to offer. The Asian can offer the opportunity to build up a business; the foreigner his capital, his technique and his connections.

Liberal socialist politics cannot take an anti-foreign form without playing into the hands of the Communists. The East needs capital which can come only by borrowing abroad or through forced savings. Only the Communists are prepared to use the terror and the starvation which alone can produce forced savings. Liberal-socialist governments cannot even attack its own business classes too much without destroying the thrift and enterprise they badly need. The Indian Government can go ahead with death duties, but it has abolished the capital gains tax, and reduced its highest sur-taxes.

Someone must be sacrificed. To some extent the minorities will be the scapegoat. They are often exploiters; they always hold jobs the majority covet; they frequently have little emotional loyalty to the State of which they claim to be citizens. The Chinese in Siam, the Indians in Burma, provide excellent scapegoats. But this is necessarily a limited policy. Some countries, like China, have no minorities to matter; some, like Indonesia, could only take action against their minorities at the expense of depriving themselves of necessary business skill, thus further impoverishing the community.

If the reformers are not to do more damage than good, the scapegoat must be one who is genuinely a parasite. Getting rid of him must immediately increase the individual incomes of many voters without diminishing the income of the nation as a whole.

The obvious candidate is the landlord; his only competitor the money-lender. Over all this area the landlord, though often person-ally a man of charm, culture, and distinction, is economically a bloodsucker. Since he takes half the crop[1] while leaving most of the expenses of cultivation to his tenant, abolishing him would

---

[1]Except where there has already been reform. In India, for instance, the rent the occupancy tenant pays to his zemindar has in most areas long been fixed, and the inflation caused by the war reduced it in general to a relatively small percentage of the crop, one-tenth or even one-twentieth.

increase his tenant's net income three, sometimes four times. The difference between £7 a year and £20 a year is much greater than that between £7 a week and £20 a week. Since, moreover, the landlord normally puts nothing back into the land he can be abolished with no fear of that loss of production which would follow the loss of the English landlord's repairs and advice.

Touching the money-lender is rather more dangerous. Peasant borrowing, particularly for social purposes, is largely a reflection of credit, not of need. If the credit is curtailed, the weddings will be less lavish. But there is a residual element which is of vital economic importance. Agriculture is an industry with a long work-in-progress period, which must be financed. It also has very high risks, and in a peasant society the easiest way of insuring against them is often not to make provision in advance, but to lend seed and maintenance after disaster has occurred. The money-lender's wings can therefore only be clipped if alternative sources of credit are provided to cover these necessary business needs. Indeed, development requires that further capital should be made available to permit of such major improvements as tube wells and better-bred cattle being financed at the banking rates which improvements can hope to earn, and not at the money-lender's rates which they can rarely bring in enough to pay.

To reduce the peasant's credit to his business needs would at the same time both reduce his rate of interest to no more than his improvements can expect to earn and compel the money-lender to invest his surplus capital elsewhere, thus freeing for productive use, in industry or trade or Government loans, money that would otherwise be frittered away on bridal jewellery and wedding parties.

The Governments have already shown their appreciation of the fact that the time they need for reconstruction can be bought only at the money-lender's and the landlord's expense. They have the fate of the one exception, Kuomintang China, as a perpetual grim reminder of what happens to a Government which will not make this sacrifice. So everywhere one finds land reform and credit reform. In North Korea the land of everyone who does not till himself has been confiscated; even those who do work themselves have not been allowed to keep more than 12½ acres. In South Korea the one-sixth of the rice land which belonged to the Japanese has been confiscated and is rented out by the State at a rent reduced to one-third the crop. In Mongolia and Manchuria and China proper, though not yet in Tibet, the Communists have been confiscating the land of Mongol Lamas and princes, Manchurian and Chinese landlords; north of the Yangtze the process is already complete, south of the Yangtze it is supposed to be finished by the end of 1952; in the North the process was easy; many landlords had either collaborated with the Japanese or fled before the Communist advance, and in North China some two-thirds of the land was in peasant hands anyway. In the South it has met with more resistence, and the social revolution involved is greater, for there had been more tenancy, and the Communist policy requires that the rented part of their holdings should be taken away even from the rich peasants. Where land still remains under tenancy rents have been reduced to one-third the crop. In Japan the occupation authorities have enforced a major land reform on the Government. Nobody has been allowed to keep more than $2\frac{1}{2}$ acres if he cultivates himself or anything at all if he does not (Law of Oct. 21, '46). Only 1,500,000 acres remain for various special reasons under tenancy, and for them rents have been reduced to 25% of the crop on rice land, 15% on upland. The compensation paid to the landlord is derisory, 40% of one year's yield at official prices, or at most one twenty-fifth of the land's 1937 value. Altogether some 5 million acres will be sold to tenants, of which about half had already been sold by the end of 1948, and the price is so low that many tenants have been able to buy in one instalment. So disheartened are the landlords, so resigned to their fate, that there has been very little attempt to sabotage the reform.[1] In Burma the Government has passed a Land Nationalisation Act providing for the taking of the land on payment of ten times the land revenue, perhaps a quarter of the value of one year's crop at present prices. In India, Acts are being passed in state after state to limit rents to one-third or one-quarter the crop, to give more and more tenants occupancy rights or at least a minimum tenure of 10 years, to impose agricultural income-tax and buy out the Zemindars, at rates of compensation varying from 14 to 3 years' purchase. As the compensation will be paid partly in cash, partly in bonds bearing interest at $2\frac{1}{2}$%, it is hoped that many Zemindars will be tempted to increase their income by using the money they receive to go into industry, just as the Chinese Communists are encouraging their landlords to do.

[1]Andrew Grad, "Land Reform in Japan", *Pacific Affairs*, New York, June 1948.

Credit reform is more difficult to devise than agrarian reform. It is true that in Japan and Korea runaway inflation has wiped out all old debt; and in India or Indonesia a more limited inflation has greatly reduced its real burden and permitted the peasant to pay off a fair proportion. In Malaya and the Philippines much was paid off in occupation currency at a time when it had become virtually valueless. In Burma, civil disorder and the flight of the Chettyars prevents collection and facilitates the quiet murder of any creditor so tactless as to press. In China the Communists have limited interest to 6% and made the money-lender go to the village council for his recoveries, so that he has every reason to limit his loans to amounts a council of peasants will not consider it unfair for fellow-peasants to have to pay.

Most interesting of all is the Indian and Pakistan legislation, whose main features are the reduction of the peasant's credit, thus removing from him his major temptation, and the checking of money-lender cheating, thus curbing the quickest method of increasing debt. Money-lenders have to take out a licence, which can be taken away from them by executive, not judicial, action for any improper behaviour. They have to give all their clients a regular statement of accounts. Interest cannot mount up to more than the original principal, nor can it be compounded. The minimum land required for the debtor's subsistence cannot be attached, old debts are conciliated, and, in some provinces, the peasant cannot charge more than the succeeding year's crop except to special creditors, normally co-operative societies. It is thus impossible for the peasant to ruin himself for unproductive purposes, since the co-operative society will not lend for such ends, and the money-lender will not lend more than he can immediately recover at harvest.

These are the main reforms with which the Governments are hoping to buy the time in which to bring prosperity into the people's lives, to earn the goodwill to enable them to ask the sacrifices Westernisation is bound to involve.

Always the Kuomintang points the moral for the rest of Asia. A Government which wishes to preserve itself from Communism must rest on the solid base of a contented peasantry,[1] it is the towns,

[1] In the Indian 1952 elections, the Communist successes were greatest in coastal Travancore-Cochin, which has the highest percentage of landless labour in the country, and in Telingana, where tenancy conditions had been particularly bad. There were very few successes amongst industrial labour. The other great Communist success, in the Andhra area of Madras, does not appear to have been primarily the result of economic causes.

not the countryside, which provide the Japanese Communists with their two million votes. The peasantry can only be kept contented if it is enabled to own its own land, to earn enough to live on and to remain free from hag-riding by debt. Therefore Asian Governments have to pursue a radical policy against landlord and money-lender; they have to make sure that the terms of trade between town and countryside are weighted in favour of the countryside; especially they have to make sure that the towns pay all, and more than all, their fair share of taxation. But since such a policy produces only temporary contentment, and, since, with an increasing population, it is necessary also to produce wealth, the Governments will have either to treat with gentle consideration the capitalists, native or foreign, who alone can provide the necessary resources, technicians, and know-how, or to squeeze the necessary resources out of their people by force and terror, since savings are not made willingly by those already down to subsistence or near it, and modernisation without know-how involves all the wastes of learning from one's own errors. The one way is the liberal, the other the Communist. There is no third. Each country must choose in its turn, as China has already chosen the Communist, India the liberal.

Chapter XXII

INDIAN FORECAST

Throughout Asia, with the one exception of Ceylon, the years since 1939 have been years of economic decline. The population has increased and production has not increased to keep pace with it; this has gone to the point where even West Pakistan on occasions imports food and Indonesia has trouble sometimes with its balance of payments. In India the population has been growing at the rate of 1.3% per year, agricultural production has remained roughly stationary and, though there has been an increase in industrial production of perhaps 30%, this is not enough, for industry is still a relatively small sector of the economy. The decline in real income during the past twenty years may be as high as 10%.[1]

The most popular Asian answer to economic difficulties is planning. Every Asian nation either has a plan or intends to have a plan. The Chinese will execute their plan in the usual Communist way. The Colombo Plan represents an attempt to put together the needs and intentions of the non-Communist countries of the area. Of these non-Communist countries, however, only India, Pakistan and Ceylon have so far produced plans on which it is possible really to work, and only India's plan as yet is a complete working document on which economic development can really be based in detail; and even the Indian plan is primarily a set of priorities for Government and Government-sponsored projects, and gives inadequate attention to, and inadequate scope for, the private sector.

Since the Indian plan is the most complete, and since India is the most important country in the area, upon whose success or failure mainly depends the future of democratic planning in Asia, we will confine ourselves to a study of future possibilities in India.

The plan itself assumes an expenditure of £1,800 million in six

[1]The United Nations' *Economic Survey of Asia and the Far East* has put it higher still, at 15.7% between 1931 and 1948–49, but 1948–49 was a particularly bad year agriculturally and this figure therefore probably overstates the case. (Ref. *Economic Survey of Asia and the Far East*, page 113, Table 9.)

years, of which the planners hope that £225 million will come from abroad, in addition to the sterling releases of £35 million a year which have already been promised. With this amount the plan hopes to be able to increase the national income by 10%, in other words, by rather more than is required to meet the increase in population. That would be quite enough to keep the Indian people satisfied. The freedom and democracy of one-sixth of the world requires an investment over six years which is less than that which Great Britain makes every year, and less than twice as large annually as the savings of Holland. The foreign aid required is only a fraction of that which has been given to England or France or Germany.

Nevertheless, carrying out the plan will be a great strain on India. India's savings have always been low, and they are now lower still. At 1949 prices they were in 1939 perhaps £450 million. In 1941–42, under the stress of war, they rose to perhaps £840 million—one-fifth of the national income—but by 1948–49 they had dropped to £150 million, of which half was undistributed business profits, and about £30 million small savings through such institutions as the Post Office Savings Banks. Since 1948–49 they have been rising again, and it might be reasonable to hope for an average of £200–250 million through the period of the plan. The easing of inflation is tempting the middle-class to save more, and the habit of re-investing profits has now become firmly fixed. The difference from before the war is that the rich, who once provided perhaps half the total savings, are now so hard hit by taxation that they provide relatively little.

At £200 million India's savings are less than one-thirtieth of the national income. By comparison, Russia during the five-year plan invested one-quarter of its national income, Japan in the 1930s, one-eighth (Table 51). India's savings are clearly not enough; they must be increased if India is not to slide into a Communism which will enforce savings by terror—a terror which seizes as ruthlessly the gold nose-stud from the peasant as it does the diamond from the Maharaja, and converts both into foreign exchange.

Some increase in voluntary savings will result if the feeling spreads that currency is now stable and that any change in the future will be in the direction of deflation, not inflation. Some increase might also result from the raising of the rate of interest, but even if both should happen together, the extra savings are not likely to be very much, perhaps of the order of £50 million a year. A large increase in the amount available for investment in India can come only from two sources—the revenue surpluses of the State, and capital from outside.

Private capital from outside is not likely to be large in quantity, though there are some individual large-scale projects, like the new oil refineries which are scheduled to have between them a capacity of over 3,000,000 tons per annum. Private investment, however, has an importance out of all proportion to its size, since it brings with it technical, marketing and managerial skills which help to change the whole economic attitude of the society, and for effective economic development attitudes are very nearly as important as money.

Foreign governmental aid will probably be on a very considerably larger scale. The sterling balance releases are, of course, only a repayment to India of money she is already owed, though the effort Great Britain is making in repaying at this time is deeply appreciated. But under the Colombo Plan there are also contributions from Canada, Australia and New Zealand which will approach £10 million per year, and there are signs that America has at last begun to realise that no form of aid either does more good or pays a higher cold war dividend than aid to India. In 1951 the American Government made a loan of $190 million in wheat and a grant of $50 million. In 1952 the Indian Government is likely to obtain a grant of $90 million, and it is possible that in future years grants might be higher. There is therefore every hope that the quite limited amounts of foreign aid required will, in fact, be forthcoming.

India does not, however, wish to be dependent for its progress upon the charity and neighbourliness of others. It is determined to do its best for itself. There has been a steady push up of taxation until it has reached very nearly the maximum which so poor an economy can bear, and probably is in real terms some 1½ times as heavy as it was in the 1930s. In obtaining this revenue, indeed, India's Governments have shown great political courage. Sales taxes, which bear hardly on those sections of the population which have already been hit by inflation, have been steadily raised; food subsidies have been almost abolished; income tax and corporation tax are little lower than in Great Britain; agricultural income taxes have been generally introduced; stiff excises have been placed on such articles of everyday consumption as cooking-fat and matches; and even the land revenue is likely to be raised in some States in the near future.

Only Pakistan in Asia, and very few countries in Europe, have shown comparable fiscal courage, and there is now very little room left for further increase. The Salt Tax might be restored, food subsidies might be completely abolished and Prohibition might be dropped, but that is all, and there are severe political difficulties in the way of any of these courses. The abolition of the Salt Tax is a heritage from Mahatma Gandhi; a final abolition of the food subsidies might mean severe agitation in the large cities; the Chief Ministers of Bombay and Madras are deeply committed to Prohibition. It would be optimistic, therefore, to assume that more than £20–30 million more could be raised in taxation, or that the total capital formation out of revenue could exceed £100 million a year over the next five years, though since this is necessarily a residual figure it could in particular circumstances be either considerably more or considerably less. Thus, in 1951–52, when export prices and therefore duties were high, the Central Finance Minister had a surplus of nearly £70 million; in 1952–53, with a drop in export prices and therefore a great reduction in export duties, there is unlikely to be a Central surplus at all.

There is, moreover, very little scope for economy. Even a settlement of the disputes with Pakistan—a settlement which is not likely to occur until the passions of 1947, already cooling, have finally died down—would probably not reduce the cost of the defence forces by more than a few million. China and Russia are sufficiently uncomfortable neighbours for India to require defence forces able to hold off at least a first attack. The only real hope of economy is the savings that will result when rehabilitation of refugees from Pakistan is completed, perhaps by 1954–55.

Finding the money for the Plan is therefore going to be a strain, but it is probable that it can just be done. Certainly nothing less than the Plan will suffice to keep the Indian people contented.

The Plan itself not only contains an introduction which is one of the best defences ever written of planning by persuasion as against planning by terror, but it also provides some very definite targets. The division of expenditure over the main heads is as follows:

	Cost (in million Rs.)	Percentage of total
Agriculture	3,984.1	17.1
Multi-purpose Projects (irrigation, power, etc.)	2,284.1	9.8
Transport and Communications	6,515.4	27.9
Fuel and Power	1,443.4	6.2
Mining and Industry	1,239.9	5.3
Social Capital and Miscellaneous	4,269.8	18.3
Unallocated yet	3,600.0	15.4
	23,336.7	100.0

There is expected to result an increase in food production of 7 million tons, in oilseeds production of 1¼ million tons,[1] in electricity production of 1.935 million K.W.

On the industrial side, for many Indian industries the Commission has thought rather in terms of working up to the full use of existing capacity than of expansion. This is probably a mistake, since it would be sometimes easier for industry than for Government to raise money. The simpler forms of industrial development often require less outside technical assistance, and the increase in the national income for any given amount of capital investment is probably larger in light industry than in any other sector of the economy. A rupee spent on expanding capacity for the production of soap will give an increase in national income perhaps half as large again as a rupee spent on multi-purpose schemes.

Otherwise the Commission appears to have chosen its priorities rightly. Transport must come first, for nothing has delayed Indian development so much in the last few years as the perpetual difficulty over obtaining waggons. Ever since Independence the Government has made rehabilitation of the railways its first care, and the results are now beginning to show in an easing of the whole flow of the country's economic life. The next priority must be agriculture, because India is at present in the impossible position of a country, most of whose population are dependent on agriculture and yet whose balance of payments is perpetually strained by the need to import food, cotton and jute. Moreover greater results can be obtained in output and employment and in the satisfaction of the people in agriculture than anywhere else.

The Planning Commission has placed its trust very largely in multi-purpose schemes. This was probably inevitable. Many of these schemes were started before the Commission began its work, and since they can only be undertaken by Government, the Plan, which is largely a determination of priorities for capital expenditure by Government, tends naturally to begin with them.

Many of the measures which require to be taken, however, need either no capital at all or very little. Ten per cent of the crop is lost in store from pests, another ten per cent in the field from weeds. The use of the pesticides and weed-killers which have been developed in the last decade or so to reduce these losses would require no investment that would not be repaid within a year. Javanese sugar

[1]This is not the Planning Commission's figure but that of the Indian Central Oilseeds Committee.

yields were raised from 15 tons an acre in 1880, the same as in India to-day, to 56 tons an acre in the late 1930s; this was by good research and the prompt application to the estates of the best seeds and the best methods; and the whole capital cost, including all the research, was only a few millions. The Coimbatore research station has already shown in a small way that the same results could be achieved in India. The spread of American types of cotton in the Punjab and Sind is as notable an example of agricultural improvement as any to be found in the world; they were first introduced only in 1910, and to-day they provide three-quarters of the Pakistan crop, fetching a price per bale three times as high as that of the old native, short staple varieties. There is no reason why American hybrid maize should not increase yields by 80% in India as it has done in Italy, or why a rust-free variety of wheat should not be found in India as it has been elsewhere, thus preventing losses that can reach a million tons in a bad year.

India's cattle offer as much scope for improvement as her crops. Her cows produce on the average 300 lbs. a lactation, as compared with 30 times as much in England. In the East Punjab the average is twelve times better than in the rest of India. It is calculated that India has only 30,000 good breeding bulls. But artificial insemination should now make it possible to utilise effectively even this small number and from them to effect a rapid improvement in the quality of cattle. Certainly whatever can be produced will be needed; India requires 4 times as much milk as she is getting.

Equally needed is a doubling of vegetable production and an increase of 50% in fruit production. Both represent a much more intense use of the land than cereals; tomatoes or oranges will usually fetch eight or ten times as much an acre as wheat and the capital investment involved is not high; for vegetables all that is needed is a well, for fruit a well and the capacity to wait until the trees come into bearing.

Most important of all improvements is fertiliser.[1] In India the use of fertiliser would result in even larger increases of crop than in Japan, since the superstition against the use of nightsoil and the absence over wide areas of any alternative to dung cake as a fuel has for centuries starved the soil of nitrogen. Before the war fertiliser was often too expensive to use, but to-day sulphate of

[1] Roughly evenly divided between nitrogenous, phosphatic and potassic fertilisers. How quickly consumption can increase is shown by the fact that Japan had used only half as much in the early 20s.

ammonia, costing perhaps £30 a ton in the village,[1] can produce three times its cost in extra crops, and there is no difficulty in selling every ton which can be got. India is able to obtain imports only of some 180,000 tons a year, and her local production, primarily from Sindri, ought to reach about 400,000 tons per annum by 1953. Sindri will, however, be followed by other factories, and imports will doubtless increase as supplies ease, for nothing else can offer India so rapid an increase in wealth as a larger use of fertiliser.

On many crops, notably rice, very little effective research has so far been done; and many of India's requirements for agricultural improvement are simply not available. This is especially true of fertiliser. A good agricultural extension service moreover takes years to organise and train, and even more years to get the peasant's full confidence.

The government appreciates the importance of all these measures and particularly of a good agriculture extension service; this is shown by the emphasis which is being placed on the new idea of Community Projects, an idea partly American in inspiration. Selected areas are being taken and on them development propaganda is being concentrated. Many more social workers are being put into villages than have ever been sent there before, and instead of each worker being engaged in only one department of husbandry, public health, or whatever it may be, each worker will be given a training in the elements of all those sciences, a combination of which is required to raise the villager's production. The first experiment at Etawah has shown that quite considerable results can be attained, e.g. the increase there in wheat production has been 25% in three years. In Sholapur, too, an inspired Collector has demonstrated how much the villager is willing to do for himself if he is only given proper leadership. The present plan is to spread these Community Projects until they cover at least one-third of the population. The money required is relatively limited. The men may be more difficult to find. But if in 10 or 15 years this programme can be achieved at a cost of, say, £150 million a year at its maximum, then the whole economic picture in India would be transformed, and India might at least have been set on the way of the beneficent spiral of better living standards, lower birth rates and slower increases in population, which has provided the West with its prosperity over the last half century.

The greatest need of the Indian countryside is, however, water, and the Plan has placed its greatest emphasis on irrigation. Thirty-

[1]Landed cost £20 per ton for English; a little more for American.

five million acres already get part or all of their water supply arti-
ficially, and the new multi-purpose schemes will add 16.5 million
acres to that. In addition, another 7 or 8 million acres may be added
by the wells the farmer digs himself, the wells the Government lends
him the money to dig, and the tube wells which the Governments
intend to dig for themselves.

Except in a few remote areas, India has very little land available to
be brought under cultivation by the traditional peasant techniques.
But there are very considerable stretches which are not amenable to
the peasant's feeble implements, but which might be more tractable
to modern methods. In the Terai, for instance, millions of acres have
been kept under jungle by the heavy incidence of malaria. In
Bundelkhand hundreds of thousands of acres are infested by
the deep-rooted weed, Kans. For such conditions, D.D.T. and
tractors now offer a remedy, and the Government's plans provide
for the reclamation of 6 million acres in 7 years at the cost of some
£100 million.

How much of the agricultural plans will be successful, it is difficult
to say. A great deal will depend on the extent to which Government
realises that neither research nor capital investment are enough by
themselves. A marketing job has to be done in the countryside—a
job of explaining to the peasant not merely that the new ways are
better, but that they will give him personally an assured profit. There
is room here for Government to make more use of the services of
private industry than it has hitherto shown itself willing to do.
Provided this marketing job is done, however, there seems no
reason why the Planning Commission's standards should not be
achieved. Table 53 shows how great an increase in production can be
brought about, even in so conservative a society as 19th-century
peasant France, by the adoption of new methods.

However great an emphasis is placed on agriculture, India must
industrialise too, because of the quick increase in the national
income which comes from properly planned industrialisation,
because of the extra employment opportunities it offers and
because, above all, India's coal and iron-ore, existing ports and
communications and ample reserve of labour make it a country
where industrialisation could be both quicker and very much more
profitable than in any other part of the unindustrialised world.

No doubt an improvement of agriculture and the extension of industry are not conflicting but complementary objectives. Industry
will provide agriculture with the workers to eat its food and the

factories to consume its raw materials. It will find in agriculture its own best markets for cloth and implements, soap and films.

India is not starting from scratch. Her industry has already reached approximately the same stage as Japan's in 1925 (see Table 54). As in Japan, development will be dependent on Government planning. Government is already undertaking a high proportion of the total enterprise of the country. Through its import licensing, coal and steel and cement allocations, and its permits for new factory-building, Government has absolute control over the fields of development still left open to private enterprise.

Japanese experience offers many hints as to the future of India. But it is not a complete guide, because all Japanese development was made with one eye on war. To every Japanese Government the object of industrialisation was power, and wealth only in so far as it meant power. There was in Japan, particularly in the 1930s, a concentration of interest on strategic industries comparable to that in Germany on the gun-making of the Ruhr. On the other hand, India's tradition is deeply pacific and, so long as she remains a member of the Commonwealth or in close association with it, she will have sufficient assurance of friends in need not to have to build up her economy for war. She will not need to make the desperate sacrifice of Russia under the first two Five-year Plans (see Table 55 for the Russian concentration on heavy industry and neglect of consumer-goods industries). Moreover because of lack of capital, India will have to concentrate on the less expensive light industries. The poverty of India, which can be measured by the fact that in some provinces the consumption of cloth is only 8 or 9 yards a year, has produced a veritable hunger for the goods which light industry produces.

The first priority in industrial development must, however, go to breaking the bottlenecks which have been strangling the Indian economy ever since 1942. Something has already been done. There is at last sufficient coal production, though not always sufficient waggons to move it. The congestion on the railways has greatly eased, and the present programme is large enough substantially to cure it by 1955 or 1956. There remain steel and urban housing. India could use perhaps one million tons more steel a year than it produces, and India was created by Nature to be a steel producer. It has coking coal, the sea, the engineering industry, and some of the world's largest reserves of high-grade iron ore, nearer together than almost anywhere else in the world. An extension of steel capacity would at one and the same time ease the foreign exchange position—India has imported 300,000 tons a year when she could get it—permit the further development of the engineering industry, whose operations lack of steel has sometimes kept down as low as 25% of capacity, and prevent the delays which at present occur in railway rehabilitation. The capacity of the two existing steel works is to be extended by some half-million tons, and Tatas are installing a tube mill and a new strip mill. But more is needed. A new steel plant near the Hirakud, for instance, a dollar-saving expansion of tinplate production, the extra capacity for pig iron of which the Government has been talking, are all urgent requirements.

The need for more urban housing is equally crying. It has been calculated that Calcutta has only $\frac{1}{2}$ sq. ft. of accommodation per person, and in all the big towns many thousands live 10 or 15 to a room, or simply on the pavements. This is not only socially disastrous. It also means that the worker has an environment so wretched that it is often impossible for him to do a day's work. Nobody can work properly who never gets a proper night's sleep, and whose family has to be left at home in the village. If industry is to progress, a contented and stable labour force must be built up; and for that nothing is more essential than adequate housing.

Next after this class of high-priority industries come those whose production saves large amounts of imports. The Indian balance of payments position is difficult, and it is worth developing import-saving industries even at some cost. One example is bicycles, where Raleighs and Tube Investments have both entered into partnership with Indian capital to manufacture in India, and there is also a third, purely Indian-owned, unit capable of producing 150,000 cycles a year. There are many other examples, the recent opening of two rayon plants, for instance, or the development of Indian production of diesel engines and transformers, or the Government telephone and cable and machine plants which should be completed in 1953 or 1954. A few sample figures will show how Indian production has already grown in industries of the type since the war:

		Monthly average 1946	Monthly average Jan.–April 1952
Diesel Engines	Nos.	39.4	663[1]
Bicycles.. ..	Nos.	422	9,488
Transformers ..	K.V.A.	3,250	17,025
Sulphuric Acid	Tons	3,400	7,073

[1]For the month of January 1952.

Beyond these high priority industries, with which ought perhaps to be included the small expansion in shipbuilding to which the Government of India is committed, it does not perhaps matter very much which way the capital which may be available for industrial development is spent. The best method would be to leave it to the decision of the individual entrepreneur. The things he finds most profitable are usually also the things where present supply least meets present demand; and it is for the consumer, not the State, to decide whether he would rather spend his money on hair oil or cloth or chocolate. Once the right to decide is given to the planners, they always produce a world with too many semi-necessities and too few minor luxuries.

No industrial development is possible without corresponding development of the ancillary services. The new industries have to have power to run them, roads and railways and ships by which to distribute their products. The electricity has been mainly provided for, partly by the multi-purpose projects, partly by the large thermal expansion (250,000 K.W.) which is to take place in Calcutta; but the power cut which had to be enforced in Bombay in 1951–52, largely because Government neither provided the electricity themselves nor permitted the supply companies to do so, is an excellent example of the danger of planning for the future without due thought for the present. The Hirakud and the Bhakra will provide Orissa and the Punjab with more electricity than they can use. The Koyna, required for Bombay's existing demand, was not included in the Plan at all. So with roads; Government has shown a surprising failure to appreciate how impossible it is either to develop a mass market or increase the production of such more valuable agricultural products as milk and vegetables, so long as village roads are as appalling as they are at present. There are few ways of spending money in India which would give as large an indirect return as road building.

Education and health will have the next claims. The public has now begun to demand them for their own sake and as symbols of India's equality in the world. Also, unless there is literacy, and unless malaria and dysentery are controlled, any great increase in India's production will be infinitely more difficult. Factory workers must be able to read standing orders, peasants must be able to understand the accounts of co-operative societies or instructions on how to use nitrogenous fertiliser. Whole areas like the Terai cannot now be brought under cultivation because the malaria incidence is too high. Land which is cultivated cannot be worked with the care and regularity needed for high yields because the farmer is too often sick.

In the past, the peasant has often not been enthusiastic for literacy. Book learning made his son want to be a clerk in the town. He has not been much interested in Western medicine which seemed less effective against dysentery than his own village remedies. In the last generation all this has changed. The peasant is clamouring for schools for he has at last realised that without education he cannot stand on his own feet in front of the great ones of his world—the village accountant, the money-lender.[1] Sulphaguanadine and penicillin, paludrine and streptomycin are beginning to give him the faith in the Western physician that he has always had in Western vaccination and surgery.

In planning a programme for education and health, the chief emphasis must be on serving the peasant direct. There must be more primary schools and technical schools. There must be more village G.P.s and rural dispensaries. The building of hospitals and colleges can be postponed, not because they are unnecessary, but because the benefits they provide are comparatively low in relation to the capital they demand. In 1938–9, some £20 million was spent on education, and about 40% of the children of school-going age were at school. Universal primary education at to-day's more than tripled prices would probably cost about £60 million above present expenditure,[2] to which must be added about another £10 million for technical education. Village G.P.'s would be definitely cheap. If they were given a subsidy of £2 per week and allowed to charge fees—the peasant at present pays his traditional herbal doctor or homeopath, dai or magician—one could have a doctor for every 5,000 people for £5 million a year; a midwife to every 10,000 might cost another £2 million. If new dispensaries and medical colleges are built and there is research into the main diseases, the amount spent might be doubled. Staff shortages are so severe that nothing like the whole of the education and health programme here sketched is possible in less than 10 years.

Table 56 shows the very great advantages which have already accrued to British exports from Indian industrialisation. It suggests how much greater advantages might result from its extension.

[1]Personal experience—The little girl who knew $2 \times 12 = 24$, when her father the Bhil headman thought it was 36, was an advertisement for education for a dozen miles around.

[2]Including £5 million or so for teachers and training, and building new schools, neither of which need be expensive under Indian conditions.

The pattern of Indian capital expenditure that has here been suggested is both crude and uncertain. The savings may have been wrongly estimated; the Government may not find it feasible to tax for a large surplus on revenue account; nationalism may demand such expensive luxuries as aeroplane factories (the Hawker-Siddeley capital block is £11¼ million), or atomic energy research; the serious minded may resent the apparent frivolity of devoting resources to these lighter consumer goods, of which lipstick is so excellent an example, where the increase in output is so particularly high in relation to the capital required.

Whatever the pattern, investment and a raising of the standard of life there must be. If it proves to be impossible the democratic way, India will try the Communist way. It is for the West to give the help which is needed for a great democratic victory.

TABLE 51

% of national income going into investment*	
The U.S. in the 1920s	15
Russia in the 1930s	25
England under Cripps	20
Holland (1949)	8*
India (1939–45)	11

*Total planned investment is 14%, but of that two-fifths will come from abroad.

TABLE 52
INDIAN PRODUCTION OF CEMENT

Year	Amount (in thousands of metric tons)
1914	1
1934	767
1942	2,220
1946	2,053

TABLE 53
INCREASE IN PRODUCTION IN FRENCH AGRICULTURE
IN THE SECOND HALF OF THE 19TH CENTURY

(a)	Yield of grain	1842 – 12 .. 1900 – 17	
	(in hectolitres per hectare)		
(b)	Number of horse hoes in use	1862 – 26,000 .. 1892 – 250,000	
(c)	Total value of agricultural		
	production	1850 – 5 milliard francs	
		1900 – 12 „ „	

N.B.—The rural population decreased by one-seventh between 1850 and 1900.

TABLE 54

COMPARISON OF JAPANESE PRODUCTION IN 1925
WITH THAT OF INDIA IN 1948

		Japanese in 1925	Indian in 1948
Finished steel	..	1,043,000 tons	854,000 tons
Coal ..	..	31,500,000 M. tons	30,271,000 M. tons
Textiles ..	..	1,000 million lbs. of yarn	1,442 million lbs. of yarn
Sulphuric acid	..	594,100 M. tons	81,500 M. tons
Soda ash ..	..	23,100 M. tons (1927)	28,700 M. tons

TABLE 55

RUSSIAN PRODUCTION

	1913	1938
Engineering (in milliard roubles of 1926–7 value)	1,446	33,613
Cotton textiles (million metres)	2,227	3,491
Rolled steel (million tons)	$3\frac{1}{2}$	$13\frac{1}{8}$
Wollen textiles (million metres)	95	114

Source: A. Baykov, *The Development of the Soviet Economic System*, Cambridge, 1946, p. 307.

TABLE 56

A. Examples of increases in British exports of machinery to India (including for 1948 Pakistan)

	1938	1948
	(in thousands of pounds)	
Generators and motors..	499	2,542
Other electrical machinery	628	2,663
Machine tools	261	2,402
Printing machinery	124	845
Refrigerating machinery	11	217
Sugar-making machinery	160	835
Textile machinery	2,673	9,140

B. Other main British exports to India and Pakistan, 1948

In thousands
of Pounds

Iron and Steel	5,176
Non-ferrous metals etc.	4,444
Woollen and worsted yarn	4,390
Cutlery, hardware	2,797
Paper, etc.	1,975
Pottery, glass etc.	1656,
Chemicals, drugs, dyes and colours	10,995
Vehicles	14,750
Electrical goods and apparatus	7,324
Internal combustion engines	2,338
Boilers	2,120

C. Main British imports from India and Pakistan, 1948.

In millions
of Pounds

Tobacco	2.9
Wool	2.7
Coir	1.7
Woollen and worsteds	1.6
Hides and skins	1.4
Seeds and nuts	9.8
Jute manufactures	15.7
Raw jute	8.9
Cotton	5.0

N.B.—(a) Imports of hides and skins from India and Pakistan were 4% of
          total British imports, from the Argentine 18%.
     (b) Imports of seeds and nuts from India and Pakistan were 7% of
          total, from the Argentine 9%.
     (c) Imports of tobacco from India and Pakistan were 7% of the
          total, from the U.S. 58%.
     (d) Imports of cotton from India and Pakistan were 5% of the
          total, from the U.S. 17%, from Brazil 11%, from Peru 4%.

Chapter XXIII

DEFENCE

In the century up to 1945 only four facts were of importance militarily in Asia.

The first was British power, which made the whole area from Hong Kong to Aden a British preserve, to which the British Navy and the Indian Army gave protection for 100 years. In all this time the only invasion which India itself had to suffer was the penetration of the Japanese into Imphal in 1942. Within the area lay also the Dutch possessions in Indonesia and the French colony of Indo-China, but France and Holland kept only small armies and smaller navies in Asia. They trusted the defence of their Asian possessions to their good relations with Britain in Europe.

The second was the weakness of China. Throughout this period China lay helpless, unable to resist any demand made upon it except by evasion, and protected from dismemberment only by the incapacity of the great powers to agree amongst themselves on who should get what.

The third was the growing power of Japan. At the time of the Meiji Restoration Japan was as weak as Burma or Thailand, but with every year that passed became more of a great power. Its rise to eminence was marked by a series of victories; over China in 1895, over Russia in 1905, over the Germans in Shantung in 1915 and over the Chinese again in the years after 1931. Japan's apogee was reached when it felt itself able to challenge the great Empires and to attack the Navy of the United States at Pearl Harbour.

The fourth was the sprawl of Russia across the North, a sprawl which spread steadily as Russia followed unremittingly what Lord Derby called its policy of "gradual aggression".

Until Pearl Harbour the system was nicely balanced. Great Britain and Russia used Persia and Afghanistan as a buffer between them. Japan had shown itself strong enough in 1905 to push Russia out of Korea and Manchuria, but not strong enough in 1922 to push Russia out of Siberia. China for many years was protected by the disagreements of its would-be conquerors. The Japanese action in Man-churia in 1931 was the beginning of that upsetting of the balance which has now become so irretrievable.

By 1950, after twenty years of war and disturbance, the picture had changed completely. British power, except for a few outposts, had gone. The Indian army was partitioned and neutral. Japan was just beginning to recover from a terrible defeat. China, after forty years of civil war, had been united by a party, the Communist party, whose first objective was to make a great power of her once again. Russia, by the steady development of its Asian provinces, by its an-nexation of South Sakhalin and the Kuriles, and by the privileges in Manchuria acquired at Yalta, had become a power in East Asia in a way it had never been before.

The defeat of Japan and the withdrawal of Great Britain have left vacuums. The conflict, which is at present going on over so much of Asia, has to decide who is to fill those vacuums.

It is gradually becoming clear who will fill the Japanese vacuum. The treaty restoring independence to Japan gives to the United States extensive rights to hold bases and station troops in Japan. It would be quite impossible for the United States to assert these rights for long against the will of the Japanese people. There are many ways in which a hostile Government can make bases untenable for a power that is unwilling to use force on a large scale in order to keep them. But the chances are that the Japanese, however much they may on occasions grumble, will in fact welcome these American forces as an assurance against attack by Russia or China, neigh-bours which once Japan was able to defeat, but both of which are rapidly becoming more powerful than Japan is ever again likely to be.

In addition the Americans have kept their base on Okinawa; they have provided by treaty for bases in the Philippines; and have the advantage of the existence of the Chinese Nationalists in Formosa. America is therefore now a power in the Western Pacific and on the eastern fringes of Asia in a way no Western power has ever been before. The control of the seas in this area—the inheritance of the Japanese Navy—has fallen to America.

The inheritance of the Japanese Army has equally clearly gone to China. The Korean war has proved that, with Russian equipment and what they can produce themselves in their Manchurian arsenals, the Chinese are now a formidable power in their own vicinity; and with the lesson of Russian experience before them, it is to be expected that they will devote as large a percentage of their savings as they possibly can to building up their heavy industry and thus their military potential. The factories left behind by the Japanese in Manchuria, and particularly the coal and steel and machinery production which the Japanese created in the Mukden area, have given them a good base from which to start. A China not rent by civil war was bound to carry weight by the sheer mass of its size and numbers. When to that is added a police state and the Communist capacity for giving large sections of the people the feeling that they have some share in decisions, there is obviously a very considerable power in the making.

What is perhaps less obvious is that in the immediate future there are very severe limitations upon the exercise of that power. China has no control over the sea around its coasts and is dependent on Russia for its air force. Its power is therefore fundamentally a land power, exercisable only across land frontiers; and China does not have many land frontiers which affect the non-Communist world. From the Pacific to the Pamirs its main frontier is with Russia, and both parties are going to make every attempt to see that no cause for dispute arises between them. On the one hand, Russia appears to have left Asia to China as her sphere, and on the other, there is no sign that the Chinese Communists have any intention of challenging the traditional leadership of the Russian Communist party in world Communism. The border that matters, therefore, is China's southern border from the Pamirs round to Formosa; and, in addition, there is the special case of Korea.

A large part of China's southern border, some 2,000 miles of it, marches with India. This fact has already resulted in India's declaring that its defence lies on the Himalayas on the other side of Nepal, and in her administering and developing much more intensively than ever in the past the tribal areas on the Assam-Tibet borders. India raised no objection to the Chinese occupation of Tibet, since it was considered that in their claims in Tibet the Chinese had a perfectly good legal case, but India will certainly resist any penetration southward, or any attempt by China to assert, for example, Tibet's shadowy rights in Bhutan. Otherwise, despite the length of the common border, it is not really very important. The country through which it passes is amongst the most difficult in the world, and it would be quite impossible to launch a full-scale invasion through it, while India would have no difficulty in dealing with any small-scale attack. There is much romance attached to the Tibetan passes and the plateau round Lake Mansarowar; but their military importance is not at present great.

China's main opportunities for southward expansion lie elsewhere. Its assistance to the Viet Minh has given it increasing influence in the Annamite areas of Indo-China, and, were the French ever to despair of this exhausting war, China's control might spread from Indo-China into Thailand, and Chinese assistance would make the already difficult British task in Malaya impossible. Burma, like India, is protected from full-scale attack by geography, but Burma's capacity to deal with even a small attack is not great, and she might be very vulnerable to assistance given to her Communist rebels.

Indonesia is protected by the sea, but otherwise over the whole south-eastern Asian area occupied by Japan at the height of her success China has inherited Japan's position as the major threat. This fact is very much more important than the position in Korea, where the Chinese and the Americans are likely to continue in a stalemate at what is the natural meeting point between the Chinese centre in Manchuria and the American base in Japan.

South-east Asia's own capacity to defend itself is limited, though this is less important than it might be for two reasons: firstly, the French in Indo-China are acting as its frontier guards, though they would probably do so more effectively if they were prepared to take more risks with Viet-Namese independence. Secondly, the Communist technique is not normally direct invasion; Korea was a very special case. They prefer to assist local Communist parties in revolt. So long, therefore, as the Indonesian or the Thai Governments are stable enough to make such revolt impossible, the risk is very much reduced.

Nevertheless, if China is not to dominate the area by the mere force of the feeling that it is the big neighbour with whom it is wisest to be on good terms, there must be some alternative source of strength to which to turn.

This source of strength can no longer be Great Britain, for Great Britain's forces are increasingly tied up in Europe, though Britain's bases in Singapore and Hong Kong will always be of assistance to any alternative champion that may be found. Nor can it be France, for France is fully occupied in Indo-China, and France, too, is unlikely to be permanently willing to divert her forces to an area of so little strategic importance to herself. Moreover, since the major countries of the area are not only independent but jealous of their

s

independence, American troops and bases are not the answer, even if the Americans were willing to extend themselves thus far. The existence of America as a power in Japan and the Philippines is a valuable reassurance, but that is all. The sentinel of this area must continue to be, as it has been for 100 years past, the governments of the Indian Sub-continent.

The role of the Sub-continent has, however, now changed its form. The Indian army, which once kept the peace from Persia to China, has been partitioned, and the two parts into which it has been split are not on the best of terms. Nor can either of the two new States afford an air force of any size. India and Pakistan cannot, therefore, in the immediate future expect to be military powers, in the way in which Russian aid is helping China to become a military power.

Even if they could, it is unlikely that this power would be placed unreservedly at the disposal of the Atlantic alliance. The foreign policy of both countries rests, if not exactly on neutrality, at least on non-belligerence. They cannot be neutral in the ideological war, for both of them are free and democratic, but they are passionately opposed to involvement in physical war, and they are by no means always convinced that on every issue the right lies with the West. Mr. Nehru did not like the United Nations' advance on the Yalu. Pakistan's sympathies are with Egypt and Iran against Britain, with the Tunisian and Moroccan nationalists against France.

It is not, however, necessary for the defence of the area that India and Pakistan should be prepared to fight for the cause of democracy in general. It is only necessary that they should be prepared to defend themselves against external attack and internal revolt. Of their willingness to do these there can be no doubt. The two countries spend as much as they can afford upon their armed forces, and take a great pride in keeping their armies, within the limits of their equipment, among the world's most effective. Of their will to suppress Communist violence, evidence has been provided by the Pakistani arrest of their Chief of Staff, and by the Indian suppression of the revolt in Telingana.

The risk does not lie in any lack of will by the present Governments. It lies in the possibility that for lack of adequate Western aid the efforts the two Governments are making to provide for their increase in population, and to give some hope of a better future to their poverty-stricken people, may not succeed. The people of the Indian Sub-continent are patient and they do not ask for much. If the standard of living goes up by even 1% per year they will be happy; but if it falls, as it could, the days of the present Governments will be numbered. If the West desires to see a stable area created in South Asia, where freedom and democracy will show themselves sufficiently successful to act as a counter-attraction to the magnet of Chinese power, then enough aid must be given to ensure that the Governments of India and Pakistan can show sufficient achievement to their people to·keep them believing that they can have both bread and freedom. The Indian general elections have shown that this is an area where to-day people are free, and democratic, and conscious, as they have never been conscious before, that it is they who make and break Governments. There are not many such areas in the world to-day, and very few indeed in that large part of the world which is still poor and unindustrialised. There could be no better expenditure of the funds of the cold war grants than to spend them on seeing that this happy state of affairs continues. For however neutral, however suspicious of aid with strings they may be, there is no greater asset in the non-Communist world's cold war balance-sheet than the freedom and democracy of India and Pakistan.

Appendix A

ASIAN TRADE

The study of the history of Europe's trade relations with Asia has long suffered from a tendency to discuss them in political and social, rather than economic terms. The very real political and social importance of these relations has thus obscured the fact that they have had until quite recently no very great economic significance. Moreover, the picturesque romance of the subject has frequently led scholars to exaggerate the political and social significance themselves.

By comparison with modern quantities and values, trade with Asia was totally unimportant until after 1850, as a few illustrations will show. At the end of the 16th century total trade between East and West was about 10,000 tons each way, and was worth about £1 million a year. In the second half of the 17th century, when the Dutch dominated the trade, their exports to the East averaged about £400,000 a year;[1] in the 18th century, the English East India Company exported only £36¾ million worth of goods to the East in the whole half century 1708–1760; in 1751 England still imported three-quarters as much from the single sugar-island of Jamaica as from the whole of Asia.

As late as 1800 the trade of all Asia with the West was not worth half as much as the U.K.'s exports of £43 million. After 1800, however, the figures begin to increase, though they remain small. Asia's total exports around 1830 were only about twice those of Belgium.[2] Europe's sales to Asia were smaller still. China took about

[1] It is an interesting sidelight on the lack of proportion between politics and economics that Dutch purchases of spices in Indonesia averaged £5,842 a year between 1662 and 1673, fetching about £35,000 in Europe and yet the fight for this trade was a considerable cause for the contemporary wars between England and Holland.

[2] Javanese exports were 24 million guilders in 1822. The East India Company's purchases in India were £1¾ million in 1826. China's exports were 20 million dollars in 1833. No other country in Asia had any export trade to matter at all. Belgium's exports were £4 million in 1831, its first year of independent existence.

14 million dollars in 1833.[1] The East India Company sold in India only £232,000 worth of goods in 1826.[2]

Even in 1850 Asian trade with the West was still of comparatively minor importance, as is shown by the figures for imports from Great Britain, then the world's dominant trading nation (Table 57). Half a dozen nations had not yet come into world trade at all and the whole area, apart from India, took less than £3 million of British exports. Trade of Asia with other Western countries was negligible—about £3 million with the U.S. or France for imports and exports added together.

The trade was so small not only because the costs were so high that the West could import from the East only luxuries, but also because the West had the utmost difficulty in finding anything to sell to the East at all. From Roman days onwards, Western payments had to be made largely in bullion. The Romans exported some £100 million worth to the East in the first two centuries A.D. and the Americans were still paying in bullion for three-quarters of their purchases in Canton in 1818. This exchange of bullion for luxuries made Western governments and economists look on the trade with a somewhat jaundiced eye, for the steady drain of precious metals both impoverished the war-chests and deflated the economy. Even such limited increase in turnover as did occur between 1500 and 1800 was made possible only by the steady replenishment of Europe's bullion stocks with silver from the New World.

The Industrial Revolution transformed the situation, because it at last provided the West with something to sell which the East wanted to buy. This something was above all cotton textiles which the new machines enabled the West to produce at prices with which the Asian craftsman could not compete. When English yarn first came to Dacca, its price was As.3 against a price of As.13 for the local hand-spun. Table 57 brings out quite clearly the dominance of textiles in European exports which resulted. Tables 58, 74 and 75 show how dominant cotton textiles continued to be right up to 1914, and how rapidly the trade in them grew.

[1] Total Chinese imports were 27½ million dollars, but nearly half was Indian opium.
[2] The East India Company paid for the goods they bought in India not out of their sales of European products but out of the £2½ million they spent in Britain on government account, such as stores and pay. It is the memory of this crucial importance of governmental expenditure in making trade possible in the early days which was responsible for much of the later belief in the advantages Great Britain obtained from its control of the Indian government.

The figures for India in Table 57 already give a hint of what has been the major development in Asia's imports in the last century. Westernisation has gradually created a demand for western machinery and metals with which to build the railways, bridges, ports and factories without which no westernisation is possible. Table 64 gives the figures for the growth of the trade in machinery.

The years from 1850 to 1913, and above all from 1880 to 1913, were thus years of unprecedented expansion in Asia's imports from the West. These new imports were mainly paid for by an equally unprecedented expansion in Asia's sales to the West. (See Tables 59, 60, 73 for the growth in trade).

Before 1850, the West had taken from the East only a few luxuries, spices, silk and tea; and prices for these luxuries in the West were so high that only the few could afford to buy them. The 19th century brought to the West both an enormous increase in population and an enormous increase in wealth, particularly amongst the new middle classes. The silk and the tea that had been the privilege of the rich became conventional necessities for all. Chinese silk exports doubled between 1868 and 1913, at the same time as a great new Japanese silk trade grew up; the main market was the United States, whose imports of silk grew from 3 million dollars in 1870 to 368 million dollars in 1928. English consumption of tea increased from 1.22 lbs. per head in 1839 to 9.5 lbs. per head in 1939[1] and Table 62 shows how Asia's tea exports grew.

The growth of Europe's requirements between 1850 and 1913 is not confined to the .traditional imports. The new industries which the Industrial Revolution had created and the new towns which had grown up around them had new demands for food and raw materials. Some of the new supplies that were needed came from Asia, though Asia never was at any stage a supplier on the scale of the United States or Canada. Indian wheat mixed very well with the harder Canadian; Indian jute made the best possible packing material for Australian wool or American maize. Indian and Chinese oil seeds helped to provide the raw material for the growing soap and margarine industries of the West. Burma and Indonesia provided a little of the oil needed by the new internal combustion engine. South-east Asia supplied rice for food and tin for tin-plate. India provided a large proportion of the hides and skins which went into the leather shoes which in the 19th century everywhere replaced clogs. And there were a host of less obvious demands, lead

[1]In 1664 England had imported two lbs. of tea, costing £2 per lb.

and linseed for paint, castor oil as a lubricant for machinery, oil seeds to make cake for animal feed. Table 61, except 61 (H) and Tables 66 and 67 give the main figures.

This steady growth of mutually beneficial exchange was interrupted by the 1914–18 war; after the war, European demand resumed in full force; there was even the growth of a great demand. The motor vehicle created a demand for rubber which was still negligible in 1913 but expanded rapidly in the twenties and thirties, making whole areas of South-east Asia vitally dependent on a crop of which they had hardly heard in 1900 (Table 61 H). But Asia's demand for European goods recovered only partly. Protectionist feeling had been stimulated by the desire no longer to be dependent on far away sources of supply for the most elementary requirements, just when the development of indigenous industries had been given a great fillip by the automatic protection of difficult supplies and very high prices during the war and the post-war boom. Industrial development in Asia was not altogether new. A few industries, notably textiles, had already been beginning to develop before 1913. The first Indian cotton and jute mills date from the 1850s, the first Chinese cotton mill from 1890; and the Japanese Government had made industrialisation a key point in its policy from the very beginning. But after 1918, the tempo speeded up, until for example, Japan and India were in 1938 bigger cotton textile producers than Great Britain, and China had become virtually self-sufficient. (Tables 69, 70, 71 and 72 give the relevant figures for cotton textiles for India and China).

This very expansion of local industry which led to so drastic a fall in the import of consumption goods, notably of cotton textiles, naturally gave an equivalent impetus to imports of machinery. (See Table 64).

This trend towards self-sufficiency in consumer goods and the import of capital goods has strengthened since the war. Every Asian country is using exchange controls and import quotas to keep down its import of consumer goods and notably of luxuries, while trying desperately to obtain as many capital goods as it can succeed in finding the suppliers and the money for. The industrialisation programme of every Asian country which is not already self-sufficient in such consumer goods as cotton textiles makes their manufacture a first priority.

The main picture, therefore, between 1850 and the present day is of the West drawing from the East certain foods and raw materials and selling to the East firstly cotton textiles and then, increasingly, machinery and all the other equipment of modern civilisation. Within and across this main current of development, however, there have been certain minor currents. Most notable is the development in Asia itself, as a result of the increase in population, of areas which are not self-sufficient in food. India, Malaya, Japan, Ceylon, and, at times, China, had all become by 1939 major rice importers. Figures for the rice trade are given in Tables 66 and 78.

Another reflection of the growth of Asia's need for food has been the expansion of Javanese sugar exports of which at their height a very large proportion went to India and China (see Table 65). These exports are an interesting case also of two other trends—the European need for overseas food already discussed, and the increasing tendency of Asia to adopt European habits. Asia only began to consume white sugar in the second half of the 19th century. To-day Indian consumption alone is about one million tons a year. There has been a similar increase in Asia's consumption of tea. India, which 100 years ago drank none, to-day drinks 150 million pounds a year and Java in 1939 was consuming one-third of its output.

The most important cross current has been the rise of Japan as Asia's major supplier of cotton textiles. Like all the rest of Asia, Japan began in the 1870s and 1880s as a textile importer and in 1913 her exports to Asia were still very small. By 1936 her total exports had reached 2,873 million yards and half went to Asia. Detailed figures are in Table 76. Nor were Japanese industrial exports confined to cotton textiles, though so far as Asia was concerned they were always the most important item. By 1939 Japan was also providing a wide range of machinery and of such durable consumer goods as bicycles. The quality was so low that Japan had hardly begun to break into the real capital goods market, but in spheres where price was of greater importance than quality, such as bicycles for the countryside or winding machinery for cotton mills, Japan's exports expanded steadily in the 1930s, and had it not been for the war, Japan would undoubtedly have become a major supplier. It is to be anticipated that it will be these lines rather than the traditional cotton textiles which will provide Japan with her main Asian market in the 1950s.

Though Asian trade only became really important economically, either to Asia or to Europe, quite recently, it had great political and social importance from the very beginning.

Its political effects are well enough known, though they are sometimes exaggerated. The Dutch wars with Portugal were the result of Portugal's union with Spain rather than Portugal's position in the Indian Ocean; the Dutch wars with England had more to do with the herring fishing than with the massacre of Amboyna; Antwerp was a bigger bone of contention in English wars with France than India.

But if the political effect on the West was limited, that in the East cannot be exaggerated. The suppression of piracy, the establishment of European Government in India and Indonesia, the creation of great areas where law and order reigned and trade was free, all grew originally from the Western need of silk and spice. The whole westernisation, which has so upset Eastern civilisation, began with trade, and has at all times been influenced by trade. It is, for example, the importance of trade which has given the port cities, Bombay, Singapore, Shanghai, their great significance in Asian society, and many of the men who first created Asian industry originally made their money as brokers or as merchants in the trade with Europe. Most important of all is the effect on Asian nationalism of the form which was taken by Asia's trade with Europe. The emphasis on handicrafts was a reaction against the predominance of cotton textiles in European exports. The appeal of a protectionism so severe as to amount almost to autarchy was due on the one hand to the consciousness of weakness produced by the need to import all arms and warlike stores from Europe, and on the other hand to the creation of widespread rural unemployment by the import of European consumer goods. The form of Asia's economic relations with Europe explains, too, the dislike for free enterprise of so much Asian nationalism. Capitalism has been in Asia a foreign institution, so that even where, as in Japan, the capitalists themselves have been native, the traditionalist sections of society as well as the industrial proletariat have been anti-capitalist; nobody called more loudly for State control in the thirties than the ultra-nationalist Japanese young officers. Over much of Asia, moreover, the capital and the capitalists themselves have been foreign too. The plantation owners, the mill-owners, the bankers, the merchant houses, the debt-holders have until recently, except in Japan, been mainly foreign, and are even now quite often foreign.[1] They were not only foreign, they were

[1]The importance of foreign interests has diminished sharply in recent years with the repatriation of so many of the British holdings in India, notably the public debt, the certificates of Japanese investments in China and Korea and the diminishing importance of Shanghai.

also privileged. The risks of Asian trade and investment have always been considerable, so capital had to be tempted if it was to come at all. The temptations varied, from the safeguards in the Government of India Act to cheap leases of State land for plantations, from extra-territoriality to the statutory limitation of tariffs, but always their effect has been to give the foreigner, and sometimes the native capitalist too, privileges which the local nationalist felt as an insult; France and England and the United States were burdened with no such special regimes for foreigners; in the nationalist mind, there-fore, no economic justification they might have could be allowed to weigh against the stigma of inferiority, the accusation of backward-ness, they entailed.

The nationalist in Asia has therefore normally been anti-European and anti-capitalist; and because he was anti-European and anti-capitalist he has found sympathy in the West mainly on the Left. The Right had too real a belief in the European mission in Asia, too keen an appreciation of what capital could do for Asia, to have any sympathy with men who appeared to them to be mere agitators, bent on destroying all that had been so painfully and so expensively built up. Independence and the rapid disappearance in recent years of privilege, may be expected to correct this Asian bias towards the European Left, but it has been a very important factor in the past and is likely to continue to be so for some time in the future.

More important even than the political effect of Western trade has been the social effect. This has been discussed at much greater length elsewhere. Here it is only necessary to emphasise again that without the economic contact with the West, the westernised middle class, the spearhead of all advance, would never have grown up, and the peasants' horizon would never have been widened from his village to the nation. So long as the village was almost self-sufficient, its inhabitants had no need to look outside, but as soon as they began to buy their cloth and sell a proportion of their crops on the world market, the world became of passionate interest to them, and they have expressed this interest very largely politically. They have come both to see themselves as part of a nation and to realise the possibilities of the vote as an instrument for improving their economic and spiritual position.

This political interest has been greatly enhanced by the vulnera-bility of Asian economies to world market trends. With the excep-tion of Japan, Asia has not gone out to sell its products to the world. The world has come to Asia to buy there the products it needs.

Often, as with rubber, or coffee, the West has actually had to introduce the commodity it wished to buy, and the first growers have very often been Europeans. The result is that Asia has exported not a wide range of miscellaneous products, but only those commodities in which its economic advantage has been very large. Nearly all Asian economies are, in consequence, dependent on one or two exports. This makes Asia much more susceptible to booms and slumps than industrialised countries, both because her exports are generally food and raw materials whose prices fluctuate much more than do those of manufactured goods, and because a change in the world demand for a single commodity can change the economic condition of a whole community, almost overnight. Rubber is an excellent example of the whole process. When it reached 4/8d. per lb. in 1925 there was a boom in South-east Asia. When it touched 2d. in 1933 whole areas were in fact bankrupt. And much of the decline in South-east Asia's economic prospects since the war is due to the increase in the price of their imports having been much greater than the increase in the price of their exports. The whole position was changed when the war in Korea sent the prices of rubber and tin and edible oils sky-high; but in 1952 the terms of trade have worsened again, so that only the rice-growers, Burma and Thailand, are still in a favourable position. It is not surprising, therefore, that the desire to use the power of the State to enforce economic diversity dominates so much of Asian economic thinking. A Malaya that was a great rice-grower as well as a great rubber-grower would be very much more stable.

From the special point of view of Great Britain, one fact stands out in the history of Asian trade, and that is the importance of the Indian sub-continent. Three-quarters of all Britain's trade with the East was with India 200 years ago, and in 1947 India still took one and a half times as much of Britain's goods as the whole of the rest of Monsoon Asia put together. Since Japan's trading position has been severely damaged by the war, since China has gone over to the Communists, and since both of them have lost most of their silk export trade through the new American preference for nylon stockings, this predominance of the Indian sub-continent, now divided into two, will undoubtedly continue, particularly as India and Pakistan are both now determined to industrialise, and much of the machinery and equipment they require for that purpose can come more cheaply from Great Britain than from anywhere else. Asian trade for Great Britain means, as it has always meant, above all, trade with the Indian sub-continent. (See Table 79 for the recent figures). In trade as in thought, the most fruitful of all Western relations with the East has been Great Britain's with India.

TABLE 57

BRITISH EXPORTS TO ASIA IN 1850

Country	Value	Principal Commodities	
India	£7,242,194	Textiles ..	£4,036,947
		Metals ..	£938,991
		(Cotton textiles 284½ million yds.)	
China and Hong Kong	£1,574,145	Textiles ..	£1,309,821
		(Cotton textiles 73¼ million yds.)	
Singapore	£562,139	Textiles ..	£379,898
		(Cotton textiles 23¼ million yds.)	
Java	£507,499	Textiles ..	£371,648
		(Cotton textiles 23¼ million yds.)	
Outer Provinces ..	Nil		
Ceylon	£218,331	Textiles ..	£109,818
		Metals ..	£37,793
		(Cotton textiles 6½ million yds.)	
Philippines	£193,269	Textiles ..	£143,883
		(Cotton textiles 8 million yds.)	
Burma	Nil		
Indo-China	Nil		
Japan	Nil		
Thailand	Nil		
Korea	Nil		
Compare Australia (excluding Tasmania)	£2,049,521		

N.B.—In cases where the figure is entered as nil, it is possible that there was some small trade, but nothing has reached the Trade and Navigation Account.

TABLE 58

INDIAN COTTON TEXTILE IMPORTS (IN LAKHS OF RUPEES)

Year					Amount
1814–5 ..	..	..	..	..	½*
1829–30 ..	..	..	..	..	52
1860–1 ..	..	..	..	..	11,00
1890–1 ..	..	..	..	..	30,00
1920–1 ..	..	..	..	..	102,00

*India still exported 85 lakhs of cotton textiles in 1814–5; this had dropped to 1 lakh in 1830.

TABLE 59

GROWTH OF EXPORTS

(a) Japan—Meiji Restoration 1868.

			Imports	Exports (in millions of pounds)
1873 ..	..	..	6	4
1892 ..	..	..	11	9
1913 ..	..	..	73	63
1935 ..	..	..	144	146

(b) Outer Provinces of Indonesia. Mainly conquered 1880—1910.

					Exports (in million guilders)
1873 ..	..	..	..	..	35
1904 ..	..	..	..	..	96
1914 ..	..	..	..	..	351
1924 ..	..	..	..	..	747
1937 ..	..	..	..	..	661

(c) Burma. Lower Burma conquered 1852, Upper Burma 1885.

					Exports (in million rupees)
1868–9	..	..	..	..	.. 32
1903–4	..	..	..	..	.. 205
1913–4	..	..	..	..	.. 386
1936–7	..	..	..	..	.. 555

(d) Indo-China. Conquest mainly 1859–1885.

					Total trade (in million of pounds)
1891	..	..	..	..	.. 5
1913	..	..	..	..	.. 26
1938	..	..	..	..	.. 39

The older territories did not lag behind as Table 60 shows.

TABLE 60
GROWTH OF TOTAL TRADE

A. Growth of Chinese Trade.

Year				Imports	Exports
				in millions of pounds)	
1864	..	..	..	17	18
1884	..	..	..	21	20
1904	..	..	..	50	25
1914	..	..	..	81	51
1933	..	..	..	73	34

B. Growth of Indian trade (in crores of rupees).

1841	..	..	..	10	14
1860–1	..	..	..	23	33
1880–1	..	..	..	50	74
1900–1	..	..	..	81	108
1913–4	..	..	..	191	249
1938–9	..	..	..	159	185

C. Growth of Javanese trade (in millions of florins)

1873	..	....	..	83	149
1904	..	..	..	119	171
1914	..	..	..	319	385
1924	..	..	..	588	1,002
1937	..	..	..	317	290

TABLE 61
INDIVIDUAL EXPORTS

A. Indian exports of hides and skins (in lakhs of rupees)

Year					Amount
1860–1	..	..	..	..	.. 66
1898–9	..	..	..	..	.. 745
1913–4	..	..	..	..	.. 1,600
1929–30	..	..	..	..	.. 1,600

B. Indian exports of oilseeds (in thousands of tons)

Year					Quantity
1840–1	..	..	..	..	Negligible
1867–8	..	..	..	..	.. 200
1894–5	..	..	..	..	.. 1,000
1913–4	..	..	..	..	.. 1,500
1938–9	..	..	..	..	.. 1,173

C. Chinese exports of oilseeds and their derivatives (in million taels)

Year					Amount
1880	..	..	..	..	Negligible
1910	..	..	..	..	.. 61
1923	..	..	..	..	.. 180

D. Indian exports of cotton (in crores of rupees)

Year					Amount
1849	..	..	..	..	.. 2
1860–1	..	..	..	..	.. 6
1913–4	..	..	..	..	.. 41

E. Indian exports of raw jute (in thousands of tons)

Year					Quantity
c. 1830	..	..	..	..	.. $\frac{1}{2}$
1857–8	..	..	..	..	.. 35
1882–3	..	..	..	..	.. 313
1909–10	..	..	..	..	.. 765
1925–9 (av.)	..	..	..	..	800

F. Burmese mineral exports (in million rupees)

	1903–4	1913–4	1936–7
Oil well products ..	22	54	194
Mineral products ..	1	6	51

G. Indonesian oil exports (in thousands of metric tons)

Year					Quantity
1880	..	..	..	..	.. Nil
1915	..	..	..	..	.. 380
1935	..	..	..	..	.. 5,140

H. South-east Asian rubber exports (in thousand tons)

Country				1900	1922	1939
Malaya	..	..	..	Nil	212	362
Indonesia	..	..	,,		103	370
Indo-China	..	..	,,		5	65
Thailand	..	..	,,		1	42
Ceylon	..	..	,,		47	62

I. South-east Asian tin production (in tons)

Siam	..	.. 1908 .. 5,000	1939 .. 20,000	
Indonesia	..	1850 .. 2,000	1900 .. 18,000	1939 .. 44,000
Malaya	..	.. 1870 .. 2,337	1900 .. 47,000	1939 .. 99,000

TABLE 62

TEA EXPORTS (in millions of lbs.)

A. India

Year			Quantity
1854	..	..	.. $\frac{1}{4}$
1885–9 (av.)	..	..	87
1900	..	..	.. 192
1927	..	..	.. 370
1947	..	..	.. 425

B. Ceylon

1880	..	..	.. $\frac{1}{6}$
1900	..	..	.. 190
1927	..	..	.. 227
1947	..	..	.. 287

C. Indonesia.

1900	..	..	.. 17
1927	..	..	.. 145

D. China*

1880	..	..	.. 280
1900	..	..	.. 185
1927	..	..	.. 116
1947	..	..	.. 361

*Chinese exports lost place because of English preference for Indian types, and because it was a peasant industry, unable to take full advantage of the drop in costs of production caused by such inventions as the mechanical roller in 1872, and the Sirocco dryer (1877) which brought Indian costs down from 10d per lb as in 1872 to 2½d as in 1913.

TABLE 63

CHINESE EXPORTS OF SILK (in millions of U.S. Dollars)

Year				Amount	% of total Chinese exports
1868	..	..	..	38	41
1898	....	..	..	38	35
1913	..	..	..	75	25
1923	..	..	..	136	23
1933	..	..	..	22	13

N.B.—The trade has now collapsed. In the first half of 1948 the U.S. took only 526 bales of raw silk from China.

TABLE 64

A. Indian imports of machinery (in millions of pounds)

Year	Amount
1861–2	$\frac{1}{2}$
1909–10	$3\frac{1}{2}$
1938–9	$7\frac{1}{2}$

B. Japanese imports of machinery (in millions of pounds)

1880	Negligible
1911	1
1926	15
1935	9

C. Chinese imports of iron, steel and machinery (in millions of pounds)

1868	$\frac{1}{3}$
1898	$\frac{2}{3}$
1930	9

TABLE 65
JAVANESE SUGAR EXPORTS (in thousand tons)

Year					Quantity
1853–7 (av.)	..	..	..	..	100*
1895	..	..	..	..	600*
1912–3	..	..	..	..	1,300
1924	..	..	..	..	2,000†
1938	..	..	..	..	1,078

*Total crop
†of which to India 500, China 130.

TABLE 66
RICE EXPORTS (in thousands of tons)

Burma	..	1850	Negligible	1881		520	1939–40	3,100
Siam	..	1860	,,	1939		1,500	1912–13	1,600
Indo-China		1860	,,	1899–1903	av. 800		1939	1,600
Korea	..	1910	,,	1938		1,500		

TABLE 67
INDIAN WHEAT EXPORTS

1870	Negligible
1914	1,300,000 tons
1930	Negligible again because of increased local demand.

TABLE 68
INDIAN EXPORTS OF JUTE GOODS (in lakhs of rupees)

Year	Quantity
1874–5	20
1890–1	560
1913–4	2,827
1938–9	2,580

TABLE 69
INDIAN HOME PRODUCTION OF COTTON TEXTILES

Year					Production* (million yds.)
1900	..	..	..	..	.. 426
1927	..	..	..	..	.. 2,189
1938	..	..	..	..	.. 3,290

*In addition handloom production rose from 1000 million yds. in 1900 to roughly 1,500 million yds. in 1938.

TABLE 70
INDIAN IMPORTS OF COTTON TEXTILES (in million yds.)

Year					Imports
1909–13 (av)	..	..	..	..	2,560
1929–30	..	..	..	..	1,812
1937–38	..	..	..	..	591

TABLE 71
CHINESE COTTON TEXTILE PRODUCTION (in million sq. yds.)

Year					Imports
1915	..	..	..	..	.. 100
1928	..	..	..	..	.. 580
1936	..	..	..	..	.. 1,219

TABLE 72
CHINESE COTTON TEXTILE IMPORTS (in million dollars)

Year					Amount
1909–13 (av)	..	..	..	..	230
1925– 9 (av)	..	..	..	..	114
1939	..	..	..	..	27

TABLE 73
BRITISH EXPORTS TO MONSOON ASIA (in millions of pounds)

Country	1880	1913
India	$30\frac{1}{2}$	$70\frac{1}{4}$
China	$8\frac{3}{4}$	$14\frac{3}{4}$
Japan	$3\frac{1}{4}$	$14\frac{1}{2}$
Indonesia	$1\frac{3}{4}$	$7\frac{1}{4}$
Malaya	$2\frac{1}{4}$	$7\frac{1}{4}$
Ceylon	1	$4\frac{1}{4}$
Philippines	$1\frac{1}{4}$	1
Indo-China	Negligible ($£13,000$)	$\frac{1}{4}$
Siam	Negligible ($£23,000$)	$1\frac{1}{4}$
Compare Australia	$13\frac{3}{4}$	$34\frac{1}{2}$

TABLE 74
PROPORTION OF BRITISH EXPORTS REPRESENTED BY COTTON TEXTILES 1880

Country	Proportion
Malaya	$\frac{3}{5}$
India	$\frac{3}{5}$
China	$\frac{3}{5}$
Indonesia	$\frac{4}{5}$
Ceylon	$\frac{1}{3}$
Philippines	$\frac{1}{2}$

TABLE 75
TEXTILES AS PROPORTION OF ALL IMPORTS IN 1909–13

Country	Proportion
China	$\frac{1}{3}$
Indonesia	$\frac{1}{4}$
Thailand	$\frac{1}{5}$
Philippines	$\frac{1}{5}$
French Indo-China	$\frac{1}{6}$

TABLE 76
IMPORTS OF JAPANESE COTTON TEXTILES 1936 (in million yds.)

Country	Quantity
India	480
Manchuria and Kwantung	351
Korea	164
Indonesia	352
China	37
Egypt	106
Straits Settlement	48
U.S.A.	73
All others	1,262
Total	2,873

TABLE 77
PHILIPPINE SUGAR EXPORTS (in million quintals)

Year	Quantity
1909–13 av.	2
1928	5
1938	9

TABLE 78
RICE IMPORTS 1938 (in thousands of tons)

Country	Quantity
India	1,100
Malaya	650*
Japan	2,000
China	400

*1940.

N.B.—Before 1914 India and Japan were normally self-sufficient, Malayan imports about one-third.

TABLE 79

BRITISH EXPORTS TO MONSOON ASIA 1936 AND 1947 (in millions of pounds)*

Country	1936	1947
India	34	91
Indonesia ..	3	6
Malaya	8	30
China	6	13
Japan and Korea	4	Negligible (£83,000)
Philippines ..	$\frac{1}{2}$	$1\frac{1}{2}$
Indo-China ..	$\frac{1}{4}$	1
Siam	$1\frac{1}{4}$	$1\frac{1}{2}$
Ceylon	3	12
Compare Australia	32	72

*Figures are given to the nearest million except where the smallness of the total would make that misleading.

Appendix B

ASIA AND DOLLARS

In the 1930s Asia's net earnings of U.S. Dollars were equal to rather more than the combined deficit of England and Holland.[1] The war has not only turned this surplus into a deficit, it has also greatly reduced Asia's capacity to export, and in many cases the only alternative source of supply is in the Dollar area.

No other single factor, not even the failure of gold to rise above its pre-war dollar price, has contributed as much to the world's present dollar difficulties. A very rough calculation will show the size of the catastrophe. This calculation can obviously be made in many different ways, using various prices and dates. No importance should therefore be attached to the exact figures. But it is clear that were Asia once more able to earn and save dollars on the pre-war scale, two-thirds of Marshall Aid would be unnecessary.

A full development of Asia's productive powers would see the end of the dollar shortage.

[1] 1937 Deficit of Gt. Britain and Holland   370 million dollars
       Asia's dollar surplus   387 million dollars

Great Britain and Holland were able to earn Asia's dollars from Asia mainly because of their large invisible earnings. Gt. Britain earned perhaps £100 million a year in Asia (half from investments, quarter from shipping) and Holland earned perhaps £20 million in Indonesia. Total British investments in Asia were nearly £100 million in 1938, over half in India.

Asia's dollar earning capacity was not new, as the following table shows

	Exports to Asia	Imports from Asia
	In millions of dollars	
1821	2	$5\frac{1}{4}$
1850	3	$12\frac{1}{2}$
1870	$5\frac{3}{4}$	$37\frac{3}{4}$
1901–5 (av.)	77	$149\frac{1}{2}$
1913	$140\frac{1}{2}$	$297\frac{1}{4}$
1928	653	1168
1937	580	967
1946	$1342\frac{1}{2}$	$881\frac{1}{4}$

Million of
dollars

Calculation [1]

Disappearance of Asia's 1937 surplus (multiplied by $2\frac{1}{2}$ to
give present values).   1000
Appearance of Asian deficit (1946)   450
Reduction in Asian exportable surplus of Oilseeds (1948
agst. 1937)   700
(Total reduction 1,384,000 tons expressed as oil, main items
(as oil), 392,000 tons soya beans, 515,000 tons groundnut,
220,000 tons coconut.)
Change in Indian cotton balance (excl. Pakistan) from 2
million bales net export to $1\frac{1}{2}$ million bales net import. ..   300
Increase in Indian food imports (excl. Pakistan) (1949 agst.
pre-war)   250
Reduction in Burmese and Indo-Chinese rice exports
(taken at the wheat price only, as they would save dollars as
alternatives to wheat).   450
Miscellaneous (e.g. Burmese lead, Indo-Chinese maize,
Javanese Sugar)   200
                                                    ————
                                                    3350

This is roughly the amount of aid demanded under the Marshall
Plan for 1950-1. Moreover, the serious deterioration in France,
Holland and the U.K's balance of payments on invisible account,
amounting to nearly £500 million in 1949, has made it necessary
for Europe to put forward a very much greater effort than before if
it is still to earn dollars in Asia.[2] Indeed Asia has been drawing on

[1]The calculations are very rough, and include not only direct dollar losses
but also reductions in exportable surplus of commodities which have otherwise to be bought for dollars.

[2]Even were Asian production to be restored, it would be more difficult for
Europe to earn dollars in Asia because of the decline in Europe's invisible
earnings, e.g. French investments in Asia in 1938 were 570 million dollars, of
which 391 were in Indo-China and 124 in China. Probably 400-500 must be
taken as lost, with a loss of income to France of perhaps 30 million a year. Gt.
Britain has lost or repatriated some £500-600 millions of her pre-war Asian
investments; and the Indian home charges have also been bought out or have
disappeared—the total reduction is perhaps £30 million a year. Holland has lost
much of its Indonesian income,though it is still too early to say exactly how much.

There has been moreover a great increase in invisible spending in Asia by
Gt. Britain, France and Holland. Sterling balance releases and Dutch, French
and British military expenditure must in total have been well over £400
million in 1949.

The total deterioration on invisible account may therefore well have been
as high as £500 million in 1949. In 1952, it will be considerably greater, for,
though Dutch military expenditure has stopped, France alone is likely to spend
£400 million or more on the Indo-Chinese War.

Europe's resources; in 1947, the worst year, India took 130 million dollars from the Sterling Area Dollar Pool, Holland had to find 87 million dollars for Indonesia, and France 21 million for Indo-China.

The restoration of the Asian position is vital. If quick results are to be obtained, however, effort must not be dissipated. The West's assistance must be given to those areas where it will have the maximum immediate effect; militarily that means Indo-China and perhaps Burma, economically it means the Indian Sub-Continent, and above all India itself. From the other countries little can be expected. Japan's great dollar export was silk. [1] To-day silk has been almost entirely replaced in the U.S. by nylon. Japan is to-day a dollar pensioner whose recovery will only bring into the field an extra competitor for non-dollar cereals and cotton, thus making the difficulties of the rest of the world worse, not better. [2] S. Korea even apart from the devastation caused by the war, is barely viable without the heavy industries and hydro-electricity of N. Korea. [3] The Philippines will have all they can do to increase their exports to the U.S. enough to make up for the ending of the flow of American grants. [4] China is making it increasingly clear that it prefers Russia and the satellites as trading partners. China's only dollar importance is that Chiang Kai Shek in Formosa should be cheaper than Chiang Kai Shek in China. [5]

In these countries a restoration of the pre-war position is not possible, or will result merely in their ceasing to be a drain on America, without any advantage to Europe.

[1]Japan's exports to the U.S. in 1937 were 639 million yen of which 403 million yen were silk and silk cloth. Total U.S. imports of raw silk which reached 368 million dollars in 1928 were 15½ million dollars in 1948.

[2]Japan's exports dropped from 204 million dollars in 1937 to 35 million in 1947. American grants have run around 400 million dollars a year.

[3]The decline in the exports of the ex-Japanese Empire seems to be an irretrievable result of the war. On the average of 1934–8 Korea and Formosa exported 1¼ million tons of rice a year; Formosa also exported 833,000 tons of sugar. In 1948 this had become a net import of cereals and an export of only 150,000 tons of sugar.

[4]In 1937 the Philippines had a visible dollar surplus of 41 million dollars. Invisible items were considerable, but there was a net earning of some millions of dollars. In 1947 there was a deficit of 278 million dollars.

[5]In 1937 China had a favourable visible balance of 54 million dollars, by 1947 this had become an adverse balance of 237 million dollars. The immediate effect of China's going Communist is that there is no need for America to find dollars to fill this adverse balance.

In Malaya and Ceylon the problem is different. Their recovery has substantially already been achieved.[1]

But their contribution to the world's dollars is likely to be lower in real terms than before the war because the real price of tin and rubber, their major exports to the U.S.,[2] has gone down to some two-thirds and one-half respectively of the pre-war level; and the large use of synthetic rubber and of electro-lytic tinplate greatly reduces the possibilities of expansion of the U.S. market.[3] Peace in Malaya would relieve the British and Malayan budgets of some millions of unproductive expenditure; it would add nothing to the 200 million dollars or so Malaya already earns net a year. Ceylon's contribution is in any case small (33 million dollars net in 1948).

Indonesia is a more complex case. Its rubber exports reached the pre-war level of some 430,000 tons in 1948, and its exports to the U.S. have always been almost entirely rubber. Its oil exports almost reached the pre-war level of 6 million tons in 1949, from a post-war low of three-quarters of a million tons. In 1949 it almost balanced its dollar accounts; in 1951 it had a large dollar surplus. The restoration of peace has relieved Holland of an obligation which, for economic and military purposes combined, was certainly over £100 million in 1949.[4]

Much has therefore already been done. But much still could be done. Another quarter of a million tons of palm oil and coconut oil[5]

[1]Malayan exports to the U.S. reached 284 million dollars as early as 1947, against 243 million in 1937. Ceylonese exports were 30 million in 1947, against 21 million in 1937.

[2]Rubber is roughly four-fifths of Ceylonese exports to the U.S. e.g. 3⅘ crores of rupees out of 4⅘ in 1937.

Rubber was pre-war two-thirds and since 1945 has been over three-quarters of Malaya's exports to the U.S.; tin and rubber together have constituted nearly the whole of Malaya's exports to the U.S. e.g. 394 million straits dollars out of 399 million in 1937, 423 million out of 439 million in 1947.

Rubber is almost the whole of Indonesia's exports to the U.S. e.g. 109 million out of 118 million guilders in 1937. (These figures exclude shipments via Singapore, but that affects only totals not percentages).

[3]Although 1949 was a boom year and the late 1930s were poor years, the U.S. consumed only 50,000 tons of tin in 1949 against 63,000 on the average of 1934-8, and U.S. consumption of natural rubber rose only from 504,000 to 577,000 tons—synthetic rubber consumption rose from nothing to 414,000.

[4]Though Holland has had to begin by granting Indonesia a loan of 200 million guilders, thus postponing full relief.

[5]The coconut oil is Coconut Oil and Copra expressed as Coconut Oil. In 1948 production was 230,000 tons against 390,000 tons in 1938. Production of Palm Oil was 49,000 tons against 221,000 tons pre-war.

should be fairly quickly obtainable. Java needs only a period of un-questioned law and order once more to export 1 million tons of sugar. [1] A further increase in oil production of 3 or 4 million tons should be possible in the next half-dozen years. If conditions are favourable to enterprise, Indonesia might, by 1955, be saving the world another 300 million dollars a year.

Thailand's direct dollar earnings are small and since they come from rubber and tin, have also been affected by the fall in the real price of those commodities. Its power to save dollars for other countries rests upon its rice exports; these are expected to be at slightly higher than the pre-war rate, in 1950 and further expansion could only be gradual.

In Indo-China and Burma all that is required is peace to enable them once more to rank amongst the world's greatest exporters of non-dollar cereals. 3 million tons of Burma maize, $1\frac{1}{2}$ million tons of Cochin-Chinese rice, $\frac{1}{2}$ million tons of Cambodian rice, would break the present price of dollar wheat and maize, and would enable Europe to divert much of its demand for grain from N. America. The saving would be of the order of 250 million dollars.

Indo-China can contribute little else but rice and maize in goods. But were the Indo-Chinese war to stop, the saving to France of 200,000 men and perhaps £400 million a year would transform Western defence, and considerably ease both the French budgetary position and the tensions within the French body politic. The defeat of Ho Chi Minh is Asia's priority No. 1.

Burma has less to offer apart from its rice, only a few million dollars worth of lead and oil when peace has been long enough established to enable the mines and wells to be restored. But the rice alone is enough to make peace between the Karens and the Burmese Government a world, as well as a Burmese, need.

Economically, incomparably the greatest opportunities are offered by India. As a direct earner of dollars it ranks only just second to Malaya. It earned 238 million dollars in 1949. Unfor-tunately, it spent 252 million dollars. [2] Yet many of the goods

---

[1] Gt. Britain alone spent £31 million in 1948 on 1 million tons of dollar sugar.

[2] In 1947 American exports to undivided India were as high as 400 million dollars. In 1937 they were only 44 million dollars. Asia's deficits have been in part the result of European productive deficiencies. (E.g. Malaya imported 21 million dollars of American textiles, India imported 99 million dollars of machinery and vehicles in 1947). As Europe recovers, so Asia's need to import from the U.S. will diminish, as can be seen both in the above Indian figures

bought in the U.S. could be produced by Europe and Australia. An increase in the Australian wheat crop would lessen Indian dependence on American cereals, while Europe makes tinplate and loco- motives and could make heavy tractors or motor trucks just as well as the U.S. Devaluation has ensured that in most cases European prices will be right; a greater effort to give the Indian market what it wants, and above all quicker delivery dates, would ensure a drop in India's U.S. purchases and thus give Western Europe an opportunity to earn dollars in India on a scale not far short of the Malayan.

But India's direct earning of dollars is only part of the story. It is a great producer of agricultural products of exactly the types of which the main supplier is to-day North America. Wheat, coarse grains, cotton, oilseeds—India is amongst the world's major producers of them all. Yet Indian yields are so low that its pre-war exports of 1,300,000 tons of oilseeds have dwindled to next to nothing, its pre-war exports of some $2\frac{1}{2}$ million bales of cotton a year have dwindled to 200,000 and it expects in 1950 to have to import perhaps $1\frac{1}{2}$ million bales of cotton, and it has been importing 3 million tons of food a year. The improvement of Indian agricul- ture to a stage where India was self-sufficient in food and exported cotton and oilseeds on the pre-war scale would save 700–800 million dollars a year to the world. The total increase in production would be of the order of 10%. This can be achieved in five years or so. All that is required is perhaps 500 million dollars and reasonable priority for fertilisers. The money would be used for schemes which are already in existence, for tube-wells, high dams, reclama- tion of weed-infested land, so that the assistance could be given as loans and not grants. How necessary the fertiliser is, is shown by the fact that in 1949–50 for India's 250 million acres there were available only 300,000 tons; Japan by contrast uses a quarter of a ton per acre.

Similar results, on the smaller scale dictated by the smaller size of the country, could be achieved in Pakistan, and Pakistan has the advantage that there irrigation can still be done by barrages, which are much cheaper than high dams. Three schemes which are already in progress, the Tal-Hareli Project and the Lower Sind and Upper Sind Barrages, all of which should be completed within five years, will bring under cultivation some seven million extra acres. Pakistani agriculture could not need a great deal of extra modernisa-

and in the reduction of the estimate for Malayan imports from the U.S. in 1950 to under half the 1948 figure.

tion to be able to produce another million bales of cotton and $1\frac{1}{2}$ million tons of wheat; and that would mean a saving of 200 million dollars for the world.

If Asia were once more to export on the pre-war scale and at the pre-war terms of trade the world's dollar problem would be solved. That is unlikely to happen. Japan's silk, Korea's rice, China's soya beans will not earn or save dollars in the next decade. The terms of trade of the rubber and tin exporting countries of S.E. Asia are unlikely to be permanently favourable; 1951 was a flash in the pan. But perhaps two-thirds of the problem could be solved if law and order could be finally restored in Burma, Indo-China and Java, and if the agricultural yields of the Indian Sub-continent could be increased by 10%. It is therefore, odd that the U.S. so long left this part of the world to the unaided efforts of impoverished Western Europe, Indo-China, Burma and Pakistan got nothing until 1951; Indonesia's first dollar loan was in 1950; the few million dollars lent India by the World Bank were lent only after the most rigorous investigation. The U.S. has preferred to spend its money on ex-enemy Japan, rickety Korea, and the disastrous Chiang Kai-shek. It has been an economic as well as a political error.[1] Fortunately, there are signs that this is now being realised. In 1952, it is likely that India will receive 90 million dollars and Pakistan 20 million, and that America will at last do something substantial to lighten the appalling burden resting upon the French in Indo-China.

[1] Japan had had some 1400 million dollars as a free gift from the U.S. by the end of 1949. The suggestion of 1000 million dollars which Mr. Chester Bowles, the American Ambassador to India, has made for India, is therefore hardly outrageous. India has over four times Japan's population, and it was the major Asian contributor to the Allied war effort.

Postscript

The book was mainly written at the beginning of 1949. In the months since then, the lines have been drawn more closely in Asia. Nationalism has finally triumphed. The peoples have shown that they will support no regime which does not give them land reform and at least the hope of a rising standard of life. The Governments, if not yet always their peoples, have realised that independence does not automatically bring the millennium. Above all, it is now definite that the conflict for the mind of Asia is to be between the two Western creeds, of Communism and democracy, and that their protagonists are to be China and India. The chance of reviving Asia's own old beliefs, of building a new continent on the basis of Confucius or even Gandhi, has died with the death of the old self-sufficient existence of the peasant village to which they were so beautifully adjusted. Asia now realises that it has to industrialise, to become scientific, to absorb all the Western concepts and ways of life without which there cannot be that increase in wealth for which Asian opinion so yearns. Whether Communism or democracy is chosen will depend not on ideologies but on facts. If the West, which in this context means the Commonwealth and the United States, wants freedom to win, then it must make sure that India offers a more successful model for imitation than China. That will be expensive, it may cost as much as £200 million a year for India alone; and the other countries will doubtless want their share. But it is much cheaper than a series of Koreas.

Asia's attainment of independence will soon be completed. Western authority remains only as an exception, almost an anomaly. Of the once great Dutch empire, only New Guinea remains, and even that is disputed. In Indo-China the need to enable Bao Dai to make head against Ho Chi Minh has steadily eroded French authority in law, though the exigencies of a war of which the French are carrying the major burden has equally steadily tended to keep it intact in fact. All the signs of power have passed to the Vietnamese. They have their single state, including Cochin China; a Vietnamese army, with Vietnamese offiers is being built up as quickly as possibly by a French command which would like to see its own troops back home, balancing the German divisions in the European Defence Community. The Vietnamese can conduct their own diplomatic relations; their magistrates try Frenchmen, the Police Commissioner of Saigon is Vietnamese. Even some of the suspicious Vietnamese are beginning to realise that the independence offered them is real, that to-day the French are no longer their overlords, but their allies in a common fight against Communism. The British territories in Asia were already vestigial in 1948; but the promise of Dominion Status for Malaya, the emphasis on the creation of a Malayan nationality, the increase in the non-official members of the Singapore Legislative Council are all pointers that freedom is not far off, once the guerillas have been crushed, and Chinese and Malays have agreed on citizenship.

As the new nationalisms have grown, it has become clearer how fundamentally 19th-century European they are in inspiration. It is not that Asia is imitative, but simply that its political development has been held up, so that much which Europe did fifty or a hundred years ago is in Asia still to do.

One can see it in many ways. The old loyalties were to a religion, a caste or a racial group. It was important that one was a Muslim, or a Brahmin, or an Ambonese. The new loyalties follow territorial boundaries. One is an Indian or an Indonesian; even in Pakistan, founded specifically to give opportunity for self-expression to a religious minority, Muslims are becoming Pakistanis. Asia, like Europe, has discovered that modern Governments can only function when all are citizens, and all citizens are of equal value. Sometimes the results are a little odd, as in the passion of the Indonesian claim to a New Guinea with which their main connection is an ex-common subjection to Dutch rule, or in the Vietnamese eagerness to take up France's "mission civilisatrice" in Cambodia and Laos. China's claim on Tibet, a non-Chinese country, is based only on a suzerainty first effectively established by the non-Chinese Manchus. But fundamentally the instinct is sound, and it is already bringing about the disappearance of one of Asia's great weaknesses, the plural society, in which the minorities could never disappear or be assimilated because they were all in one way or another privileged. In Burma the Indians who are left have had to take Burmese citizenship if they wish to earn a living, in Ceylon the Government is undertaking a campaign of Ceylonisation of industry and commerce—and it is significant that the word is Ceylonisation, not Sinhalisation, though it is admittedly largely the Indians who are hit. The test is not a man's race, but his citizenship. The Chinese, too, is losing his privileged status. Whether in Indonesia or Siam or Viet Nam, his separateness, his fierce loyalty to his motherland, is found less and less tolerable. His capacity for hard work, his business ability make him in some ways a coveted citizen, but it is becoming steadily clearer that the price of acceptance will be transference of loyalty to his new country. The Indian Muslim, the East Pakistan Hindu, the Ambonese, all are losing, sometimes rather unpleasantly, the privileged position which imperial rule, and also their own merits, produced for them.

Nationalism struck Asian society with hurricane force; now another European idea, equality, is shaking it with the shock of an earthquake. Liberté has come; now the common man of Asia, a citizen for the first time, is demanding Egalité and Fraternité too.

Everywhere feminism makes headway, in Muslim Pakistan Begum Liaquat Ali's women National Guards have brought women from the seclusion of purdah into the most male of occupations, their country's defence. In India untouchability has been made an offence under the Constitution. In Indonesia the new unitary State will for the first time give the members of the Javanese electorate their full political weight. In Malaya the Malay is beginning to assert himself economically, the Chinese to claim his rights as Malayan born. Everywhere the once ruling European must submit to the whims of native Governments, and their sometimes very raw officials.

The new equality can sometimes be very tiresome, for it has come quickly, and can be heady for the half-educated, but it is very real. No Government in Asia to-day can ignore its electorate, can count on the age-old apathy of the governed to accept exploitation and misery in the way they have always been accepted.

Most notable example of the new refusal is the growing urgency of land reform. No Government in Asia to-day can tolerate absentee landlordism and avoid civil war. The failure to enforce such reform was one of the causes of Chiang Kai-shek's ruin, so that even the Kuomintang in Formosa is beginning to put a little conviction into its talk of land redistribution; and the North Koreans' most effective weapon against Syngman Rhee has been their readiness to give the land to the peasant. In India and East Pakistan zemindars are being abolished, conservatively, reluctantly, litigiously and slowly, but abolished, if only because the parties in power know that failure to do so would give the rural vote to their left wing enemies. In India the Constitution was changed to make legal the terms on which the abolition is taking place. In the Philippines where nothing has been done, the Hukbalahap guerillas have increased their strength on Luzon and not long ago they were able to raid towns within a few miles of Manila, despite the millions in help which America has given the Government. In Japan, by contrast, land reform has been real and effective and the foundation has thus been laid on which a conservative democracy can be built.[1] Government. In Japan, by contrast, land reform has been real and effective and the foundation has thus been laid on which a conservative democracy can be built.[1]

With land reform has gone the curbing of the money-lender. Not only in China has his power been broken. In India interest on rural debt is now estimated at £20 million a year, perhaps a seventh or an eighth in real terms, of what it was pre-war. In Indonesia the rural money-lender was usually Chinese, and during the war with the Dutch the Chinese on the whole supported the Dutch, so the money-lender just did not get paid. Equally in Burma and Indo-China civil commotion has offered an excellent opportunity for repudiating one's debts, sometimes even for destroying one's promissory note or liquidating one's creditors.

These changes in the countryside do not, however, mean that Asia is moving Left. It is not. Outside the Communist area it is moving Right at about the same pace as Western Europe, and for very similar reasons the Congress which won the Indian 1952 elections had become a Conservative party. Indeed, Asia and Europe are becoming one so rapidly that changes in European political thought, and the lessons of European political experience, now take effect in Asia almost at once.

In Asia as in Europe the bright hopes of 1945 have been brought down to earth. The first call on all budgets is the armed forces. Everywhere administrators and technicians are lacking. Nowhere is there enough capital to do much more than provide for depreciation. In the main countries, India, China, Pakistan, Japan, Java, an increasing population presses ever more heavily on the means of subsistence. Governments are moving Right therefore of necessity. With savings so hopelessly inadequate, the few capitalists must be conciliated, foreign capital must be reassured, nationalisation must

[1]General MacArthur's claim to have made Japan a real democracy already is only a useful propaganda exaggeration.

be relegated to limbo. Governments which cannot borrow and which have not the force (or the will) to compel saving, cannot take the economic initiative. Governments which have not the administrators to plan or the managers to nationalise must perforce turn to the despised entrepreneur for salvation. The story is everywhere the same, in Pakistan or Burma, Ceylon or Indonesia.

Only the degree of resultant disillusionment varies. Countries can prosper on a belief in democracy and free enterprise, as America shows; countries can increase their economic power by planning backed by terror, as Russia shows. And in either case success will bring passive acceptance, if not active support, from the majority. But regimes which have had to move Right, while not only their public but they themselves still think Left, are in no such happy position. The country has gone against its convictions and the resultant sour taste can be sweetened only by success.

This mood may not last. In India the expectations of a bright new world are already forgotten; the people have accepted the thesis of their Five-Year Plan, that prosperity can be won only slowly, by hard work and sacrifice. Yet for these countries success by their own unaided efforts is difficult. Local free enterprise is all too often a mockery, for the local capitalist all too often confines his enterprise to speculation. Promises to foreign capital are kept so vague by the continuing suspicions of local public opinion, that only the long established, or firms with a strong sense of their duty to undeveloped countries, will venture. There is so much talk of equal distribution and profit sharing, taxes are so high and labour opposition to rationalisation is so fierce, that capital finds it more profitable to stay at home. Why invest in Asia when one can get as much as 10% by buying equities on the New York Stock Exchange?

But without an influx not only of capital, but of the ways of thought of a true capitalist society, there is no hope for democracy in Asia. Enterprise must sweep away the stagnancies of the traditional economies. Profits must be made so that there will be something to tax for education and health. The worker must be provided with mechanical servants—each American worker has the equivalent of 30, each English worker of 13—which will relieve him of degrading and brutalising tasks and enable him to produce enough to be clean, to pay for a decent house, and to educate his children. The equality of the United States or France is not possible in societies where the majority do not earn enough to keep body and soul together. Levelling down would only reduce the governing

U

classes to a level where they could neither govern nor manage, and there simply is not the production in these economies, where income per head is still declining, to level up.

Only one Asian economy, Japan, has hitherto been able to raise itself by its own bootstraps, and that required savings of the order of 40% of the natural income over many years. Such economies as India or Indonesia or Pakistan do well if they save 6 or 7%. This is not even enough to provide for the natural increase in their populations, let alone to provide for an improvement in the standard of living, and it must be remembered that they only reach this level in a good year. It is doubtful whether to-day, if American aid were withdrawn, even Japan could provide for its annual increase out of its own savings.

The economies of Asia have been running down since 1938. Their new democracies have taken over under the most difficult conditions. Old administrators and technicians have been withdrawn, the ravages of war and inflation have to be repaired, the vicious spiral of deteriorating welfare has to be reversed, law and order itself is sometimes most uncertain. The nationalist has been successful in obtaining the independence of the West from which all good things were to flow, and now he has to explain to his constituents why the millennium has not arrived. One has only to listen to Nehru to-day to see how good his arguments are; but to understand the active dissatisfaction of so much of the Indian electorate one has only to read the glowing promises of Nehru's speeches before he came into office. Democracy nowadays is everywhere judged by the economic advance it produces; it means the comfortable watch chains of Victorian England, the refrigerators of contemporary America. The East does not see why in Asia alone democracy should mean economic retrogression.

It might have been left to find the answer for itself, had it not been for the challenge of Communism, which in the future will mean particularly Chinese Communism. Communism has shown in Russia that with whatever brutality, it can build factories and drain the surplus population off the land. If it repeats the experience in China, then it will be no answer to the starving Bengali or Javanese peasant that democracy and free enterprise have done everything that Russia or China have done, but better and less brutally, in America and Western Europe. He will judge on his own experience, on his own democracy and his own capitalists. If the West wants Asia not to go Communist, it is no use distributing pictures of

English Council Houses or the electric stoves of negro share-croppers. The West will have to see that Indian workers get at least a one-room tenement, that Tonkinese rice farmers get at least enough rice to eat. It will have to help the new democracies of the East to repeat the miracles which freedom and saving, risk-taking and ingenuity, capital and integrity have wrought in the last century in the West.

The challenge which has to be faced is not to be lightly esteemed. To the Asian, fear of Russia is an ambivalent emotion; he recognises how much there is in Russian society to be afraid of but he also feels that a system which could bring Russia from the impotence of the early 1920s to the terrifying power of to-day must have something to teach the weakness of his own country, under which he so chafes.

A successful Communist China would be more dangerous still. For two generations China has been the very definition of weakness. Every Asian knows that the Chinese Communists are starting with a society even more poverty stricken, even more ruined by war and inflation, even more lacking in all the instruments of modern life from railways to schools, than his own. Already the Chinese have shown that they can fight the West on level terms; already many Asian visitors are impressed by Chinese discipline and enthusiasm; if the Chinese should also be able to raise the standard of living of their people, and there is no corresponding success on the democratic side, then the attractive force of Communism will be irresistible. Theories are judged by results; if Chinese Communism butters parsnips and Indian and Pakistani and Indonesian democracies do not, then democracy and free enterprise will be dismissed as fine words which the East is too poor to afford.

It is indeed more in this possibility of their economic success than in their military strength that lies the Chinese Communist challenge to the free world. Despite the threat they offer in Korea and Indo-China, it will be some time before they matter militarily in areas to which they are not contiguous. But as a Communist revolution, they have the unique advantages of Chiang Kai-shek and the American Republicans.

Chiang Kai-shek and the Kuomintang were an advantage in two ways. They were just a revolutionary party and a successful political general with no deep roots in traditional China, there clung to them none of the aura of hoary sanctity which gave the Tsar and the Orthodox Church their hold. They themselves were, in a less consistent way, as determined to change China as the Communists. They were, moreover, that easiest of all Governments to replace, a revolutionary government whose revolutionary élan had been lost in corruption and self seeking. The Communists have little opposition because by the end everybody had despaired of the Kuomintang. Even democrats accepted the Communists as the lesser evil. The Communists do not, now they are in power, have to face a civil war as the Russian Revolutionaries did. Nor do they have to have a terror on the Russian scale, for they do not have the same massive opposition to repress. They can get full credit for the honesty and the good discipline which usually go with the beginnings of a revolutionary regime, without the shootings amongst the revolutionaries themselves that so rapidly make revolutions conspiratorial, frightened and ruthless. The two million they have liquidated have been killed out of neatness not necessity.

Even economically, to begin with at any rate, the Communists can hardly fail to have some success. The cessation of civil war, partial demobilisation, the restoration of the railways and the currency, the end of inflation—all these are bound to lead to a considerable economic revival, a revival which the repair of Manchuria will further increase. The difficulty will come when they have to get out of China's intolerably poor society the surplus to make industrialisation possible; and then their reforms, and the intolerable conditions so recently endured, may well make it possible for them to squeeze out of their peasantry much more than is possible for, say, an Indian Government with a past of law and order and an election to win. Chinese Five Year Plans have at least an even chance of coming off.

The American Republicans have been the most invaluable of opponents. Their insistence on help for Chiang gave the Communists their modern armaments; and the loudness of their support made it possible for the Communists to discredit Chiang as an American running-dog. After the Communist victory, their continued hostility, their refusal to contemplate recognition, the importance they attached to Formosa gave the Communists exactly that state of crisis abroad which produces a ready acceptance of sacrifices at home. As between the Communists and the Americans, even Kuomintang Chinese have repeatedly shown a preference for the Communists. China has always been an impossibly xenophobic country. And the Communists got all these advantages without risks. They knew perfectly well that America was not going to attack them. The Korean war, and General MacArthur's advance to the Yalu, finally enabled them to paint the Americans to their people as imperialists interfering in an area where for many hundreds of years Chinese influence had been dominant.[1] No position could be more convenient for a new revolutionary regime with sacrifices to ask for. If the "China Lobby" did not exist, Mao Tse Tung's propaganda machine could doubtless invent it; but how fortunate for him that he finds it ready-made!

The Communists may succeed. The quality of the Chinese and North Korean armies shows how effective their ruthless Westernisation can be when applied to an Eastern society—for it must never be forgotten that in the East, Communism's contempt for the past, Communism's respect for machines and productivity and proletariats, above all Communism's materialism, are all powerful engines of Westernisation. The ideas of Victorian Germany and continental exiles in the British Museum are substituted for Confucius and Buddha, Gandhi and Mohammed.

What can the West do to meet the challenge? It can see that Eastern States have enough arms to face direct Communist attack, and help them if they are attacked, as the Americans are doing in Korea, or the French in Indo-China. But this is only a beginning. Most Asian States are not threatened, as yet at least, with Communist aggression; Communist internal violence is important only in Burma and Malaya; in India the armed revolt in Telingana was called off at the end of 1951. That is not the threat. Indeed in some cases, India or Indonesia for example, further arming might itself be a danger, because of the diversion of resources from investment it would involve. The true danger is a slow decline in the standard of life, disillusioning electorate and politicians alike in their high hopes of freedom and democracy. The disillusioned politicians become corrupt; the disillusioned voter is fair game for the demagogue. The result may not be Communism, but it is certainly the end of democracy. Immediately there might only be chaos of the type China knew after 1911; but chaos is always the totalitarian's best opportunity. Once chaos had come, other people in Asia might feel that China's way out was the only way.

[1] There can be no question that President Truman was right to act as he did in Korea; and a very good case can be made for the whole MacArthur policy, though it may have involved more risks than it was worth. But it was to be expected that the result would be a closing of Chinese ranks against democracy and the West; and this has in fact happened.

At all costs, therefore, in those States which are free and democratic, this disillusionment must be prevented. That means large doses of Western capital and Western free enterprise given in such a way that Asia will not lose its self-respect. One of the best ways would be to put the American dollar behind the Commonwealth six-year plan for South Asia, which was produced at the Sydney and London conferences. The importance of this plan can be very great. Another way would be straight dollar loans by the American government to the Asian governments. One of Asia's great difficulties is the disappearance of the great European capital markets where overseas governments could borrow at 3% or 4%. Wall Street prefers direct investments; and there cannot be a direct American investment in an Indian multi-purpose scheme or a Burmese railway. Gifts are good, but only if intermixed with loans. It is good for no one to live on charity and the development which needs to be done in Asia should pay for itself. A school or a hospital is appropriately given; if a railway or a steel plant cannot pay 3% it should not be built.

In this use of Western capital to build up Eastern democracy the key country is India, and, on a smaller scale, Pakistan. The smaller countries could not absorb large amounts of capital nor have most of them the large Western-educated middle class from which to draw the technicians and administrators, the accountants and the sales managers which any extensive investment requires. India has coal and iron and hydro-electricity, it has an existing industry as large as Japan's in the early 1920s, a fair communications net, large urban populations, a middle class in its second or third generation of Western education. It would respond immediately to investment, but the sums it requires are considerable, though small in relation to Western programmes. £100–£200 million a year from outside would be enough to bring life to the stagnating Indian economy and hope to the frustrated Indian electorate. (The sum envisaged in the Commonwealth plan is rather larger than this.) Compared with what the United States spends at home on investment, it is nothing —perhaps a hundredth part; it is only a fraction of what the U.S. has spent on those much less worthy causes, Japan and Germany and Chiang Kai-shek—even the little Philippines have had 2 billion dollars. Certainly nothing less will do. The 35 million dollars of Point Four is a mere token that it is recognised that a problem exists. It is very striking that while America has invested so much in other parts of the world since the end of the war, it has neglected South

Asia almost completely, the Philippines excepted. The perpetual talk that what Asia needs is technicians and not capital, is equally futile. Indian railway and irrigation engineers, Indian health experts and electricity engineers have already drawn up perfectly good schemes to cost hundreds of millions. What they need to carry them out is not advice from experts who know nothing of India but, primarily, a great deal of money, and secondarily, a quite limited number of men on the job itself.

The Americans may justifiably feel that this is only another example of the tendency of the rest of the free world to throw its problems in their laps. But for good or evil, they are already committed in Asia, in Korea, in Japan, in the Philippines, temporarily at least in Formosa. And they have only to ask themselves what would happen to democracy in Asia if the tradition of Gandhi and Nehru were to be discredited by economic failure, and what freedom could hope to save from the wreck of its position in Asia if India were to follow China into Communism or anarchy.

Glossary

ADVAITA VEDANTA: The metaphysical theories of early Hindu philosophers culminating in the work of SANKAR ACHARIYA.

BANIA: Hindu trader or, usually, money-lender.

CHAMPA: Kingdom of eastern Indo-China, absorbed by the Annamites in the 15th century.

CHO: Japanese unit of area-measurement, about $2\frac{1}{2}$ acres.

CHETTYAR: Money-lending and mercantile community, hailing from South India.

CRORE: Ten million. A crore of rupees at present exchange rates is £750,000.

GUPTA: An imperial dynasty of North India, in power from about A.D. 300 to 480.

KOKU: Japanese unit of capacity, about 5 bushels.

LAKH: One hundred thousand. A lakh of rupees, at present exchange rates, is £7,500.

MALGUZARI: The payment of rent, on land upon which revenue is raised.

MEIJI: Emperor of Japan from 1867 to 1912, during whose reign Japan was transformed into a modern state.

MOW: Chinese unit of area-measurement, about $\frac{1}{6}$ acre.

PICUL: Chinese unit of weight, about $133\frac{1}{3}$ lbs.

RYOT: Indian peasant (literally "subject").

SAMURAI: Warrior caste of pre-Meiji Japan.

SRI VIJAYA: Great Indonesian empire, based on Sumatra, which flourished from about the 7th to the 11th centuries.

SUNG: Chinese dynasty, lasting from A.D. 960–1278.

SANKAR ACHARIYA: One of the most famous Hindu theologians. A.D. 789–820; see "Advaita Vedanta".

TAN: Japanese unit of area, about 830 sq. yds. 10 tan = 1 cho.

TAEL: Chinese unit of weight (about $\frac{1}{3}$ oz.) for measuring silver; hence a unit of value.

TALUQDAR: Great landowner in United Provinces of India.

UPANISHADS: Philosophical writings of ancient Hindu literature.

YUAN: Chinese dollar.

ZAIBATSU: The great monopolist entrepreneurs of Japan.

ZEMINDAR: A landowner who pays his revenue direct to the central authority.

INDEX